The Expository Pulpit Series

ROMANS

From Ruin To Redemption

by

Dr. Glen Spencer Jr.

I0140258

SPENCER'S EVANGELISTIC MINISTRIES
15 Pine Ridge Road – Tunkhannock, Pa 18657
EMAIL: GraceForLiving@epix.net

Romans: Man's Ruin and Redemption

Copyright © 2009 by Glen Spencer Jr.

All Scripture Quotations From The **King James Bible**

Contents

Recommendations From Our Readers

Pastor Spencer is not only a gifted preacher, but a gifted writer as well. As a fundamentalist and pastor, I am careful about the books I endorse, but Dr. Spencer is at the top of my list of writers. So, it is with great honor that I recommend his Expository Pulpit Series to you.

Michael D. McClary, Th.D,
Pastor, Community-Bainbridge Baptist Church,
Founder/Executive Director, Good Samaritan Ministries

I have enjoyed reading your books in the past and look forward to getting newer ones. The thing I enjoyed about your books were that when I read them I said, "I have to teach this to my people. I want others to know this". I appreciate your study, work and insight.

Dr. Jeff Fugate
Pastor, Clays Mill Road Baptist Church
President of Commonwealth Baptist College

Dr. Glen Spencer's Bible commentaries are valuable for today. They are expository, edifying and exciting in aiding the Christian, the teacher and the preacher to understand the mind of God and to become victorious in their daily lives. I will use the complete set.

Dr. Bruce Miller, Evangelist
President of Atlantic Coast Baptist College

It is with great delight that I recommend to you, "The Expository Pulpit Commentary Series." Dr. Glen Spencer Jr. combines years of exhaustive research and practical ministry experience to bring to the church, the pastor, the teacher, and the student of the Scriptures a sound, in-depth and yet very practical set of study tools. This ongoing verse by commentary series will be a great addition to your library. This is not just more rehashed information but wise insight from a seasoned Bible Scholar. I know Dr. Glen Spencer Jr. the man and have found him to be a great Christian, a compassionate pastor and a true champion of the authorized King James Bible, believing it to be God's Preserved Word For English speaking people.

This trustworthy commentary series is, Dispensational in theology, pre-Tribulation and pre-millennial in its eschatology, literal in its hermeneutical approach and expository in its format. I am thrilled that this good work is now available to you and I as we seek to benefit from its invaluable help to deepen our knowledge of God's perfect, preserved word.

Dr. Jon M. Jenkins,
Pastor, Grace Baptist Church
President of Grace Baptist College

"You have written an excellent study on the Book of Revelation. This will be a great help to preachers and teachers everywhere. This work is informative, inspiring, and encouraging. Your alliterative outlines are excellent! Your study of this book will be a great help to many, many Christians."

Dr. Lee Roberson
Founder of Tennessee Temple University

The Gospel Of God

There is no greater subject than Christ and His gospel. The word gospel means *"good news"* and good news it is. The gospel is the good news that Jesus Christ came to this old sin darkened world to redeem sinful man.

THE SERVANT AND THE GOSPEL

Paul, a servant of Jesus Christ, called to be an apostle, separated unto the gospel of God. (Romans 1:1) Paul introduces himself to the Roman Christians by describing himself and his work in three ways.

Paul Was A Servant Of God

Paul, a servant of Jesus Christ... This was Paul's signature—he was a servant of Jesus Christ. There is a great lesson in the way Paul introduces himself. Paul had studied and received his education at Jerusalem under Gamaliel, the greatest Jewish teacher of his time (Acts 22:3). Upon the completion of his education, Paul joined the sect called the Pharisees. They were proud and authoritative religionists who held strictly to their brand of the law. He was later a member of the great Sanhedrin. Paul could have introduced himself as *"Saul the distinguished theologian."* His Hebrew name was Saul, meaning *"one who is sought after or asked for."* It signified someone who was prominent and much in demand But he used his Roman name Paul, which means *"small or little."* Here is a man who was once a proud Pharisee, glorying in his pedigree, his education and his religion, now he signs his letters Paul, the little one. He did not try to exalt himself. The days of trying to be a big shot were over for Paul. Paul was little, the Lord was great.

Furthermore, he introduces himself as a **servant.** This is very significant. The religious leaders of his day who used such terms as *"Rabbi"* and *"Master,"* and who sought the **uppermost rooms at feasts, and the chief seats in the synagogues. (Matthew 23:6)** But when Paul introduced himself to the Roman Christians, he didn't begin by magnifying himself. Instead he identified himself as a lowly servant or slave. By this term he does not mean that he is forced against his will to be a slave to someone. The word servant carries the idea of a bondservant. The Mosaic law allowed a servant to voluntarily become a permanent bondservant of his master. **And if the servant shall plainly say, I love my master, my wife, and my children; I will not go out free: Then his master shall bring him unto the judges; he shall also bring him to the door, or unto the door post; and his master shall bore his ear through with an aul; and he shall serve him for ever. (Exodus 21:5-6)** A bondservant is one who voluntarily surrenders his life to the will and service of another. In essence this is what Paul had done. He had voluntarily given himself wholeheartedly to the Lord Jesus Christ with all of his life.

In doing so Paul was following the example of his Saviour. **For even the Son of man came not to be ministered unto, but to minister, and to give his life a ransom for many. (Mark 10:45)** No greater Servant ever lived than Christ. **But made himself of no reputation, and took upon him the form of a servant, and was made in the likeness of men. (Philippians 2:7)** Just think about it. Jesus Christ could have come to earth and sit upon the throne as King of kings and Lord of lords. When He possessed every right to supreme authority, he took the role of a servant. The Creator voluntarily chose to serve his creatures. Jesus said, **I am among you as he that serveth. (Luke 22:27)** To understand this idea of being a bondservant is to get down to the very heart of the Christian experience. Every child of God ought to be a bondservant, one who voluntarily gives himself to the Lord Jesus Christ for life.

Paul Was Summons By God

Paul was **called to be an apostle.** Paul became an apostle when he saw the Lord Jesus Christ on the Damascus road (Acts 9). It was there on that dusty road that he was converted and called into the gospel ministry. The word **apostle** means *"sent one"* and carries the idea of a *"commissioned emissary or messenger."* Paul establishes the authority for his ministry. In declaring his authority Paul was not being proud and pushy. In his letter to the Corinthians Paul declared, **For I am the least of the apostles, that am not meet to be called an apostle, because I persecuted the church of God. (1 Corinthians 15:9)** Paul was not flaunting his credentials as many do today, but was simply declaring the fact that he spoke with the authority of Christ.

Paul Was Separated Unto God

Paul says that he was **separated unto the gospel of God.** Paul was a separated man. Notice that his emphasis was not on what he had separated from, but what he was separated unto. The word **separated** means *"to mark off from others."* It carries the idea of setting boundaries. So far as Paul was concerned, there was no other purpose for his existence. His life was to be spent within the boundaries of the gospel. He never stepped outside of his boundary. Everything he did was in service to his Saviour for the purpose of propagating the gospel. Paul's life purpose is summed up in his words, **For to me to live is Christ. (Philippians 1:21)**

THE SCRIPTURES AND THE GOSPEL

Which he had promised afore by his prophets in the holy scriptures. (Romans 1:2) God always works according to His word. Paul was making it clear that the gospel was not some alternative plan that God had to come up with because the Jews had rejected their Messiah. His message was not to proclaim some new theology. Paul's message was as old as the word of God. The gospel was in the Old Testament Scriptures. **For I delivered unto you first of all that which I also received, how that Christ died for our sins according to the scriptures. (1 Corinthians 15:3)** The Old Testament had clearly revealed the person and work of Christ. The ceremonies, rituals and even many of the people of the Old Testament serve as types and point to Christ. From the time of man's fall he looked for the Messiah (Genesis 3:15). Every type, every promise and every prophecy of the Saviour was fulfilled in the person of Jesus Christ.

THE SAVIOUR AND THE GOSPEL

Concerning his Son Jesus Christ our Lord, which was made of the seed of David according to the flesh; And declared to be the Son of God with power, according to the spirit of holiness, by the resurrection from the dead. (Romans 1:3-4) Previously Paul had stated that he was separated unto the **gospel of God.** Now we come to the person that the gospel is all about—Jesus Christ. **For God is my witness, whom I serve with my spirit in the gospel of his Son, that without ceasing I make mention of you always in my prayers. (Romans 1:9)** Our gospel is a Christ centered gospel. Paul, by inspiration offered a strong warning to those who pervert the gospel. **... If any man preach any other gospel unto you than that ye have received, let him be accursed. (Galatians 1:9)**

Paul wrote this warning concerning the Judaizers who were gospel by mixing works with grace. The word **gospel** means *"good news."* Noah Webster defines gospel as:

> "The history of the birth, life, actions, death, resurrection, ascension and doctrines of Jesus Christ; or a revelation of the grace of God to fallen man through a mediator, including the character, actions, and doctrines of Christ, with the whole scheme of salvation, as revealed by Christ and his apostles."

The gospel is all about Jesus Christ. Any preaching that is not Christ centered is not true gospel preaching.

His Incarnation

Concerning his Son Jesus Christ our Lord, which was made of the seed of David according to the flesh. (Romans 1:3) Christ as born as a descendant of David. The word **made** comes from *"ginomia"* and carries the idea of a *"transition from one state or form to another."* This is what happened at the Virgin Birth when the Christ took on a human nature. He was **made of the seed of David according to the flesh.**

Notice He does not say, He was born of the seed of David, but He was **made of the seed of David according to the flesh.** Paul uses the same terminology in the book of Galatians, **But when the fulness of the time was come, God sent forth his Son, made of a woman, made under the law. (Galatians 4:4)**. John also used the same expression, **And the Word was made flesh, and dwelt among us, and we beheld his glory, the glory as of the only begotten of the Father, full of grace and truth. (John 1:14)** He was not born flesh but made flesh. Ordinary humans are born flesh every day, that requires no miracle. But Jesus Christ was made flesh. This is the Virgin Birth. It is important to understand that Christ is not simply 50% man and 50% God, He was 100% man and 100% God. Christ did not simply become human, but became a unique person, fully God, and at the same time, fully man. This is what theologians often refer to as the Hypostatic union.

He was **made of the seed of David according to the flesh.** Jesus' natural mother, Mary, and legal father, Joseph, were descendants of David (Matthew 1:6, 16; Luke 1:27). In order to fulfill prophecy the Messiah had to be a descendant of David (2 Samuel, 7:12-13; Psalm 89:3-4, 19, 24; Isaiah. 11:1-5; Jeremiah 23:5-6). In the opening sentence of the New Testament we read, **The book of the generation of Jesus Christ, the son of David, the son of Abraham. (Matthew 1:1)** And when we come to the closing chapter of the New Testament, Jesus says, **I Jesus have sent mine angel to testify unto you these things in the churches. I am the root and the offspring of David, and the bright and morning star. (Revelation 22:16)** Jesus perfectly fulfilled all the Messianic prophecies of the Old Testament. As the descendant of David, Jesus inherited the right to reclaim, restore, and to rule David's kingdom.

His Infallibility

And declared to be the Son of God with power, according to the spirit of holiness ... (Romans 1:4) The term **Son of God** points to the Deity of Christ. The Jews of the first century understood the term **Son of God** to mean deity, **But Jesus answered them, My Father worketh hitherto, and I work. Therefore the Jews sought the more to kill him, because he not only had broken the sabbath, but said also that God was his Father, making himself equal with God. (John 5:17-18)** The Bible gives many references to Christ's Deity. Looking down from Heaven God said, **This is my beloved Son, in whom I am well pleased. (Matthew 3:17)** Jesus said, **he that hath seen me hath seen the Father. (John 14:9)** God the Father refers to His Son as God, **But unto the Son he saith, Thy throne, O God, is for ever and ever: a sceptre of righteousness is the sceptre of thy kingdom. (Hebrews 1:8)**

Don't miss the contrast here between His humanity and His deity. He is seed of David **according to the flesh.** But He is the Son of God **according to the spirit of holiness.** The phrase **spirit of holiness** is not a reference to the Holy Spirit. It is speaking of the very essence of God, and Holy is what Jesus is. This is His testimony according to the Scriptures. Over and over the word of God declares Jesus to be without sin.

- He was made **to be sin for us, who knew no sin. (2 Corinthians 5:21)**

- He was high priest who **was in all points tempted like as we are, yet without sin. (Hebrews 4:15)**

- He was **holy, harmless, undefiled, separate from sinners, and made higher than the heavens. (Hebrews 7:26)**

- He is described as **a lamb without blemish and without spot. (1 Peter 1:19)**

- The Bible says that He **did no sin, neither was guile found in his mouth. (1 Peter 2:22)**

The Lord Jesus Christ fully met the righteous requirements of the Law. He was perfectly holy because He was the Son of God

His Invincibility

Next Paul says, **by the resurrection from the dead. (Romans 1:4b)** Jesus was victorious over death further proving His deity. Jesus had promised **Destroy this temple, and in three days I will raise it up. (John 2:19)** He explained further, **But he spake of the temple of his body. (John 2:21)** That prophecy was never fully understood by the disciples until Christ's resurrection. But three days after His crucifixion, when He rolled away the stone and stepped forth in resurrection glory, the disciples got the picture. **When therefore he was risen from the dead, his disciples remembered that he had said this unto them; and they believed the scripture, and the word which Jesus had said. (John 2:22)** Just as His righteous life proved His Deity, so does His resurrection from the dead. Death could lay no claim upon Jesus. Jesus is God and God does not die. Jesus died only because He submitted to death in our place. Jesus said, **… I lay down my life, that I might take it again. No man taketh it from me, but I lay it down of myself. I have power to lay it down, and I have power to take it again. This commandment have I received of my Father. (John 10:17-18)** Jesus is the only One Who ever died and conquered death. He said, **I am he that liveth, and was dead; and, behold, I am alive for evermore, Amen; and have the keys of hell and of death. (Revelation 1:18)**

Paul said, **For I delivered unto you first of all that which I also received, how that Christ died for our sins according to the scriptures; And that he was buried, and that he rose again the third day according to the scriptures. (1 Corinthians 15:3-4)** Paul clearly defines the Gospel message as the death, burial, and resurrection of Christ. Paul makes it clear that Jesus literally lived, He literally died, and He literally rose from the dead. The resurrection of Christ is essential to the gospel. After all, what good is a dead Saviour? **And if Christ be not raised, your faith is vain; ye are yet in your sins. (1 Corinthians 15:17)** Praise God! Jesus Christ came of the grave and is **alive for evermore.**

The devil hates the doctrine of Christ's resurrection because it is where He was defeated. What a death blow the resurrection dealt to Satan. Satan tried throughout the Old Testament to stop the prophecy of Genesis 3:15 from being fulfilled. Even at Christ's birth Satan tried to get Him killed and throughout His ministry Satan constantly moved against Him. When Christ was pronounced dead Satan thought he had won the war. The death of Adam was Satan's handiwork. God had assured Adam that if he disobeyed and partook of the fruit of the tree of the knowledge of good and evil that he would die. Satan's temptation led to Adam's disobedience.

With Adam's disobedience came both his spiritual and physical death. Satan put Adam in the grave. Up until the resurrection of Christ Satan could claim every grave as his own possession. But when Jesus stepped out of that grave, Genesis 3:15 was fulfilled and Death was Conquered and the Devil was Crushed

His Intent

By whom we have received grace and apostleship, for obedience to the faith among all nations, for his name: Among whom are ye also the called of Jesus Christ. (Romans 1:5-6) Paul had been a recipient of God's grace on the Damascus road. It was during that time that he also received his apostleship. **... for obedience to the faith among all nations, for his name.** The word **for** speaks of "intent or purpose." That intent is **obedience to the faith among all nations.** God saved and called Paul with the intention and for the purpose of preaching Christ. Paul says, **Among whom are ye also the called of Jesus Christ.** It is not just Paul's job. It's not just the work of the preacher, but it is everyone's responsibility to get God's message out.

THE SAINTS AND THE GOSPEL

To all that be in Rome, beloved of God, called to be saints: Grace to you and peace from God our Father, and the Lord Jesus Christ. (Romans 1:7) Paul was interested in **all** that was in Rome. He wanted to get the gospel to everyone. **Grace and peace** are Paul's favorite expression in greeting those to whom he writes. A **saint** is one who has been set apart and separated unto the service of Christ. Every believer is a saint, but sometimes believers do not live very saintly.

Paul's Heart For The Romans
Romans 1:8-17

Here we get an idea of Paul's heart for the Roman Christians. Rome was a sinful place, but in spite of the surrounding wickedness, many of the Roman believers had excelled in the faith. So much so that they were known throughout the entire Roman empire. Paul commended them and rejoiced in their faithfulness.

PAUL'S PRAISE

First, I thank my God through Jesus Christ for you all, that your faith is spoken of throughout the whole world. (Romans 1:8) Paul gave thanks to God **through Jesus Christ.** Christ is the one Mediator between God and man. Jesus said, **I am the way, the truth, and the life: no man cometh unto the Father, but by me. (John 14:6)** Christ has made the way to God possible for us. **For there is one God, and one mediator between God and men, the man Christ Jesus. (1 Timothy 2:5)** Because of His work as a mediator we have access to the Father and we can at any time **come boldly unto the throne of grace... (Hebrews 4:16)** Paul never forgot that it was only by Christ's work that anyone could come before God.

Paul was thankful for their faith. He said, **your faith is spoken of throughout the whole world. (Romans 1:8b)** The Church at Rome was a great Church with a testimony of faith and faithfulness. So great was their faith that it was **spoken of throughout the whole world.** By faith Paul was not talking about their saving faith in Christ. It wasn't the faith that brings salvation, but it was their persevering faith that Paul was commending. It was the kind of faith that brought persecution. Remember, this is Rome we are talking about. Christians were hated there. They were persecuted and put to death over a mere profession of faith. Their deaths they were made the subjects of sport as they were eaten by lions in the coliseums while thousands watched and cheered. Many were covered with animal skins and ripped apart by wild dogs. It was common for believers to be covered with tar and set on fire to serve as human torches to light Nero's gardens at night.

Some churches are famous because of their pastor. Others are known for their architecture. Yet others for their size and wealth. But the Church at Rome was known for its faith. Jesus said to His disciples, **Have faith in God. (Mark 11:22)** Paul said that without faith it is impossible to please God (Hebrews 11:6). God is honored and pleased when we exhibit great faith. These Christians were famous for their faith. God give us such a faith.

PAUL'S PRAYER

For God is my witness, whom I serve with my spirit in the gospel of his Son, that without ceasing I make mention of you always in my prayers. (Romans 1:9) Paul's Pastoral heart really shows through here. Notice that Paul's praying was **without ceasing** and **always.** We miss out on one of the greatest resources God has given us. That is prayer. Notice that didn't say *"without ceasing and always I preach."* He didn't say, *"without ceasing and always I go soul-winning."* He didn't say, *"without ceasing and always I study."* But he did say **without ceasing** and **always** I pray. There are times when we can't preach. There are times when we can't win souls. But we can always pray. This was a way of life for Paul. He was dedicated in his prayer life. Paul believed he ought to **Pray without ceasing. (1 Thessalonians 5:17)**

Paul said to the Thessalonians, **We give thanks to God always for you all, making mention of you in our prayers. (1 Thessalonians 1:2)** Notice the phrase, **for you all.** Paul thanked God for all of the people in the Church at Thessalonica, not for just a few. Everyone is part of the ministry and Paul prayed for everyone. Giving thanks and praying for each other ought to be one of the things that we are known for—it ought to be our reputation. Paul said to the Philippians, **Be careful for nothing; but in every thing by prayer and supplication with thanksgiving let your requests be made known unto God And the peace of God, which passeth all understanding, shall keep your hearts and minds through Christ Jesus. (Philippians 4:6-7)**

Notice how Paul said, **I make mention of you always in my prayers.** This is the ministry of intercessory prayer—praying on the behalf of others. The prophet Samuel said, **Moreover as for me, God forbid that I should sin against the LORD in ceasing to pray for you... (1 Samuel 12:23)** Samuel considered his failure to pray for others as a sin against the Lord. I have read numerous times of John Welch, the Scotch preacher who was known for his fervent prayer life. He wrote that he considered his day to be ill spent if he did not pray at least eight or ten hours. At night, he kept an extra blanket by the bed so that if God gave him a burden during the night, he could get up and pray. His wife once complained when she found him on the floor weeping in the middle of the night, to which he replied, "*O woman, I have the souls of 3,000 to answer for, and I know not how it is with many of them.*" Read the biography of any great Preacher or Christian and you will find that one thing they had in common was a fervent prayer life.

Every Christian can pray! Pray for your Pastor, pray for your Sunday-school teacher, Pray for the leaders, the Bible Institute, yourself, your spouse, your children, etc There is no shortage of people to pray for—PRAY!

PAUL'S PRIORITY

Making request, if by any means now at length I might have a prosperous journey by the will of God to come unto you. (Romans 1:10) Paul had a great desire to visit Rome and minister to the believers there. Paul was **Making request**, that is, he was praying fervently for the opportunity to visit Rome. But notice how Paul prayed for **the will of God**. Paul's life and ministry was always directed by God's will. That is the divine formula for prayer. **And this is the confidence that we have in him, that, if we ask any thing according to his will, he heareth us. (1 John 5:14)** Every child of God needs to know and do the will of God. Too many Christians mess around with the will of God. Some ignore it altogether and live according their own will. Others manipulate and maneuver around circumstances in attempt to control what they call the will of God. Few be they that actually seek and settle into the will of God. Christ is our example in being surrendered to the will of God. Even though it meant terrible pain, suffering and separation from God. He said, **...Father, if thou be willing, remove this cup**

from me: nevertheless not my will, but thine, be done. (Luke 22:42) The priority of Christ's life was to obey the perfect will of God. Jesus was able to say, **for I do always those things that please him. (1 John 8:29)** What a testimony we would have if we would simply set our hearts to do the will of God. Someone has well said, *"To know the will of God is the greatest knowledge. To find the will of God is the greatest discovery. To do the will of God is the greatest achievement."*

PAUL'S PURPOSE

For I long to see you, that I may impart unto you some spiritual gift, to the end ye may be established; That is, that I may be comforted together with you by the mutual faith both of you and me. (Romans 1:11-12) The word for **long** carries the idea of *"an intense carving and earnest desire."* Paul's purpose for wanting to go to Rome was two-fold.

It was for their Edification

Paul says, **that I may impart unto you some spiritual gift, to the end ye may be established. (Romans 1:11)** Paul desires to impart **some spiritual gift.** The word for gift is *charisma* and is used in Romans 12 and 1 Corinthians 12 in reference to the gifts of the Holy Spirit for service. Since we know that such gifts are imparted by God and not by man Paul is probably talking about exercising his own preaching and edifying them. The primary meaning of edify is to build up. Noah Webster says, *"To instruct and improve the mind in knowledge generally, and particularly in moral and religious knowledge, in faith and holiness."* Paul's desire was to build them up in the faith. This seems to be the point in Paul saying, **to the end ye may be established**

It was for their Encouragement

Next Paul says, **that I may be comforted together with you by the mutual faith both of you and me. (Romans 1:12)** Paul realized the importance of fellowshipping with other believers. He talked about being **comforted together** by their **mutual faith.** Paul emphasizes the reciprocal nature of Christian fellowship. So many believers give up and wash out when trials and heartaches come their way and a lot of times it is because of their failure to draw upon the strength and wisdom of others. It is amazing that the first thing most believers do when hardship hits is withdraw from the Church and other Christians. This they do to their own destruction. Paul not only realized that he could be a great blessing to the Christians at Rome, but that they could be a blessing to him. We need one another. **Not forsaking the assembling of ourselves together, as the manner of some is; but exhorting one another: and so much the more, as ye see the day approaching. (Hebrews 10:25)** The fellowship and encouragement are two great benefits of cooperate worship.

PAUL'S PROBLEM

Now I would not have you ignorant, brethren, that oftentimes I purposed to come unto you, but was let hitherto, that I might have some fruit among you also, even as among other Gentiles. (Romans 1:13) Paul's desire and plan to visit was hindered time and time again. Near the close of this book Paul again says, **I have been much**

hindered from coming to you. (Romans 15:22) Paul wrote to the Thessalonians, **Wherefore we would have come unto you, even I Paul, once and again; but Satan hindered us. (1 Thessalonians 2:18)** How often we can identify with the same problem, **but Satan hindered us.** Satan is a very real enemy and will stop at nothing to thwart our work. The name **Satan** means *opponent* or *adversary* and is used over fifty times in the Bible. Satan and his forces are set on hindering the work and will of God. Paul experienced it, many other Bible men and women experienced it, and so will we. Paul said, **Satan hindered us.** The word **hindered** is a military term that means to *cut off* or *to make a road impassable.* It carries the idea of *cutting into and impeding one's course by cutting off his way.* It referred to cutting up the road to stop an enemy's advance. We will face the hindrances of Satan in our work, but let us never forget the words of John, **Ye are of God, little children, and have overcome them: because greater is he that is in you, than he that is in the world. (John 4:4)**

PAUL'S PREACHING

Paul's preaching was driven by a great burden to preach the gospel.

The Duty of Preaching

I am debtor both to the Greeks and to the Barbarians, both to the wise and to the unwise, (Romans 1:14) The word **debt** means to owe something. It carries the idea of being under an obligation. **For though I preach the gospel, I have nothing to glory of: for necessity is laid upon me; yea, woe is unto me, if I preach not the gospel! (1**

Corinthians 9:16) The ministry is not a profession for Paul. It was the work that God had called him into. Paul said **for necessity is laid upon me.** This was a Divine compulsion to preach the Word of God. Paul had been apprehended by God, and the obligation was such that he had no choice but to preach.

The Desire of Preaching

So, as much as in me is, I am ready to preach the gospel to you that are at Rome also. (Romans 1:15) The word **ready** comes from *"prothymos"* and means prepared and willing. Paul had a desire and was ready to preach. Later Paul would exhort Timothy to, **Preach the word; be instant in season, out of season... (2 Timothy 4:2)** To be **instant in season, out of season** is to be ready and available at all times. The word **instant** means to *"stand by,"* or *"to be ready at all times."* Paul didn't need a notice, only an opportunity.

The Defense of Preaching

For I am not ashamed of the gospel of Christ: (Romans 1:16a) Too many are ashamed of the Saviour and His gospel. They are embarrassed and uncomfortable with speaking up for and being identified with Christ. Jesus said, **For whosoever shall be ashamed of me and of my words, of him shall the Son of man be ashamed, when he shall come in his own glory, and in his Father's, and of the holy angels. (Luke 9:26)** In his second letter to Timothy Paul warned the young preacher, **Be not thou therefore ashamed of the testimony of our Lord, nor of me his prisoner: but be thou partaker of the afflictions of the gospel according**

to the power of God. (2 Timothy 1:8) Many are ashamed and deny Christ because peer pressure and intimidation. They are concerned about what others might say. They speak of sports, politics and world events, but they are silent concerning Christ. God help us to speak up for Christ. Paul went on to say, **Whereunto I am appointed a preacher, and an apostle, and a teacher of the Gentiles. For the which cause I also suffer these things: nevertheless I am not ashamed: for I know whom I have believed, and am persuaded that he is able to keep that which I have committed unto him against that day. (2 Timothy 1:11-12)** Paul stood for Christ with a holy boldness because of his unwavering trust in Him.

The Dynamic of Preaching

... for it is the power of God (Romans 1:16b) The word **power** comes from *"dynamis"* from which we get the word dynamite. Paul preached the gospel because of its power to save sinners. **For the preaching of the cross is to them that perish foolishness; but unto us which are saved it is the power of God. (1 Corinthians 1:18)** There is no other message on earth that has such power.

The Design of Preaching

... unto salvation to every one that believeth; to the Jew first, and also to the Greek. (Romans 1:16c) Paul's purpose in preaching was to bring the lost to Christ. Notice the word **everyone**. Everyone who believes will be saved. There are no outcasts. Jesus said, **... him that cometh to me I will in no wise cast out. (John 6:37)** All one has to do when he hears the gospel is to believe and by faith call upon the Lord. (John 1:12, Romans 10:13).

For therein is the righteousness of God revealed from faith to faith: as it is written, The just shall live by faith. (Romans 1:17) Through the preaching of the gospel, **righteousness of God revealed**. The gospel teaches us that God is holy and we are sinners. As sinner's we are helpless to save ourselves. Therefore, God gave His Son to provide salvation for whosoever would believe. However, faith is not only the method of entering into salvation, but faith is also how we are to live. Paul says, ... **the righteousness of God revealed from faith to faith: as it is written, The just shall live by faith.** We go from faith to faith. That is, as we live by faith, the righteousness of God is continually revealed. Saving faith is more than a fire escape, it is the way our life is to be lived.

The Awful Pit Of Depravity
Romans 1:18-32

The Book of Romans is all about the good news of the gospel. However, the negative side must also be preached. Before man is ready for salvation he must see his need for salvation. Paul points out that we need God's righteousness (vs.17) but we deserve God's wrath (vs.18) In presenting the gospel Paul takes us down into the pit of depravity and shows us what man really is apart from Christ.

THE RETRIBUTION OF GOD

For the wrath of God is revealed from heaven against all ungodliness and unrighteousness of men, who hold the truth in unrighteousness. (Romans 1:18) What a solemn thought! **The wrath of God.** The fact that every individual will someday stand before the righteous God of Heaven ought to sober us. The doctrine of God's wrath is tragically ignored in most religious circles today. There is a great deal of preaching on God's love, but very little is said about God's wrath. People confuse God's love with their own sentimentalism and fail to balance God's love with His other attributes. God's love must be balanced with His holiness and justice. Certainly we know that **God is love. (1 John 4:8, 16),** but at the same time, God is Holy and demands our holiness. **But as he which hath called you is holy, so be ye holy in all manner of conversation; Because it is written, Be ye holy; for I am holy. (1 Peter 1:15-16) God is love,** but He is also a **consuming fire. (Deuteronomy 4:24, 9:3; Hebrews 12:29)** We must realize that God will not wink at and ignore our sin. He is going to deal with it according to His righteous nature.

THE REVELATION OF GOD

Here Paul states that fallen man has a revelation of God and therefore will stand **without excuse** in the day of judgment. In the context Paul lists two ways that God is revealed to man.

Man's Conscience

Because that which may be known of God is manifest in them; for God hath shewed it unto them. (Romans 1:19) Notice that the things which may be known of God is revealed **in them.** Here we see that within the heart of every man is an awareness of right and wrong. This is further stated in the next chapter. **For when the Gentiles, which have not the law, do by nature the things contained in the law, these, having not the law, are a law unto themselves: Which shew the work of the law written in their hearts, their conscience also bearing witness, and their thoughts the mean while accusing or else excusing one another. (Romans 2:14-15)** This is a biblical fact. Man has a conscience that tells him what is right and wrong. In the account of Paul's shipwreck in Acts 28, you will remember how Paul was gathering wood for the fire when a poisonous snake bit him. The Bible says, **And when the barbarians saw the venomous beast hang on his hand, they said among themselves, No doubt this man is a murderer, whom, though he hath escaped the sea, yet vengeance suffereth not to live. (Acts 28:4)** Notice how the pagan natives concluded that Paul was being punished by God for his sin. They had a conscious knowledge that there is right and wrong and God punishes man for his evil deeds. You say, But preacher, there were no missionaries and no preachers on that island. How did the barbarians have such knowledge? God put it there. Here in Romans, Paul tells us that such knowledge is in the heart of every man. David Livingston and other missionaries have testified that down in the deepest and darkest jungles of the world they do not find atheists, but rather they find men and women who are conscious of the difference between right and wrong and aware of the fact that they must answer to God.

God's Creation

For the invisible things of him from the creation of the world are clearly seen, being understood by the things that are made, even his eternal power and Godhead; so that they are without excuse. (Romans 1:20) Not only is God revealed in the conscience, but also in creation. Creation testifies of God's sovereign power at work.

> **The heavens declare the glory of God; and the firmament sheweth his handywork. Day unto day uttereth speech, and night unto night sheweth knowledge. There is no speech nor language, where their voice is not heard Their line is gone out through all the earth, and their words to the end of the world In them hath he set a tabernacle for the sun, Which is as a bridegroom coming out of his chamber, and rejoiceth as a strong man to run a race. His going forth is from the end of the heaven, and his circuit unto the ends of it: and there is nothing hid from the heat thereof (Psalms 19:1-6)**

God has left the indelible mark of His fingerprints all across the face of the universe. When the heathen sees creation all around him—the mountains, the sky, the stars, the trees, the flowers, fruit, animals—he knows that such a work is not of man. What Paul is saying is that when man looks at creation he must conclude that there is a God.

THE RESPONSE TO GOD

They Responded With Indifference

Because that, when they knew God, they glorified him not as God. (Romans 1:21a) Wicked man wants nothing to do with God. Notice the text says, **when they knew God**. God had made Himself known (Romans 1:19-20), but man willfully rejected His revelation. When we go back to Adam we see that mankind started with the knowledge of the one True God. Adam had the knowledge of God. Noah and his family had the knowledge of God. As did Abraham and others. However, somewhere along the way man begin to reject God's revelation. By man's choice **they glorified him not as God**. Hence, man's plunge into darkness started.

They Responded With Ingratitude

Neither were thankful. (Romans 1:21b) They had no appreciation of God. Our society is marked by this kind of unthankfulness. As God's people we are to be thankful. **Enter into his gates with thanksgiving, and into his courts with praise: be thankful unto him, and bless his name. (Psalm 100:4)** Ingratitude is a step away from God.

They responded with Ignorance

They **became vain in their imaginations, and their foolish heart was darkened. (Romans 1:21c)** The word **imaginations** speaks of the thought process. It carries the idea of deliberating and coming to a conclusion. The word **vain** means *empty, futile, worthless.* The word **darkened** speaks of the absence of light. As a result of pushing God out of their life they lost the God given ability to reason and come up with a sensible conclusion concerning the things of God. The further they moved away from God the more vain they became and the deeper into darkness they went. The tragedy is that lost men love the darkness. Jesus said, **And this is the condemnation, that light is come into the world, and men loved darkness rather than light, because their deeds were evil. (John 3:19)**

They Responded With Intellectualism

Professing themselves to be wise, they became fools. (Romans 1:22) While rejecting revelation and denying God these men profess themselves to be wise. Because they have rejected God and His truth they are fools. Twice the Bible declares that **The fool hath said in his heart, There is no God. (Psalms 14:1; 53:1)** The word **fool** in our text does not mean that they were mentally deficient, but describes someone who has moved from God's light into darkness and therefore, has no spiritual discernment. **But the natural man receiveth not the things of the Spirit of God: for they are foolishness unto him: neither can he know them... (1 Corinthians 2:14a)** Jesus said, **O fools, and slow of heart to believe all that the prophets have spoken. (Luke 24:25)** We are dealing with an intellectualism today that is cultic. Men seem to worship the brain. Dr. Martyn Lloyd Jones wrote:

> "The whole drift toward modernism that has blighted the church of God and nearly destroyed its living gospel may be traced to an hour when men began to turn from revelation to philosophy."

Such is the problem with prideful intellectualism. Solomon said, **The fear of the Lord is the beginning of wisdom. (Proverbs 9:10)** Without God wicked men are void of spiritual understanding and become fools. Men with a string of degrees after their names declare themselves to be wise even as they continue to plunge into darkness.

They Responded With Idolatry

And changed the glory of the uncorruptible God into an image made like to corruptible man, and to birds, and fourfooted beasts, and creeping things. (Romans 1:23) When man rejects God he does not cease to be religious. He simply creates his own god, many times he creates god in his own image. Man is a religious creature, so he will worship. According to the 1986 World Almanac, 26 million people in the world have a religious affiliation of some sort. Hindus have over 330 million gods. They also worship cows and countless other animals that they consider to be sacred. However, notice it is clear that the true God is **uncorruptible** which means that God *is "unchanging and not capable of corruption."* The One true God always has been, and always will be. **Now unto the King eternal, immortal, invisible, the only wise God, be honour and glory for ever and ever. Amen. (1 Timothy 1:17)**

They Responded With Insult

They **changed the truth of God into a lie. (Romans 1:25)** What an insult to throw into the face of Almighty God! To change His truth into a lie. The Psalmists said that God had magnified His word above His name (Psalm 138:2). Yet, man doesn't like what God says, so he changes it. This is man's way. Hence, the hordes of modern translations.

THE REJECTION BY GOD

It is tragic, but a fact! When man in his stubbornness and rebellion chooses sin over God he can become so hardened that God gives him up. Three times this truth is unmistakably stated

> **Wherefore God also gave them up ...** (Romans 1:24a)

> **For this cause God gave them up...** (Romans 1:26a)

> **God gave them over to a reprobate mind..** (Romans 1:28)

The phrases translated **gave them up** and **gave them over** comes from a word that carries the idea of *handing over,* or *delivering to another.* Douglas Moo said, *"Like a judge who hands over a prisoner to the punishment his crime has earned, God hands over the sinner to the terrible cycle of ever-increasing sin."* Because of their rebellion against God, God in effect says, Have it your way. Do your own thing. When God gives the sinner up, He withdraws His Divine restraint, allowing him to hopelessly sink deeper and deeper into the moral quagmire he has chosen for himself. This isn't God's choice. It is the sinner's choice.

A lot of folks don't like to accept the fact that sinners can cross the deadline and the God of love and mercy give up on them. Their problem is that they can't get past their own sentimental idea of love. God's love is just and righteous. When God gives a sinner over and rejects him it is righteous retribution (Proverbs 1:24-31).

They have had their chance. They have chosen their own way and said no to God. They crossed the deadline and passed the point of no return. God simply let them have their own way and follow the path they have chosen. They will go to Hell for certain.

THE REPROBATION APART FROM GOD

Man left to himself is on a downward spiral and when God withdraws himself, that downward plunge only accelerates.

Their Wicked Companionships

The Bible says that they **dishonour their own bodies between themselves ... For this cause God gave them up unto vile affections: for even their women did change the natural use into that which is against nature: And likewise also the men, leaving the natural use of the woman, burned in their lust one toward another; men with men working that which is unseemly, and receiving in themselves that recompence of their error which was meet. (Romans 1:24b, 26-27)** One of the signs that many have been given up by God is the flood of homosexuality that is so widespread in our land. It is amazing that a sin so wicked could be so accepted in modern society. According to the book of Romans, homosexuality is the natural result of a society that refuses to honor God and recognize His truth (vs. 18 and 21). America has gone so far with this sin that Christians often have to defend their position that homosexuality is sinful and unacceptable to God. However, the Bible clearly calls homosexuality a sin and refers to it as an abomination.

In the beginning God did not bring a man to Adam. When God saw that it was not good for man to be alone, He gave him a woman. It was Adam and Eve, not Adam and Steve. Paul said, **the woman for the man. (1 Corinthians 11:9)** God established the first home by giving Adam a wife, not another man. Over and over in the word of God the sin of homosexuality is seen as the wickedest of sin. **But the men of Sodom were wicked and sinners before the LORD exceedingly. (Genesis 13:13)** Notice the word **exceedingly.** The sin of homosexuality exceeds all other sins. God judged and destroyed Sodom because of this sin (Genesis 18-19). And again, **Thou shalt not lie with mankind, as with womankind: it is abomination. (Leviticus 18:22) If a man also lie with mankind, as he lieth with a woman, both of them have committed an abomination: they shall surely be put to death; their blood shall be upon them. (Leviticus 20:13)**

This passage here in Romans contains the clearest teaching in the New Testament on the sin of homosexuality. In this section Paul, under inspiration of the Holy Spirit, describes homosexuality as **vile, uncleaness, dishonour, against nature,** and **lust.** No amount of theological sleight of hand can present homosexuality as acceptable. Notice the use of such terms as **natural use** and **against nature. (vs. 26-27)** These people abandon the **natural use** of the body and do those things which are **against nature.** The words **natural** and **nature** speak of that which is inborn, that which governs us—our instincts. It speaks of the instincts that God has given us. What Paul is saying here is that homosexuality and lesbianism is unnatural. It goes against the very nature that God has given us.

Many of these homosexuals and lesbians have been given over by God **to a reprobate mind, to do those things which are not convenient. (Romans 1:28)** The word **reprobate** means to be *disapproved, rejected, and cast away.* It carries the idea of being abandoned to wickedness and eternal damnation. Webster's New World Dictionary say, *To reject and abandon as beyond salvation; depraved; corrupt; unprincipled; rejected by God; excluded from salvation and lost in sin.* It is a word that was used of metal that did not pass the test and was discarded. Three characteristics of a reprobate are:

First, they are **_Rejected_** of God. **Reprobate silver shall men call them, because the LORD hath rejected them. (Jeremiah 6:30)** A reprobate is rejected of God and forever doomed and damned to Hell. Once God withdraws from the sinner there will be no conviction, no concern and no coming back.

Second, they **_Resist_** the truth. **Now as Jannes and Jambres withstood Moses, so do these also resist the truth: men of corrupt minds, reprobate concerning the faith. (2 Timothy 3:8)** No one hates the word of God and resists the truth like the homosexual movement. They particularly hate the King James Bible because it addresses them from God's perspective. The modern translations watered their sin down and in some cases imply that it is OK.

Third, they are sometimes **_Religious_. They profess that they know God; but in works they deny him, being abominable, and disobedient, and unto every good work reprobate. (Titus 1:16)** As absurd as it is many who are reprobate claim to **know God**. They are deceived of course—they do not know Him. I have witnessed to homosexuals who argue that their lifestyle is OK and that they are Christians. However, actions speak louder than words. They profess with their lips to know God, but by their **abominable and disobedient** lifestyle they prove that they are reprobate and rejected of God.

Homosexuality and lesbianism is the most shameful and the most abnormal form of immorality and God meets it with His judgment and rejection.

Their Wicked Character

Character is one of the missing virtues in this world. Paul description reads like the daily newspaper.

First, ***they are Controlled***. Paul describes them as being **... filled with all unrighteousness ... wickedness. (vs. 29)** Righteousness speaks of that which is right and holy. God is the source of all true righteousness. These sinners apart from God are described not only as **unrighteous** and **wicked**, but **filled with all unrighteousness.** The word **unrighteousness** means *injustice, wrongdoing, evildoing, every kind of evil.* It is the act of living one's life as his depraved nature dictates. When God withdraws the depraved nature takes complete control and wickedness floods the heart and life.

Second, ***they are Covetous***. They are described as being full of **covetousness (vs. 29)** and **envy. (vs. 29)** Webster defines **covetousness** as *"Inordinately desirous; excessively eager to obtain and possess; directed to money or goods, avaricious."* Thayer says, *"one eager to have more, especially what belongs to others... greedy of gain."* This speaks of those who are never satisfied with what they have—they always want more. Paul said of covetousness, **let it not be once named among you, as becometh saints**.

(Ephesians 5:3) Envy goes beyond **covetousness**. It is the spirit that not only covets what someone else has, it resents the fact that the other person has it.

*Third, **they are Cruel**.* They are filled with **maliciousness. (vs. 29)** This word means *"malice, viciousness, ill-will, spite, grudge, desire to injure."* They are further described as **implacable** and **unmerciful. (vs. 31)** The word **implacable** speaks of the unwillingness to forgive and make peace. The word **unmerciful** describes them as people who have no pity or compassion toward others.

*Fourth, **they are Crafty**.* The word **deceit (vs. 29)** means *"to bait, snare, mislead, beguile; to be crafty and deceitful; to mislead or to give a false impression by word, act, or influence."* This word describes those who are crooked and stoop to underhanded methods for getting their own way.

*Fifth, **they are Calloused*** They have become so hardhearted and unreasonable that they are **haters of God. (vs. 30)** These are people who hate God and the principles that He represents. They hate the very One who loved them so much that He sent His Son to die for them. This is hatred at its height.

*Sixth, **they are Crude**.* They are **without natural affection. (vs. 31)** They are crude and unnatural. This speaks again of sexual perversion. Men with men and women with women. Homosexuality and lesbianism. It is unnatural.

Their Wicked Conduct

Character will eventually show up in conduct. This section reads like the morning newspaper.

First, **_their Debauchery_.** **Fornication. (vs. 29)** The word **Fornication** speaks of unlawful sexual activity. It describes sexual immorality in general. Webster defines **fornication** as:

> "The incontinence [no restraint, free or uncontrolled indulgence of the passions] or lewdness of unmarried persons, male or female; also, the criminal conversation [behavior] of a married man with an unmarried woman."

It is the word from which we get pornography, and refers to any illicit sexual activity. Paul says that one who habitually practices this sin will not go to Heaven—he is unsaved. **Fornicators ...shall not inherit the kingdom of God. (1 Corinthians 6:9)** A child of God has no business involved in such sin. **For his is the will of God, even your sanctification, that ye should abstain from fornication. (1 Thessalonians 4:3)**

Second, **_their Disregard_.** Next on list is **murder. (vs. 29)** These people have no concern for the sanctity of life. Murder is the act of maliciously taking another's life. It is the breaking of the sixth commandment. It is a great offence to God who is the giver of all life. It speaks of the vast disregard for human life that we see so much of today. This can be applied to abortion—the murder of the unborn.

Third, **_their Deficit_.** Paul uses the word **malignity. (vs. 29)** This is a word that means *"ill character"* and speaks of bad character in general. Such people have a serious deficiency. They are void of character. There is certainly a lack of godly character in today's world.

Fourth, **_their Disobedience_**. They are **disobedient to parents. (vs. 30)** This sin is so widespread that you can't go out without seeing it. It is everywhere. Paul names this sin as one of the signs that the end times are upon us (2 Timothy 3:1-5). If young people will not respect and obey their parents, they will not respect and obey God! We live in a day when young people disdain, disregard and defy parental authority without even giving it a thought. Much of the blame lies at the feet of the parents for their failure in bringing the children up in the nurture and admonition of the Lord. A nation that loses its children is on a downhill slide to the pit of Hell!

Fifth, **_their Deceit_**. They are **covenantbreakers. (vs. 31)** This speaks of those who don't keep their word. Such people are liars. They think nothing of breaking agreements, whether in business or religion. The Bible says, **... all liars, shall have their part in the lake which burneth with fire and brimstone: which is the second death. (Revelation 21:8)** This certainly can be applied to the epidemic of divorce today. Men and women think nothing of standing before God and making vows only to break them when things get a little tough. **When thou vowest a vow unto God, defer not to pay it; for he hath no pleasure in fools: pay that which thou hast vowed. (Ecclesiastes 5:4)**

Their Wicked Conversation

James said that the tongue is, **an unruly evil, full of deadly poison. (James 3:8)** Harry Ironside referred to the tongue *"the index of the heart."* What man is in his heart is revealed by his tongue. Notice how these people speak.

First, **_their Contention_**. They love to **debate**. **(vs. 29)** This word means *"strife, discord, contention, fighting, struggling, quarreling, dissension, wrangling."* This word speaks of those who are always in a fuss with someone. They will not accept facts. They just want to argue. They question authority and argue against established truth.

Second, **_their Chatter_**. They are **whisperers (vs. 29)** and **backbiters. (vs. 30)** They can't keep quiet. These are gossipers and slanderers who make it their business to tell all they know. They delight in smearing reputations and slamming the character of others.

Third, **_their Conceit_**. They are **boasters. (vs. 30)** This speaks of braggarts. It defines those who are full of themselves. Someone said, *"Pride hides a man's faults to himself and magnifies them to everyone else."* Solomon said, **These six things doth the LORD hate: yea, seven are an abomination unto him: (Proverbs 6:16)** And look at what tops the list! **A proud look ... (Proverbs 6:17a)** These **boasters** are prideful glory mongers who go about building themselves up and seeking their own glory. Jesus said, **He that speaketh of himself seeketh his own glory. (John 7:18)**

Their Wicked Concepts

Without God man's thinking is messed up and he constantly dwells on wicked things. His concepts become more and more wicked.

First, they have **_No Reasoning_**. Paul describes them as being **without understanding. (vs. 31)** They have lost the ability to reason things out. It speaks of a thought process apart from God. It is the absence of comprehension pertaining to the things of God. God commanded man to

Come now, and let us reason together... (Isaiah 1:18) But once man sins beyond repentance and God withdraws, man looses the ability to reason concerning spiritual matters.

Second, they have **No Restraint**. They are **inventors of evil things. (vs. 30)** This speaks of those who are bored by the usual ways of sinning. They are always looking for something new and more depraved. They are looking for some new way by which sin can be committed. We live in an age of invention, but today's inventions are more evil than ever before.

Third, they have **No Redemption**. Paul drives the final nail into the coffin. **Who knowing the judgment of God, that they which commit such things are worthy of death, not only do the same, but have pleasure in them that do them. (Romans 1:32)** The old saying *Misery Loves Company* is certainly true here. Not only do such people commit these sins, ruin their own lives and go to a Devil's Hell, but they encourage others to commit them and drag them to Hell along with themselves.

Judgment Of The Self-Righteous
Romans 2:1-16

Paul now moves from the heathen to the self-righteous man. This is the man who has tried to live right. He has never murdered anyone. He has never been divorced. He has not been involved in the sexual perversion of the heathen. He has been a good citizen and so on. He is a pretty good man so far as this world is concerned. But when searched by God, he was found to be just as wicked inwardly as the heathen was outwardly. Therefore, he is just as condemned and will be judged by the same standard. When his judgment comes …

THERE WILL BE NO EXCUSE

When the lost stand before the righteous Judge of Heaven there will be no defense.

<u>Each will be judged according to His Position</u>

Therefore thou art inexcusable, O man… (Romans 2:1a) In the last chapter the heathen was declared to be **without excuse. (Romans 1:20)** Now, the self-righteous man is told that he is **inexcusable**. The word carries the idea of being *without an answer of defense.* There is no excuse that will be heard by the Judge. No possible reason can be conjured up that will stay the hand of judgment. This word pictures a criminal standing before the Judge with no possible defense.

<u>Each will be judged according to His Performance</u>

Paul says, **whosoever thou art that judgest: for wherein thou judgest another, thou condemnest thyself; for thou** that judgest doest the same things. (Romans 2:1b) The self-righteous man is quick to point everyone else's failure. The self-righteous would never commit murder, but the Bible says, **Whosoever hateth his brother is a murderer... (1 John 3:15)** The self-righteous wouldn't commit adultery, but Jesus said, **That whosoever looketh on a woman to lust after her hath committed adultery with her already in his heart. (Matthew 5:28)** This idea is simple. The self-righteous man condemns himself because he does the same things that the heathen does. He sins and comes short of the glory of God (Romans 3:23) just as the man he judges.

Remember the account of David and Bathsheba. David committed the sin of adultery. David's sin escalated when she sent him word that she was pregnant. He slyly tried to cover his sin by getting her husband Uriah drunk and sending him home to sleep with his wife. When this did not work, he arranged for Uriah's murder.

David thought that the entire matter was buried, but one day the prophet Nathan showed up and told David a story. There was in his kingdom a poor man with a lamb which was considered to be a part of his family. There was also a rich man who owned many flocks. This rich man took the poor man's lamb and killed it to provide for a meal. As David heard the story, he boiled with anger. David quickly passed judgment. **And David's anger was greatly kindled against the man; and he said to Nathan, As the LORD liveth, the man that hath done this thing shall surely die: And he shall restore the lamb fourfold, because he did this thing, and because he had no pity. (2 Samuel 12:5-6)** Immediately

Nathan pointed at David and declared **Thou art the man. (2 Samuel 12:7)** That is exactly what God says here.

Each will be judged according to Holy Principle

But we are sure that the judgment of God is according to truth against them which commit such things. (Romans 2:2) Notice that the **judgment of God is according to truth.** The application here can be two-fold.

First, the truth of the ***Sinner's Wickedness***. When God judges nothing will be hidden from Him. **All things are naked and opened unto the eyes of Him with whom they have to do. (Hebrews 4:13)** It seems that truth is the missing element in many court cases today. Human judges are limited when it comes to knowing the true facts of any case. He must depend upon the testimony of men and the arguments of attorneys. Men lie and attorneys often warp the truth. However, the judge in this case is the Almighty, All-knowing God of the universe. He knows the truth and the details of every case. Every lie will be met with the truth and there will be no slick lawyers to twist the facts and jump through loop holes. Nothing can be hid from Him! **For God shall bring every work into judgment, with every secret thing, whether it be good, or whether it be evil. (Ecclesiastes 12:14)** Nothing, not even the smallest detail, will escape His scrutiny. **For the ways of man are before the eyes of the LORD, and he pondereth all his goings. (Proverbs 5:21)** God knows everything about us, every detail, every thought, every word, every work, every secret. Every sin will be revealed and judged when man stands before God.

Second, the truth of the **_Saviour's Word_**. The standard of judgment is the same for all men. There is no evasion of truth. The Bible will be at every sinner's judgment. The very Bible that God gave to man to instruct him, will be opened to convict and damn him. All sixty-six books will be there to testify of every man's sin. **In the day when God shall judge the secrets of men by Jesus Christ according to my gospel. (Romans 2:16)** Jesus said, **He that rejecteth me, and receiveth not my words, hath one that judgeth him: the word that I have spoken, the same shall judge him in the last day. (John 12:48)** Sinful man runs from the word of God all of his life only to face it on the judgment day.

THERE WILL BE NO ESCAPE

And thinkest thou this, O man, that judgest them which do such things, and doest the same, that thou shalt escape the judgment of God? (Romans 2:3) There is no excuse that can be offered, neither will there be any escape. God's judgment is certain. Both, the heathen and the self-righteous man has experienced the **goodness and forbearance and longsuffering** of God. But how was God's grace received? It wasn't received, it was despised. **Or despisest thou the riches of his goodness and forbearance and longsuffering; not knowing that the goodness of God leadeth thee to repentance? (Romans 2:4)** The word **despisest** means *to make of no account, to regard as nothing, to despise utterly, to treat with contempt.* The heathen despised the **goodness and forbearance and longsuffering** of God by saying I don't want it, I want my sin instead. The self-righteous man despised the **goodness and forbearance and longsuffering** of God by saying *I don't need that, I am OK.*

Paul said, **not knowing that the goodness of God leadeth thee to repentance?** God's goodness and forbearance and longsuffering should lead men to repentance. When they realize how wonderful He is, they ought to run to Him seeking His forgiveness. Instead many despise Him.

But after thy hardness and impenitent heart treasurest up unto thyself wrath against the day of wrath and revelation of the righteous judgment of God. (Romans 2:5) Notice the word **impenitent,** speaking of their refusal to repent. Prideful and stubborn man despises God's grace until finally his heart is hardened beyond repentance. **He, that being often reproved hardeneth his neck, shall suddenly be destroyed, and that without remedy. (Proverbs 29:1)** This illustration of hardening the neck is taken from the stubborn ox that turns away from and stiffens his neck to avoid surrendering to the yoke. This aptly pictures stubborn men who continually refuse to heed God's word and repent. When the time of judgment comes there will be no <u>Excuse</u>, there will be no <u>Escape</u> and …

THERE WILL BE NO EXONERATION

Sadly, for this crowd the day of mercy and pardon will be long passed. The only option will be to face the Judge and accept the sentence. There are three characteristics of this judgment.

<u>It will be Fair in its Character</u>

Who will render to every man according to his deeds. (Romans 2:6) Lost man at the judgment of God will get exactly what he has coming. Paul gives two examples of man's deeds.

First, the **_Continuing Saint_**. **To them who by patient continuance in well doing seek for glory and honour and immortality, eternal life. (Romans 2:7)** The word **continuance** means *"a cheerful and hopeful endurance."* Here is a group of people who continue in the things of God cheerfully. This describes those who have trusted Christ and are saved.

Second, the **_Contentious Sinner_**. **But unto them that are contentious, and do not obey the truth, but obey unrighteousness, indignation and wrath. (Romans 2:8)** This is a different crowd Paul says is **contentious, and do not obey the truth.** The word **contentious** speaks of wrangling and disputing. This is the man who, instead of receiving the truth, he contends against it. They are servants of self and want their own way, therefore they argue and wrangle against God's requirements.

This speaks of two different reactions to God. Man will react to God's grace in one of two ways—he will either **Repent** or He will **Rebel**. Therefore, there are two different results. For the man who Rebels there is **tribulation and anguish. (Romans 2:9)** For the man who Repents there is **glory, honour, and peace. (Romans 2:10)** Man reaps what he sows.

Paul is not teaching works salvation. We know that man is not saved by doing good. The Bible is clear that, **by the deeds of the law there shall no flesh be justified in his sight. (Romans 3:20)** No one will escape the wrath of God because of Good deeds. However, deeds reflect character. The saved man, because he has the power of the Holy Spirit will seek to continue in well doing. When he sins, the Holy Spirit convicts and he repents, bringing his life back in line with God's word. The self-serving contentious man rebels and contends against God's conviction. One repents, one rebels and each will be judged accordingly. **For there is no respect of persons with God**. (Romans 2:11) God's judgment will be **Fair in its Character**.

It will be Full in its Coverage

God is always just and fair in His judgment. He will judge man based on the knowledge he has.

First, those with the Law will be ***Judged By The Law***. **For as many as have sinned without law shall also perish without law: and as many as have sinned in the law shall be judged by the law; For not the hearers of the law are just before God, but the doers of the law shall be justified**. (Romans 2:12-13) The man who has heard the law of God will be judged according to the law. America is full of people who know right from wrong, yet refuse to submit to God. They live on in their sin enjoying its pleasures for a season. They know it is wrong, but they snub God and do as they will. One day they will stand before the One they snubbed and **It is a fearful thing to fall into the hands of the living God**. (Hebrews 10:31)

Second, those without the Law will be ***Judged By The Light***. **For when the Gentiles, which have not the law, do by nature the things contained in the law, these, having not the law, are a law unto themselves: Which shew the work of the law written in their hearts, their conscience also bearing witness, and their thoughts the mean while accusing or else excusing one another;** (Romans 2:14-15) People often ask, What about the heathen who has never heard the gospel? Is he lost? Of course He is lost. God will be fair in His judgment, but no one goes to Heaven without a personal relationship with Jesus Christ. God will be perfectly fair and judge him according to the light that he has—his conscience. J. Vernon McGee said, "*Some folk think because the heathen do not have the revelation of God that they will escape God's judgment. But the fact is that they are not living up to the light they have. God will judge them on that basis.*" God's judgment will be **Fair in its Character**, it will be **Full in its Coverage**.

It will be Fierce in its Condemnation

In the day when God shall judge the secrets of men by Jesus Christ according to my gospel. (Romans 2:16) That is one of the most frightening thoughts imaginable. **I the LORD search the heart, I try the reins, even to give every man according to his ways, and according to the fruit of his doings. (Jeremiah 17:10)** The God Who knows the heart and works of all men will search and try them. Daniel Webster, in answer to the question: "*What is the greatest thought that ever entered your mind?*" said, at once, "*My responsibility to my Maker!*"

Judgment Of The Religious Man
Romans 2:17-29

In chapter one the **Heathen** is shown to be without excuse. In the first part of chapter two the **Hypocrite** is dealt with and proven to be inexcusable. Now Paul comes to the **Hebrews** and they are also found to be lost and without excuse.

HIS PRIVILEGES EXAMINED

The Jews were a people of great privilege. They were the apple of God's eye. They were His chosen people. The entire history of Israel is one of a unique and privileged relationship with God. No other nation had been called the people of God as were the Jews. Paul examines the blessed privileges of the Hebrew and shows that even the religious man is lost if he doesn't know Christ.

Their Hebrew Pedigree

Behold, thou art called a Jew... (Romans 2:17a) The Jews took great pride in the fact that they were children of Abraham. Jesus rebuked the Jews for making their empty boast. **Then said Jesus to those Jews which believed on him, If ye continue in my word, then are ye my disciples indeed; And ye shall know the truth, and the truth shall make you free. (John 8:31-32)** When the Jewish leaders heard those words, they were greatly offended and snapped back, **We be Abraham's seed, and were never in bondage to any man: how sayest thou, Ye shall be made free? (John**

8:33) So Jesus brought it down to their everyday life. **Jesus answered them, Verily, verily, I say unto you, Whosoever committeth sin is the servant of sin. (John 8:34)** Were they descendents of Abraham? Yes. But were they children of God? No. The Saviour went on to explain to them who was really their father.

> **Jesus said unto them, If God were your Father, ye would love me: for I proceeded forth and came from God; neither came I of myself, but he sent me. Why do ye not understand my speech? even because ye cannot hear my word Ye are of your father the devil, and the lusts of your father ye will do. He was a murderer from the beginning, and abode not in the truth, because there is no truth in him. When he speaketh a lie, he speaketh of his own: for he is a liar, and the father of it. (John 8:42-44)**

Being Abraham's physical descendants did not make them his spiritual descendants.

... and makest thy boast of God. (Romans 2:17c) The Jews were a high and haughty bunch. The word **boast** means *"to glory, to feel proud."* Their boast was that they were God's chosen people. But it was just that—an empty boast. There was no substance to it. The Jews thought that they were guaranteed a place in Heaven based on their covenantal ties with God (Genesis 12:3). However, Paul argues that being a Jew does not make them just before God.

Their Holy Principle

Paul says, **and restest in the law. (Romans 2:17b)** The Jews believed that because the law had been revealed to them they had some sort of special standing with God. The trouble is, they had the law but they didn't honor it. Jesus spoke of this when He said, **This people draweth nigh unto me with their mouth, and honoureth me with their lips; but their heart is far from me. (Matthew 15:8)**

Had the Jews honored the law they would have accepted Christ as their Messiah. Paul said, **Wherefore the law was our schoolmaster to bring us unto Christ, that we might be justified by faith. (Galatians 3:24) Anyone who will truly follow the law will be led to Christ.**

Their Heavenly Purpose

And knowest his will, and approvest the things that are more excellent, being instructed out of the law. (Romans 2:18) The foolish pagans bowed down to gods of wood and stone, but the Jew knew the revealed will of God. They had an awareness of what God expected of them.

Their High Privilege

And art confident that thou thyself art a guide of the blind, a light of them which are in darkness, An instructor of the foolish, a teacher of babes, which hast the form of knowledge and of the truth in the law. (Romans 2:19-20) Here is another failure on the Jew's part. They were **confident** that they were the spiritual elite. They considered themselves the cream of the crop. They were the ones who could set everyone else strait. The trouble was, they weren't living up to their lips. Because they had been given so much, they were not only responsible for themselves, but for others also. However, their unfaithfulness to God and disobedience to His Word disqualified them as examples and teachers to the Gentiles.

HIS PRACTICES EXPOSED

Thou therefore which teachest another, teachest thou not thyself? (Romans 2:21a) These Jews were good at telling everyone else how to live, but they had failed in living up to their own preaching. They boasted of a superior standing with God, but consistently broke the very law they gloried in. Paul points out the example and the effect of such a lifestyle.

The Example of their Living

It is always tragic when our life does not match our profession. Paul reaches into their everyday life an gives three examples of their inconsistent lifestyle.

First, ***the Example of Stealing.*** Paul says **thou that preachest a man should not steal, dost thou steal? (Romans 2:21b)** This is an interesting one to start with. Throughout the ancient world, the Jew was looked upon as a thief. He used every method he could to get a few extra pennies from his customers. The Jew was known for being sneaky and shrewd in his business practices. This got them in trouble with God **He is a merchant, the balances of deceit are in his hand: he loveth to oppress. (Hosea 12:7)** The Jews of the Old Testament wouldn't dare go out and steal something. The law was clear. **Thou shalt not steal. (Exodus 20:15)** However, they were like a lot of folks today. They would get dishonest gain in their business dealings and shrug it off as *"I'm just making a living."* Paul points out that while they taught others not to steal, they themselves were crooks.

Second, **_the Example of Adultery_**. **Thou that sayest a man should not commit adultery, dost thou commit adultery? (Romans 2:22a)** Paul really hits them where they were living. A large number of Jewish men were living in adultery. It was common for a Jewish man to divorce his wife simply because he was tired of her or he wanted another woman. This was his way of manipulating the law and maneuvering around his responsibility to be faithful to his wife. However, Jesus made it clear that divorce for any ole reason was unacceptable. **But I say unto you, That whosoever shall put away his wife, saving for the cause of fornication, causeth her to commit adultery: and whosoever shall marry her that is divorced committeth adultery. (Matthew 5:32)** He repeated this same teaching later. **And I say unto you, Whosoever shall put away his wife, except it be for fornication, and shall marry another, committeth adultery: and whoso marrieth her which is put away doth commit adultery. (Matthew 19:9)** Jesus made it clear that a marriage can end in divorce and the innocent party be free only if it is on the basis of sexual immorality. So then, all of these guys who divorced their wives because they were tired of them or for any other unscriptural reason, were living in adultery. To add problems to their mess, Jesus had said that, **whosoever looketh on a woman to lust after her hath committed adultery with her already in his heart. (Matthew 5:28)** These puffed up Jews must have been deflated by this point.

Third, **_the Example of Idolatry_**. Paul says, … **thou that abhorrest idols, dost thou commit sacrilege? (Romans**

2:22) We think of idols as statues or false gods and that is true. However, it goes much further than that. An idol is anything that takes the place of God in your life. It could be your work, food, books, education, possessions, television, or fashion. Your family can be an idol. The bottom line is, anything that squeezes God out of first place in your life is an idol. Paul basically said, *"You won't go down to the pagan temple and worship false gods, but what do you do with your tithes and offerings."* Paul asked, **dost thou commit sacrilege?** The word **sacrilege** carries the idea of, *"taking for one's own private use what is consecrated to God."* This wicked practice was a major sin of the Jew. **Will a man rob God? Yet ye have robbed me. But ye say, Wherein have we robbed thee? In tithes and offerings. Ye are cursed with a curse: for ye have robbed me, even this whole nation. (Malachi 3:8-9)** These religious Jews abhorred idolatry, but they committed the worst kind of idolatry. They became their own gods. They put themselves above God by robbing Him and using His tithes and offerings for their own purposes.

The Effect On The Lost

Thou that makest thy boast of the law, through breaking the law dishonourest thou God? For the name of God is blasphemed among the Gentiles through you, as it is written. (Romans 2:23-24) What a tragedy! When we fail to live up to our profession we help send others to Hell. These religious Jews proudly boasted an exclusive relationship with God, but they failed to reflect His purity, goodness and compassion in their lives. The God of the Jews meant nothing to the Gentile world because of what it saw in those who claimed to be His people. Instead of embracing the God of Heaven, the world blasphemed Him. Jesus said, **But woe unto you, scribes and Pharisees, hypocrites! for ye shut up the kingdom of heaven against men: for ye neither go in yourselves, neither suffer ye them that are entering to go in. Woe unto you, scribes and Pharisees, hypocrites! for ye devour widows' houses, and for a pretence make long prayer: therefore ye shall receive the greater damnation. Woe unto you, scribes and Pharisees, hypocrites! for ye compass sea and land to make one proselyte, and when he is made, ye make him twofold more the child of hell than yourselves. (Matthew 23:13-15)** These people who were so privileged were not only going to Hell themselves, they were taking the world with them. What a reproach to the dear name of God. Their very lives contradicted their profession. The world can spot a fake and they see enough of it. The lost want nothing to do with a religion that has no power in the lives of those who profess it.

HIS POSITION EXPLAINED

Paul deals with another matter that was very important to the Jew—circumcision. The Jews connected circumcision with salvation. God had instituted circumcision as a mark of His covenant with Abraham and his descendants. **This is my covenant, which ye shall keep, between me and you and thy seed after thee; Every man child among you shall be circumcised And ye shall circumcise the flesh of your foreskin; and it shall be a token of the covenant betwixt me and you. And he that is eight days old shall be circumcised among you, every man child in your generations, he that is born in the house, or bought with money of any stranger, which is not of thy seed. (Genesis 17:10-12)** The Jews prided themselves in the rite of circumcision. Paul says, **For circumcision verily profiteth, if thou keep the law: but if thou be a breaker of the law, thy circumcision is made uncircumcision. (Romans 2:25)** Paul points out that circumcision is only profitable if the Jew keeps the Law. If the Law is broken, the external symbol becomes worthless.

But he is a Jew, which is one inwardly; and circumcision is that of the heart, in the spirit, and not in the letter; whose praise is not of men, but of God. (Romans 2:29) Paul explains that circumcision was a symbol of what had happened inside of a man. The Jews had missed their relationship with God and let the ceremony itself become their religion.

The Verdict Is In
Romans 3:1-19

In chapter one God dealt with the **Heathen** and proved him to be without excuse. In the first part of chapter two the **Hypocrite** is dealt with and proven to be inexcusable. In the last part of chapter two Paul confronted the **Hebrews** and they are also found to be lost and without excuse. Now in chapter three he lumps all **Humanity** together and proves their lost condition apart from Christ.

THEIR COMPLAINT IS ANSWERED

As noted these chapters present a courtroom scene. God the Judge is upon His throne and all the world has been summoned to court. The charges have been clearly stated—all are sinners. Before the case is closed however, the Jews raised four objections. Paul answers these objections.

The First Objection: **What advantage then hath the Jew? or what profit is there of circumcision? (Romans 3:1)** Back at the end of chapter two Paul made the point that circumcision is inward, and not outward. It is not a ritual of the flesh, but the righteousness of the heart that God is looking for. Their argument is that if both Jews and Gentiles are lost sinners, then what is the advantage of being a Jew?

The Answer: **Much every way: chiefly, because that unto them were committed the oracles of God. (Romans 3:2)** The word **oracles** speaks of the supernatural utterances of God. The word God word was committed to the Jew. The word **committed** comes from *"pisteuo"* and means *"to committ, put in trust with, to entrusted."* The Jews were to be the custodians of God's Word (Deuteronomy 4:7-8, Psalm 147:19-20). Paul's argument is that the Jews have enjoyed a tremendous advantage because they had the word of God and that was the greatest advantage of all.

The Second Objection: **For what if some did not believe? shall their unbelief make the faith of God without effect? (Romans 3:3)** The argument here is that since some have failed does that mean that God has cast away the entire Jewish nation? In essence what they are asking is, Will Jewish unbelief cancel out the faithfulness of God?

The Answer: **God forbid: yea, let God be true, but every man a liar; as it is written, That thou mightest be justified in thy sayings, and mightest overcome when thou art judged. (Romans 3:4)** This is a strong and emphatic answer. The phrase **God forbid** is the strongest negative Greek expression and carries the idea of an absolute impossibility. The fact is that no one will ever be able to charge God with being unfaithful. If there is any untruth, it is on man's side.

The Third Objection: **But if our unrighteousness commend the righteousness of God, what shall we say? Is God unrighteous who taketh vengeance? I speak as a man. (Romans 3:5)** This is a clever but unreasonable argument. **But if our unrighteousness commend the righteousness of God.** Their argument is that their disobedience gives God an opportunity to show his righteousness. Therefore, their sin was really a good thing. Talk about Scripture twisting!

The Answer: **God forbid: for then how shall God judge the world? (Romans 3:6)** Paul's answer is an emphatic no! God is the judge of all the world. For God to be just, He must punish sin. God will judge all the lost justly.

The Fourth Objection: **For if the truth of God hath more abounded through my lie unto his glory; why yet am I also judged as a sinner? (Romans 3:7)** Here the claim is made that the truth of God is exalted when contrasted to man's lies. Again, they are trying to justify their sins on the basis that God is glorified through the forgiveness of sin.

The Answer: **And not rather, as we be slanderously reported, and as some affirm that we say, Let us do evil, that good may come? whose damnation is just. (Romans 3:8)** Paul branded as slanderous the reports that he advocated such a position that good comes from doing evil. Paul concludes that those who were spreading such lies were deserving of the damnation they had coming.

THEIR CONDITION IS AFFIRMED

What then? are we better than they? No, in no wise: for we have before proved both Jews and Gentiles, that they are all under sin. (Romans 3:9) Both Jew and Gentile come under the same heading. Paul declares that *"We are no better than they."* We are all lost. **As it is written, There is none righteous, no, not one. (Romans 3:10)** None of us are anything but sinners in the sight of God, and to make it worse we don't even understand nor do we seek after God.

THEIR CONDUCT IS ASSESSED

Paul continues the indictment with more evidence. He assesses their conduct and it to further prove their lost condition before God. The case is summed up.

They are all gone out of the way. (Romans 3:12a) This phrase carries the idea of *leaning the wrong way*. The idea is that we do not stay on the right path. Our tendency is to wander astray. This phrase was used in the military to describe someone who went AWOL.

Paul says, **they are together become unprofitable. (Romans 3:12b)** The word **unprofitable** is an interesting word. It comes from the Greek *"achreioo"* and means *"to spoil, render useless, to become unprofitable."* It was used to describe food that had soured or meat that had spoiled. It speaks of an irreversible process. Man is so far gone, that in his unregenerate state, he is not profitable to God. What an apt description of man's depravity.

Next, **there is none that doeth good, no, not one. (Romans 3:12c)** This is a blow to man's pride. Most men would claim that they are all bad. Surely we can find some good things about people if we look for them. God says, no you cannot. The truth of the matter is, the best man can produce apart from God is nothing more than filthy rags. **But we are all as an unclean thing, and all our righteousnesses are as filthy rags; and we all do fade as a leaf; and our iniquities, like the wind, have taken us away. (Isaiah 64:6)**

Their throat is an open sepulcher. (Romans 3:13a) The grave is a place of corruption and stench. Imagine coming upon an open grave with the smell of a rotting corpse rising up into your face. This is what man's throat is compared to.

With their tongues they have used deceit. (Romans 3:13b) Deceit comes from a word that carries the idea of *luring with bait.* It means to mislead someone by making him believe something that's not true. Men constantly deceive by using flattery, smooth words and lies.

Next Paul says, **the poison of asps is under their lips. (Romans 3:13c)** The asp is a snake whose poison is contained in a small sac at the base of the tongue. The tongue is seen as a serpent that strikes at and poisons everything in sight. James says that the tongue is **an unruly evil, full of deadly poison (James 3:8)**

Whose mouth is full of cursing and bitterness. (Romans 3:14) Cursing speaks of blasphemous language. Just listen to people talk and you will understand what Paul was saying. The vile everyday language that is commonly used in America today is a disgrace.

Not only is the mouth full of cursing, it is also full of **bitterness.** Bitterness is self pitying, suppressed anger that stews and smolders deep down inside a person and eventually that sours the whole life. Such a person is so poisoned inside that every time he opens his mouth bitterness spews forth.

Their feet are swift to shed blood. **(Romans 3:15)** Man in our day has little or no respect for life. Think about it. The first child born into this world murdered his own brother. Things haven't gotten any better.

Destruction and misery are in their ways. (Romans 3:16) Man left to himself is miserable and destructive. He never really improves things. He make it worse.

And the way of peace have they not known. (Romans 3:17) We hear a lot about peace today, but there has never been more war. **For when they shall say, Peace and safety; then sudden destruction cometh upon them, as travail upon a woman with child; and they shall not escape. (1 Thessalonians 5:3)**

There is no fear of God before their eyes. (Romans 3:18) Here is the root problem. There is no fear of God. Solomon said, **The fear of the LORD is the beginning of knowledge: but fools despise wisdom and instruction. (Proverbs 1:7)** Webster defines fear as, *"an unpleasant often strong emotion caused by anticipation or awareness of danger."* The word fear in relation to God also carries the idea of *"reverence, awe, great respect."* Genuine fear of the Lord is always seen in obedience to the Word of God. The reason there is so much sin and wickedness is due to man's lack of reverence and awe of God. The world as a whole has no respect whatsoever for God. They ridicule His existence. They mock at the thought of judgment and puny man shakes his fist at Heaven with no fear of God's wrath. But it is not over. Those who are so bold as to mock God will someday shutter before Him. The Bible says, **It is a fearful thing to fall into the hands of the living God. (Hebrews 10:31)**

THEIR CASE IS ADJOURNED

Now we know that what things soever the law saith, it saith to them who are under the law: that every mouth may be stopped, and all the world may become guilty before God Therefore by the deeds of the law there shall no flesh be justified in his sight: for by the law is the knowledge of sin. (Romans 3:19-20) The whole world has been indicted, the evidence has been presented, the arguments heard and the judgment has been handed down. The whole world, regardless of color, creed or class is guilty. Man now knows that he is a sinner and he has no excuse for his sin. He is lost and on his way to Hell and there is nothing he can do about it.

Hope For The Hopeless
Romans 3:21-31

Up to this point, we have clearly seen the fact that man is lost. The heathen, the Jew and the Gentile are in the same fix. All are by nature depraved and guilty before God. If there is going to be any hope for him it must come from God. Paul now turns to the good news.

The words **But now** introduce God's answer to our dilemma. Those are words of grace! Paul has taken us to the depth of depravity and shown us what miserable and hopeless sinners we are. Praise God, He does not leave us in the pit. With the words **but now**, new hope breaks onto the scene. God has provided a Saviour and through Him He will impute to us righteousness.

THE TESTIMONY OF OUR SITUATION

But now the righteousness of God without the law is manifested... (Romans 3:21a) Paul points out that there is a righteousness apart from the law. He declares that righteousness doesn't come by **Behaving**, but by **Believing**. This is imputed righteousness and it is obtained by faith in the finished work of Christ. Paul refers to it as the **righteousness of God without the law.** The Law only reveals the righteousness of God. **Wherefore the law is holy, and the commandment holy, and just, and good. (Romans 7:12)** The law revealed the righteousness of God and made known God's righteous requirements for man. Paul pointed this out earlier, **for by the law is the knowledge of sin. (Romans**

3:20) The law cannot save. It only points out man's sinfulness and condemns him.

This would be hard for a Jew to swallow, but Paul says that this truth was, ...**witnessed by the law and the prophets; Even the righteousness of God which is by faith of Jesus Christ unto all and upon all them that believe: for there is no difference. (Romans 3:21b-22)** Paul points out that Jews have no argument because their Old Testament and their Prophets declared this truth. The law and the Prophets spoke of the Messiah that would come. Beginning with the first prophecy of the Messiah in (Genesis 3:15), and continuing throughout the Old Testament was the teaching of salvation by faith in Christ. Such passages as (Psalm 22) and (Isaiah 53) spoke clearly of Christ's sacrifice for lost man. His redemptive work in seen in the types and offerings of Scripture. This is why Jesus could say, **Search the scriptures; for in them ye think ye have eternal life: and they are they which testify of me. (John 5:39)**

THE TRAGEDY OF OUR SIN

For all have sinned, and come short of the glory of God. (Romans 3:23) Everything Paul has said about man's sinfulness and depravity is driven home in this one verse. Man is lost and he does not even seek God and if he did he couldn't get to Him. Isaiah said it this way: **But we are all as an unclean thing, and all our righteousnesses are as filthy rags; and we all do fade as a leaf; and our iniquities, like the wind, have taken us away. (Isaiah 64:6)** Oh how familiar are these verses and how real their message. **All have sinned and come short...** Notice the tenses here. The **all**

have sinned is past tense while **come short** is present tense. Sinners is what we are and the consequences are continual. We are sinners and we will always come short of the glory of God. The Pharisees tried to and failed. Jesus said, **For I say unto you, That except your righteousness shall exceed the righteousness of the scribes and Pharisees, ye shall in no case enter into the kingdom of heaven. (Matthew 5:20)** The Bible is clear that God demands perfect righteousness and He will not settle for anything less. His justice demands it. To **come short** means to *"come behind, be destitute, fail, lack, suffer need, be in want, be the worse."* In other words, no matter how much work and effort we put into it we will never meet God's standard of perfect righteousness. We will always come behind.

THE TREASURE OF OUR STANDING

It is an amazing truth that sinners can stand justified before God. We are sinful creatures. Even God's people, redeemed and saved by the blood, still have to battle the flesh and pursue holiness. But so far as our stand, God sees us as just as if we never sinned.

The Position Of The Saint

Being justified… (Romans 3:24a) The word **justified** means *"to be declared righteous."* Noah Webster defines justification as meaning *"to pardon and clear form guilt; to absolve or acquit from guilt and merited punishment, and to accept as righteous on account of the merits of the Savior, or by the application of Christ's atonement to the offender."* Justification is the act of God whereby He declares the forgiven sinner to be righteous. What a precious truth. There is no area of the believer's life that justification has not dealt with.

> **But he, whom God raised again, saw no corruption. Be it known unto you therefore, men and brethren, that through this man is preached unto you the forgiveness of sins: And by him all that believe are justified from all things, from which ye could not be justified by the law of Moses. (Acts 13:37-39)**

Yes! We are justified from all things by the precious blood of Christ. To be justified is to stand before God just as if we had never sinned. Please get a hold of this truth. Justification before God is far more than forgiveness. If your son goes throws a ball through your window and breaks it, you can forgive him, but he is still guilty. No amount of forgiveness can change the fact that he broke the window. In other words, you can forgive him, but you can't justify him. When a sinner comes to Christ, God does both. He forgives and justifies. Forgiveness removes the penalty, but justification removes the guilt. Justification means that you are not merely a forgiven criminal, but that you are righteous.

> **But God commendeth his love toward us, in that, while we were yet sinners, Christ died for us. Much more then, being now justified by his blood, we shall be saved from wrath through him. (Romans 5:8-9)**

The Christian has been declared righteous by God Himself. By merit of Christ's blood the forgiven sinner is justified, and stands just as if he had never sinned. Paul asked the rhetorical question, **Who shall lay any thing to the charge of God's elect? It is God that justifieth. (Romans 8:33)** There is no charge that can be brought against the Christian—God has declared him innocent and justified.

The Price Of The Salvation

Our justification is given **freely by his grace. (Romans 3:24b)** The word **freely** here is a very important word that takes us beyond the power of money. We have heard it said that if a man has enough money he can buy anything. Well, that is not true. A few things are of great value and have no price attached to them—they are priceless. Our justification is like that—it is priceless. This word **freely** carries the idea of *without a cause.* Christ used this word when He said, **They hated me without a cause. (John 15:25)** Jesus Christ never did anything to deserve the hatred of men, yet they hated him *without a cause.* And, by the same token, although we, as sinners, never could deserve, or merit, justification, God has bestowed upon us **without a cause** by His grace. Not only was there no price that could be paid for it. But there was no work, no merit, no barter, no negotiation—nothing outside of God's grace was involved any way.

The Provision Of The Saviour

This provision was made **through the redemption that is in Christ Jesus: Whom God hath set forth** to **be a propitiation through faith in his blood Romans. (3:24c-25a)** There are two important words used here.

First, **the Payment was Offered**. The word **redemption** speaks volumes. To redeem means to pay a satisfactory price for a person or thing. The word was used in the Bible of purchasing a slave from the auction block. That slave was in bondage. He had nothing. He could not purchase his own freedom. He was bound to whoever paid the price for him. That is a picture of us. Mankind is helplessly bound by sin. He can do nothing to obtain freedom. He is a slave. The sinner himself cannot make a satisfactory payment for his sin. The curse of the law rests heavy upon us all—we were under the bondage of sin. **Cursed is every one that continueth not in all things which are written in the book of the law to do them. (Galatians 3:10)** How impossible it is for sinful and fallen man to obey the law of God. The curse was upon us all for **all have sinned and come short of the glory of God.** (Romans **3:23)** The debt of sin must be paid and we being sinners cannot pay the price. What a sad picture, but Christ stepped in and paid the redemptive price and redeemed us. The purchase price was His blood.

> **Forasmuch as ye know that ye were not redeemed with corruptible things, as silver and gold, from your vain conversation received by tradition from your fathers; But with the precious blood of Christ, as of a lamb without blemish and without spot. (1 Peter 1:18-19)**

Jesus Christ purchased redemption for man by paying the price demanded and satisfying the demands of the law.

Second, **Propitiation was the Outcome**. Our redemption is in ... **Christ Jesus: Whom God hath set forth to be a**

propitiation through faith in his blood. (Romans 3:25a) The word **propitiation** carries the idea of satisfaction. Noah Webster defines **propitiation** as: *"The act of appeasing wrath and conciliating the favor of an offended person; the act of making propitious."* Relating to salvation propitiation means that Christ met and satisfied the righteous demands of God. The same word is used for **propitiation** in (Romans 3:25) and for **mercyseat** in (Hebrews 9:5). This takes us back to the Tabernacle in the wilderness. The tabernacle was set in a courtyard 150 feet long and 75 feet wide—it was built according to the specific plans as given to Moses from God. In the court was the brazen altar for sacrificing and the laver where the priests cleansed themselves before entering into the presence of God. The sanctuary was in the court and was divided into two parts: the holy place and the holy of holies Most Holy Place. Two veils were hung, one in front of the holy of holies and the other was over the entrance into the holy place. Only the priests were allowed to enter into the holy place, the congregation had no access into it. Only the high priest could enter the holy of holies and that only once a year on the day of Atonement. For anyone else to attempt access it meant sudden and sure death.

In the holy of holies the central piece of furniture was the ark of the covenant (Exodus 25:10-22). The ark was an oblong chest measuring 45 x 27 x 27 inches. It was made of acacia wood and overlaid inside and out with gold. Inside the ark were the tables of the law and Aaron's rod that budded. The lid of the ark, made of solid gold, was called the mercy seat. It was on the lid of the ark, is the Mercy Seat, that the atoning blood was applied (Leviticus 16:14-15). It is the place where God met man. God said to Moses, **And there I will meet with thee, and I will commune with thee from above the mercy seat. (Exodus 25:22)** The only place where God could meet and hold communion with man has always been and always will be over the blood-sprinkled mercy seat. There is no other meeting place, just as there is no other atonement.

The law demands of every man perfect obedience, or death. Jesus Christ covered that demand and became the believer's Mercy Seat. As the High Priest, He entered into Heaven with His own blood satisfying the righteous demands of Almighty God. Jesus Christ is our Mercy Seat. He is our **propitiation.** Christ, as the Mercy seat, is the One who has covered the law, and satisfied all of its demands. What a Saviour!

The Passing Of Our Sentence

Paul says, **... to declare his righteousness for the remission of sins that are past, through the forbearance of God To declare, I say, at this time his righteousness: that he might be just, and the justifier of him which believeth in Jesus. (Romans 3:25b)** God being fully satisfied with Christ's payment for sin means that the sin debt is paid in full. God requires nothing else. When we come to Christ and trust Him as our Saviour he forgives us. The word **remission** means, *"to pass over."* In mercy God withheld His judgment. The idea here is not that God ignores our sin, but He passes over it because the payment has been made. It is a matter of **forbearance.**

To declare, I say, at this time his righteousness: that he might be just, and the justifier of him which believeth in Jesus. (Romans 3:26) Because sin was judged, and payment made, God is indeed just. Because Jesus took our place under the wrath of God, He is able to justify our sins through Jesus.

THE TRUTH OF OUR SALVATION

A long as man insists of making his way to Heaven by his works, he is lost and defeated by his sin. Man must come to the place that he realizes himself to be hopeless and helpless apart from Christ.

Pride Is Eliminated

Where is boasting then? It is excluded By what law? of works? Nay: but by the law of faith. Therefore we conclude that a man is justified by faith without the deeds of the law. (Romans 3:27-28) Our salvation and standing before God is not based on anything we have done. It is in no way of our own merits. We have nothing to brag about. In fact we ought to be shameful and repentant. This ought to eliminate our pride.

Prejudice Is Excluded

Is he the God of the Jews only? is he not also of the Gentiles? Yes, of the Gentiles also: Seeing it is one God, which shall justify the circumcision by faith, and uncircumcision through faith. (Romans 3:29-30) The Jews looked down with contempt upon the Gentile. They considered themselves to be the elite of God. The Jews could not say, "Our God is the God of the Jews only." God's justification is offered to whosever will. Any man, woman or child regardless of creed, color, or class—if they will turn from their sin and call upon Christ for salvation, God will forgive and such a one will stand before God forgiven and justified

Principle Is Established

Do we then make void the law through faith? God forbid: yea, we establish the law. (Romans 3:31) Salvation and justification by faith does not destroy the law, but establishes it. The gospel does not replace the law because the law was never a means of salvation. The law was given to show us God's perfect standards of holiness and to show us that those standards are impossible to satisfy. The law's purpose was teaching, not saving. **Wherefore the law was our schoolmaster to bring us unto Christ, that we might be justified by faith. (Galatians 3:24)** God makes it clear that the law saves no one. **Therefore by the deeds of the law there shall no flesh be justified in his sight: for by the law is the knowledge of sin. (Romans 3:19-20)** All you have to do is break one law and you're done. **For whosoever shall keep the whole law, and yet offend in one point, he is guilty of all. (James 2:10)** Justification and salvation by faith does not destroy the law, but establishes it because when a sinner sees his need of the Saviour and turns to Him for salvation, that is exactly what the law was meant to do— show man his need of a Saviour.

Two Old Testament Witnesses
Romans 4:1-12

Paul continues to offer argument after argument for the doctrine of justification by faith. He argues with the Jews based upon the lives of their own heroes.

THE TESTIMONY CONCERNING JUSTIFICATION

The Law required that all things be established by two or three witnesses. Therefore, Paul draws upon the lives of two Old Testament witnesses to prove that justification in the Old Testament was through faith.

The Testimony Of Abraham

What shall we say then that Abraham our father, as pertaining to the flesh, hath found? (Romans 4:1) Abraham was the physical father of the entire Jewish race. He was the Patriarch of the Patriarchs. There could be no greater or more influential witness than Abraham. **For if Abraham were justified by works, he hath whereof to glory; but not before God. (Romans 4:2)** Performance is the basis for boasting in oneself. If Abraham's works were the basis of his righteousness he would have grounds for boasting. He could brag about his accomplishments. Paul says, **but not before God**. Prideful man can work and boast all he wants to, but God still sees nothing good in him. Boasting is completely excluded from genuine salvation. **Where is boasting then? It is excluded By what law? of works? Nay: but by the law of faith. (Romans 3:27)** We are saved by grace, through faith, **Not of works, lest any man should boast. (Ephesians 2:9)**

The Jews pride in their law, ceremony and status had blinded them to the fact that the only way to be justified before God is by faith. The Bible is clear that **no flesh should glory in his presence. (1 Corinthians 1:29)** Sinful man has nothing of himself that he can boast about. We must brag on God **He that glorieth, let him glory in the Lord. (1 Corinthians 1:31)**

For what saith the scripture? Abraham believed God, and it was counted unto him for righteousness. (Romans 4:3) Paul drives his point home with a direct quote from the Old Testament (Genesis 15:6). This Scripture clearly teaches that Abraham was justified by faith. **He believed God** and that is how he was justified.

Now to him that worketh is the reward not reckoned of grace, but of debt. (Romans 4:4) Any plan of salvation that includes works destroys God's grace. The person who works expects a reward for his work. When you go out and work at your job, you expect a paycheck because you've earned it. When your employer gives you the paycheck there is no grace involved. You have earned the paycheck—it is rightfully yours. The employer is just paying a debt. The point Paul is making is, if works are involved in salvation God isn't giving you anything. If you earn your salvation God is simply a debtor paying His bill.

But to him that worketh not, but believeth on him that justifieth the ungodly, his faith is counted for righteousness. (Romans 4:5) The words **count, impute,** and **reckon** all come from the same word. This is a word that comes from the business and legal world that means *"to credit to an account."* I would be like going to the bank and depositing $ 10000. The bank applies that money to your account. So Abraham believed God, and God in effect got out His book and put it down to Abraham's account as righteousness. This is imputed righteousness. When we believe God and by faith trust in Christ, God takes out the book and credits Christ's righteousness to our account. **For he hath made him to be sin for us, who knew no sin; that we might be made the righteousness of God in him. (2 Corinthians 5:21)** That is how He saved Abraham and that is how He saves today.

The Testimony Of David

Even as David also describeth the blessedness of the man, unto whom God imputeth righteousness without works, Saying, Blessed are they whose iniquities are forgiven, and whose sins are covered Blessed is the man to whom the Lord will not impute sin. (Romans 4:6-8) David lived under the dispensation of law. How was he saved? By keeping God's law? No! Did he stay saved by keeping the law? Absolutely not! In fact, David was a law-breaker. He was an adulterer (2 Samuel 11). However, he was a saved man. David was saved the same way that Abraham was saved—by grace through faith.

David's testimony is taken from Psalms 32:1-2. **Blessed is he whose transgression is forgiven, whose sin is covered Blessed is the man unto whom the LORD imputeth not iniquity, and in whose spirit there is no guile. (Psalms 32:1-2)** This Psalm is most likely a companion to Psalm 51, in which David confesses his sin of adultery with Bathsheba. These verses show that David was justified freely without any works or merit of his own. Here in Psalm 32, David used three words to describe his sin. David used the same three words in Psalm 51:1-2. Let us look at these three words:

The first word used is **transgression. Transgression** is the overstepping of a line, going beyond the boundaries. It means to go beyond that which the law allows. For example, when the speed limit is 55 MPH, you go 65 MPH, you are transgressing the law.

Next, we have the word **sin.** Sin is *missing the mark.* **For all have sinned, and come short of the glory of God. (Romans 3:23)** The mark that God has set is perfect righteousness and we have all missed it. Sin is the failure to fulfill God's purpose. We always fall short.

Lastly, the word **iniquity.** Iniquity is the inborn tendency of human nature to sin. **Behold, I was shapen in iniquity; and in sin did my mother conceive me. (Psalms 51:5)** From birth we are depraved and sinful. We are bent toward sin. Sinners is what we are.

David was certainly a sinner and God's law condemned him. There was nothing that he could do to redeem himself. He had broken the law. The law condemned him and he was to die for his **transgression,** for his **sin,** and for his **iniquity.** God was his only help. David said, **Blessed is the man to whom the Lord will not impute sin. (Romans 4:8)** Remember that the word impute means *to credit to an account.* When David responded to Nathan's message and repented God forgave him. **And David said unto Nathan, I have sinned against the LORD And Nathan said unto David, The LORD also hath put away thy sin; thou shalt**

not die. (2 Samuel 12:13) God no longer imputed David's sin to his account. Instead God imputed righteousness to David Just like Abraham, David was saved by grace through faith.

Note that both of Paul's proof texts comes from the Old Testament. Salvation by grace through faith has always been God's method of saving and justifying the lost. Unfortunately, the ultra-dispensationalists teach that man was saved by works in the Old Testament and by grace in the New Testament. They make God a respecter of persons. Abraham lived before the law, David lived during the dispensation of law and both were saved by grace through faith. God's method of salvation has been the same in every age.

THE TIMING CONCERNING JUSTIFICATION

Cometh this blessedness then upon the circumcision only, or upon the uncircumcision also? for we say that faith was reckoned to Abraham for righteousness. (Romans 4:9) Paul anticipates another argument and, as it were, heads them off at the pass. It is true that Abraham was saved by faith before the law and David was saved by faith during the dispensation of the law. However, the Jews might argue both of them were circumcised which was the symbol of God's covenant with His chosen people (Genesis 17:9-14). Paul asks, **How was it then reckoned? when he was in circumcision, or in uncircumcision? Not in circumcision, but in uncircumcision. (Romans 4:10)** Paul is dealing with the timing of Abraham's circumcision in relation to his being declared righteous. In other words, when was Abraham counted righteousness? Before circumcision or upon being circumcised? This presents a big problem for the Jew.

And he received the sign of circumcision, a seal of the righteousness of the faith which he had yet being uncircumcised: that he might be the father of all them that believe, though they be not circumcised; that righteousness might be imputed unto them also. (Romans 4:11) Faith was credited to Abraham while he was yet uncircumcised. Righteousness was imputed to Abraham in (Genesis 15:6). However, he was not circumcised until (Genesis 17). Abraham had righteousness imputed to him fourteen years before he was circumcised. Paul concludes that circumcision had nothing whatsoever to do with the imputation of righteousness to Abraham. He was saved by grace.

Abraham: Saved By Faith
Romans 4:13-25

Paul now comes to another major point in this passage. He has just argued that Abraham was not justified by circumcision. Now Paul argues that man is not justified by keeping the Law. Paul contrasts the promise to Abraham with the Law.

THE CASE OF ABRAHAM'S FAITH

For the promise, that he should be the heir of the world, was not to Abraham, or to his seed, through the law, but through the righteousness of faith. (Romans 4:13) Paul is saying that God's promise to Abraham had no conditions attached to it. It was not **through the law, but through the righteousness of faith.** Paul wrote in Galatians, **And this I say, that the covenant, that was confirmed before of God in Christ, the law, which was four hundred and thirty years after, cannot disannul, that it should make the promise of none effect. (Galatians 3:17)** The Law came four hundred and thirty years after Abraham was made heir to the promise by faith. Therefore, the law could in no way have any bearing on Abraham's justification. To make the promise conditional on obedience to the Law, which was not in effect when the promise was given, would **disannul** the whole promise.

For if they which are of the law be heirs, faith is made void, and the promise made of none effect. (Romans 4:14) The word **void** means to *"be empty, void, of none effect."*

The Law voids the promise and makes it of none effect, because if we have to keep the Law to receive the promise, the promise will never be fulfilled. We can't keep the law. But Faith, on the other hand, is able to receive anything God promises.

Because the law worketh wrath: for where no law is, there is no transgression. (Romans 4:15) Paul simply states that the law **worketh wrath.** The law doesn't justify man, it condemns him and results in the wrath of God. **For whosoever shall keep the whole law, and yet offend in one point, he is guilty of all. (James 2:10)** Anyone who is trusting in the law to get to Heaven is in a hopeless situation.

THE CHARACTERISTICS OF ABRAHAM'S FAITH

The Principle of Abraham's Faith

Therefore it is of faith, that it might be by grace. (Romans 4:16a) Abraham's justification was of faith so that it could be by grace. The flesh works, but faith believes. We are powerless to keep the Law. The flesh cannot accomplish what God requires. Faith accepts the fact that salvation must come by the grace of God, or it will never happen. Grace is *"the unmerited favor of God to sinners."* Grace is God doing for us that which we cannot do for our self. When we come to Christ by faith we are saved by His grace.

The Promise of Abraham's Faith

Paul says, **to the end the promise might be sure to all the seed. (Romans 4:16b)** If the promise was dependent on

Abraham's works, it would have stopped there, for Abraham didn't kept the law. Because Abraham failed the promise would never had been handed down to his seed.

The Potential of Abraham's Faith

Paul says, **not to that only which is of the law, but to that also which is of the faith of Abraham; who is the father of us all, As it is written, I have made thee a father of many nations, (Romans 4:16c-17a)** The reach of salvation through faith extends far beyond the Jews. When God promised Abraham that he would be **a father of many nations. (Genesis 17:4)**, He wasn't just speaking of the Jewish peoples. These promises to Abraham go beyond the bloodline of Abraham and encompass all.

The Person of Abraham's Faith

Paul said, **before him whom he believed, even God, who quickeneth the dead, and calleth those things which be not as though they were. (Romans 4:17b)** Abraham's justification was entirely the work of God. Abraham's faith was in God's ability to what He had promised. Abraham lived the faith life just as we are to do today. No one is saved apart from faith. (Ephesians 2:8-9) Abraham's faith was in the coming Messiah. (Genesis 3:15) We vividly see his faith in the account of his offering Isaac on Moriah. **And Abraham said, My son, God will provide himself a lamb for a burnt offering: so they went both of them together. (Genesis 22:8)** There is more in Abraham's statement than just a lamb for Moriah that day. Mount Moriah was Abraham's Calvary. Abraham was speaking prophetically of the Lamb that would be smitten of God (Isaiah 53:4), to take away the sins of the world (John 1:29). Abraham saw ahead to the day, when God himself would become the lamb offered for man's sin. **By faith Abraham, when he was tried, offered up Isaac: and he that had received the promises offered up his only begotten son, Of whom it was said, That in Isaac shall thy seed be called: Accounting that God was able to raise him up, even from the dead; from whence also he received him in a figure. (Hebrews 11:17-19)** Abraham did not go up on Moriah that day expecting God to provide a lamb to sacrifice in place of Isaac. He fully expected to sacrifice Isaac and God raise him from the dead. That is what Jesus was talking about when He said to the Jews, **Your father Abraham rejoiced to see my day: and he saw it, and was glad. (John 8:56)** Abraham's faith was in the Lamb of God—Jesus Christ the Saviour.

THE CONQUEST OF ABRAHAM'S FAITH

Abraham had a victorious faith. He believed and persevered when many would have given up.

Abraham's Faith Conquered Impossibility

Who against hope believed in hope, that he might become the father of many nations, according to that which was spoken, So shall thy seed be. (Romans 4:18) By faith Abraham had hope when there was no human reason to hope. If Abraham were to look at Sarah and look at his situation and circumstances, he would have no choice but to say, This is a hopeless situation. Every circumstance was totally against the promise of a son and there was no way the flesh could produce it. There was nothing he could do to bring about a child of himself and Sarah. However, Abraham looked at Almighty God and by faith rested in God's sure promise. He knew that God could perform that which He had promised. Jesus said, **The things which are impossible with men are possible with God. (Luke 18:27)** Abraham was looking in the right place.

Abraham's Faith Conquered Inadequacy

And being not weak in faith, he considered not his own body now dead, when he was about an hundred years old, neither yet the deadness of Sara's womb. (Romans 4:19) At an age when everyone knew that child bearing was long over, Abraham believed that he and Sarah would have a child because God said so. Where most would have failed Abraham had faith. Notice that the words **dead** and **deadness** are used to speak of Abraham and Sarah's ability to conceive. Abraham was powerless but it did not diminish his faith because he served the all-powerful God of Heaven. He served the God who created man. Such a God would certainly have no problem in fulfilling His promise.

Abraham's Faith Conquered Inconsistency

He staggered not at the promise of God through unbelief; but was strong in faith, giving glory to God. (Romans 4:20) Inconsistency is an awful thing. One minute we believe, the next we are wondering if God can get the job done. Abraham **staggered not at the promise of God through unbelief.** That means that he did not waver in his faith. He did not bounce back and forth between believing

God and not believing God. His faith had staying power. Abraham stayed the course.

Abraham's Faith Conquered Infidelity

And being fully persuaded that, what he had promised, he was able also to perform. (Romans 4:21) Notice it says that Abraham was **fully persuaded**. There was no doubt that God would do what He said. **And therefore it was imputed to him for righteousness. (Romans 4:22)**

THE CONCLUSION OF ABRAHAM'S FAITH

Now it was not written for his sake alone, that it was imputed to him; But for us also, to whom it shall be imputed, if we believe on him that raised up Jesus our Lord from the dead; Who was delivered for our offences, and was raised again for our justification. (Romans 4:23-25) The account of Abraham's justification **was not written for his sake alone.** Paul brings the whole message home to the Church. The promise is also for us **to whom it shall be imputed, if we believe on him that raised up Jesus our Lord from the dead**. The promise boils down to one Person—the Lord Jesus Christ. All that Abraham had was a promise. But that promise was anchored to the infallible word of the unchanging God. We are saved the same way Abraham was. We too are justified when we put our faith in the risen Saviour.

The Benefits Of Our New Standing
Romans 5:1-11

Up to now Paul had dealt largely with man's depravity and need for salvation. We have clearly seen his sinful state and the fact that he abides under the wrath of God. Chapter five begins a new section where Paul begins to point out several benefits of our salvation.

A PEACE FOR OUR SITUATION

Therefore being justified by faith, we have peace with God through our Lord Jesus Christ. (Romans 5:1) Paul declares that because we are justified **we have peace with God.** Lost man is at war with God. He is an enemy of God and resides under condemnation. Jesus said, **he that believeth not is condemned already, because he hath not believed in the name of the only begotten Son of God.** **(John 3:18)** Just a few verses later He said, **he that believeth not the Son shall not see life; but the wrath of God abideth on him. (John 3:36)** What an awful state of enmity that once existed between me and God.

- God's wrath was against me. **For the wrath of God is revealed from heaven against all ungodliness and unrighteousness of men, who hold the truth in unrighteousness. (Romans 1:18)**

- God's judgment was against me. **But we are sure that the judgment of God is according to truth against them which commit such things. (Romans 2:2)**

- God was constantly angry with me. **God is angry with the wicked every day. (Psalms 7:11)**

- Anything good and religious that I tried to do was unacceptable to God. **The sacrifice of the wicked is an abomination to the LORD. (Proverbs 15:8)**

- I could not please Him. **So then they that are in the flesh cannot please God. (Romans 8:8)**

Yes, I was God's enemy because I was wicked. (Romans 5:10, Colossians 1:21). The Bible says, **There is no peace, saith the LORD, unto the wicked. (Isaiah 48:22)** However, as a result of salvation the believer is no longer at enmity with God. The war is over and **we have peace with God through our Lord Jesus Christ.** Peace with God comes with salvation and is the result of the shed blood of Christ and His reconciling work on the cross. **And, having made peace through the blood of his cross, by him to reconcile all things unto himself; by him, I say, whether they be things in earth, or things in heaven. And you, that were sometime alienated and enemies in your mind by wicked works, yet now hath he reconciled. (Colossians 1:20-21)** No longer is God against me, He is for me. Paul said, **If God be for us, who can be against us? (Romans 8:31)** Like David, we can say **The LORD is on my side... (Psalms 118:6)**

A POSITION FOR OUR STANDING

By whom also we have access by faith into this grace wherein we stand, and rejoice in hope of the glory of God. (Romans 5:2) As believers we have a new standing in Jesus Christ. This standing is attained not by any work or ritual of our own but simply through the grace of God. Notice three facts concerning our standing.

Our Provider

The **by whom** refers to Jesus Christ. It is through our Lord Jesus Christ that we **have access by faith into this grace wherein we stand**. Although faith is necessary for salvation, it is Jesus Christ and His grace, not the believer's faith, that has the power to save and to keep saved. We have **access by faith into this grace** because we have been pardoned from our sins. The word **access** comes from *"prosagogueay"* and means a *"leading or bringing into the presence of."* It carries the idea of being lead into the presence of and being presented to the King. At the court of a king in Bible days there was an official called the Prosagogeus. He could either grant or deny access to the king. He decided who would be admitted into the king's presence. In other words he held the power of access to the king's presence. For the sinner Jesus Christ is the Prosagogeus. He alone holds the power of access into the Father's presence. **For through him we both have access by one Spirit unto the Father. (Ephesians 2:18)** Jesus Christ gives us access into the presence of God. **For there is one God, and one mediator between God and men, the man Christ Jesus. (1 Timothy 2:5)** Jesus died in man's place to reconcile him to God.

Our Position

Paul says **wherein we stand.** This speaks of our standing as God has declared it. We are in Christ by the grace of God. There are two great truths here.

First, our standing is a **_Present Position_**. It is not something we hope to gain, it is something that we already have. **Beloved, now are we the sons of God... (1 John 3:2)** Those who have come to Christ for salvation are children of God now and forever. Remember, justification is the act of God whereby He declares the forgiven sinner to be righteous. To be justified is to stand before God just as if we had never sinned. Justification means that you are not merely a forgiven criminal, but that you are righteous. This is our standing. When God looks at us He sees us as righteous.

Second, our standing is also a **_Permanent Position_**. It is something that we cannot lose. The word **stand** carries the idea of standing firm and immovable. It speaks of the permanence of our salvation—our eternal security. Jesus said, **And I give unto them eternal life; and they shall never perish, neither shall any man pluck them out of my hand. (John 10:28)** Arthur Pink said:

> "It is utterly and absolutely impossible that the sentence of the divine Judge should ever be revoked or reversed Sooner shall the lightnings of omnipotence shiver the Rock of Ages than those sheltering in Him again be brought under condemnation."

Once a person comes to Christ there will never be a time from that day forward in which he is not saved. He cannot lose his salvation. It cannot be taken from him. He cannot sin it away. He is secure for eternity. This is a guarantee of the Saviour. **Being confident of this very thing, that he which hath begun a good work in you will perform it until** the day of Jesus Christ. **(Philippians 1:6)** Our justification is a permanent position in which we stand.

Our Praise

Justification allows us to **rejoice in hope of the glory of God.** The word **hope** speaks of something yet in the future, a future expectancy. **For we are saved by hope: but hope that is seen is not hope: for what a man seeth, why doth he yet hope for? (Romans 8:24)** We do not hope for that which we already have. We hope for things yet to come. Hope is looking forward to a good thing. When people use the word **hope** today it often carries with it the connotation of uncertainty. They say, I hope I have enough money to pay my bills. I hope I get a good report from the doctor. However, in the Bible the word **hope** carries the idea of certainty because when God says something is going to happen we can expect it to happen without any doubt. As believers we have the hope that because we stand justified, we will someday be glorified.

> **Behold, I shew you a mystery; We shall not all sleep, but we shall all be changed, In a moment, in the twinkling of an eye, at the last trump: for the trumpet shall sound, and the dead shall be raised incorruptible, and we shall be changed For this corruptible must put on incorruption, and this mortal must put on immortality. So when this corruptible shall have put on incorruption, and this mortal shall have put on immortality, then shall be brought to pass the saying that is written, Death is swallowed up in victory. (1 Corinthians 15:51-54)**

Notice that Paul said, **we shall all be changed, this mortal must put on immortality,** and **this corruptible shall have put on incorruption.** This refers to the Rapture when all believers will be glorified. John said, **Beloved, now are we the sons of God, and it doth not yet appear what we shall be: but we know that, when he shall appear, we shall be like him; for we shall see him as he is. (1 John 3:2)** Because we are His and He loves us, He is coming back for us and when He catches us away in the rapture we are going to receive our glorified bodies. We will be like Jesus. John said, **we shall be like him.** God's desire for every believer will be realized at last. The glorification of the Christian. **For whom he did foreknow, he also did predestinate to be conformed to the image of his Son, that he might be the firstborn among many brethren. (Romans 8:29)** When that day comes we will be like Christ. So many people have no hope in their hearts; there is no expectation of great and glorious things to come. There is only a fear and heartache. But the person who is saved and justified looks forward to the future glory awaiting him. Isaiah spoke of the future when **Thine eyes shall see the king in his beauty: they shall behold the land that is very far off. (Isaiah 33:17)** What a hope! Someday we will see Jesus in all of His beauty. We will share in the splendor of Heaven. In that day **we shall be like him.** No wonder Paul said we can **rejoice in hope of the glory of God.**

A PATIENCE FOR OUR STRUGGLES

And not only so, but we glory in tribulations also: knowing that tribulation worketh patience; And patience,

experience; and experience, hope: (Romans 5:3-4) Notice that Paul didn't say anything about trying to escape trouble. Instead he said, **we glory** in it. The word **glory** means to "*boast, rejoice, or to be glad.*" That is the opposite of whining and complaining. Paul said, **Do all things without murmurings and disputings: (Philippians 2:14)** That would include tribulations. We know that our tribulations will not destroy us, but if we respond correctly they will only make us better.

The Problems

The **tribulations (Romans 5:3a)** of which Paul is speaking are not the everyday troubles that are common to all men, but the troubles and trials that Christians suffer for the sake of their Lord. Jesus said, **In the world ye shall have tribulation: but be of good cheer; I have overcome the world. (John 16:33)** The Christian who has determined to live all out for God will have tribulations. **Yea, and all that will live godly in Christ Jesus shall suffer persecution .(2 Timothy 3:12)**

The word **tribulations** comes from a word that means "*to press, squash, or to squeeze.*" It was used in Bible days to describe the squeezing of olives to produce oil and the squeezing of grapes to produce wine. When tribulations come the pressure is on and we get squeezed. Tribulations aren't fun, but they are necessary. When you squeeze an olive you get oil. When you squeeze a grape you get juice. God allows tribulation to squeeze us so that He can get something out of us. Paul said, **For our light affliction, which is but for a moment, worketh for us a far more exceeding and eternal weight of glory. (2 Corinthians 4:17)**

The idea is that product produced is far greater than the problems we have to endure. While troubles and tribulation are not pleasant, they nevertheless result in greater fruit being produced to God's glory. The Bible says, **We must through much tribulation enter into the kingdom of God**. **(Acts 14:22)**

The Patience

The word **patience (Romans 5:3b)** means "*the ability to wait and endure.*" This is a word that speaks of patience and endurance under affliction and provocation. It is the ability to keep on keeping on even against strong opposition and obstacles. It carries the idea of staying under and enduring the load. A lot of people today deal with tribulation and trouble by just quitting. It is a lot easier to quit than it is to endure. But the Bible exhorts us to **endure hardness, as a good soldier of Jesus Christ. (2 Timothy 2:3)** One of the greatest needs in Christianity today is for people to just stay by the stuff. We have too many quitters in our churches— they don't persevere. **If thou faint in the day of adversity, thy strength is small. (Proverbs 24:10)** Bob Jones Sr. said, "*The test of your character is what it takes to stop you.*" Don't quit short of your potential.

The Practice

The next benefit Paul mentions is **experience. (Romans 5:4a) Experience** comes from the word "*dokeemay.*" It was a word used to describe the refining process of metal. In order to make the metal purer and stronger it would be melted down and the dross burned away. This word is used to describe the Christian who stays by the stuff. He endures the trials and tribulation and as a result he is purer and stronger for it. Just like the refined metal gains purity and strength from the fire, so we are strengthened and purified in our trials. This is what Job was talking about when he said, **when he hath tried me, I shall come forth as gold**. **(Job 23:10)**

The Prospect

Out of all of this there is **hope. (Romans 5:4)** Again, Job is an example. **And though after my skin worms destroy this body, yet in my flesh shall I see God. (Job 19:26)** Job didn't understand everything he was going through. But he did trust God. He knew that even if he died he would see God. Such is the believer's hope. **Which hope we have as an anchor of the soul, both sure and stedfast, and which entereth into that within the veil; (Hebrews 6:19)**

A PROMISE FOR OUR SATISFACTION

Satisfaction is a great benefit of salvation. Too many folks bounce around like a BB in a box car. They seem to moving from one place to another, from ministry to ministry, from Church to Church, even from doctrine to doctrine, never finding satisfaction and contentment. Paul said, **But godliness with contentment is great gain. (1 Timothy 6:6)** God intends for His people to be contented and in this one verse we have two great aids to satisfaction.

Never Disappointed in the Lord

And hope maketh not ashamed. (Romans 5:5a) We are assured that this **hope** we have **maketh not ashamed.** The word **ashamed** carries the idea of being "*disappointed, shamed, or confounded.*" Our hope is grounded upon Jesus

Christ, therefore, we will never be **ashamed. For the scripture saith, Whosoever believeth on him shall not be ashamed**. (Romans 10:11) This is a guarantee that not only are we saved now, but we will still be saved when we stand before God. As a believer I can have full assurance of salvation. The God Who saved me will complete it. Paul said, **Being confident of this very thing, that he which hath begun a good work in you will perform it until the day of Jesus Christ. (Philippians 1:6)** What a promise! We are promised that our Lord Who begins the work of salvation in us will continue to **perform** that work. The word **perform** means to, "*bring to an end, accomplish, perfect, and complete.*" There is not even the slightest possibility of failure or of partial fulfillment. Every believer is an ongoing work. We will never be disappointed in His work. We can be certain that God will fully complete His work of salvation in us. Jesus is not only the author, but also the **finisher of our faith. (Hebrews 12:2)** Our great God and Saviour is not going to stop short of what He has started in us. That is Bible assurance.

Never Depleted Of His Love

Paul says, **because the love of God is shed abroad in our hearts by the Holy Ghost which is given unto us. (Romans 5:5b)** The love of God changes everything! God's love was **shed abroad in our hearts** at the time of our salvation. The phrase **shed abroad** carries the idea of being *"poured forth or gushed out."* Our hope is backed up by the love of God. This is where it all started. **For God so loved the world, that he gave his only begotten Son, that whosoever believeth in him should not perish, but have everlasting life. (John**

3:16) If it were not for the sacrificial love of God there would be no hope of salvation.

John said, **In this was manifested the love of God toward us, because that God sent his only begotten Son into the world, that we might live through him. Herein is love, not that we loved God, but that he loved us, and sent his Son to be the propitiation for our sins. (1 John 4:9-10)** The word **manifested** means to *"make visible."* God has shown us what true love looks like. He made His love visible on Calvary. In Jesus Christ and His atoning work we see the depth of God's love for us. **But God commendeth his love toward us, in that, while we were yet sinners, Christ died for us. (Romans 5:8)** The word **commendeth** means to *"show, prove, establish, exhibit."* God demonstrated and presented His love to us by giving His only begotten Son to die on Calvary's cross for our sin.

Not only did God love us and send Christ to die for us, but Paul says, **while we were yet sinners, Christ died for us**. Notice it does not say, "while we were good, Christ died for us." It does not say, "while we were trying our best, Christ died for us." it does not say, "because we were worth so much, Christ died for us." But while we were yet sinners, God gave His Son to die in our place. What love that has been **shed abroad,** poured forth and gush out into our hearts. What amazing love! God's love! A love that is never depleted! Our hope is a sure thing because it is grounded upon the love of God.

A PAYMENT FOR OUR SIN

For when we were yet without strength, in due time Christ died for the ungodly. For scarcely for a righteous

man will one die: yet peradventure for a good man some would even dare to die. But God commendeth his love toward us, in that, while we were yet sinners, Christ died for us. (Romans 5:6-8) Paul stresses the depth and magnitude of God's love for us.

We were Helpless

For when we were yet without strength. (Romans 5:6a) The phrase **without strength** carries the idea of being *"feeble, weak, and powerless."* The idea is that sinful man is utterly helpless when it comes to his salvation. We are sinners before God and we are powerless to change that.

We were Horrible

Christ died for the ungodly. (Romans 5:6b) The general meaning is to be *"impious, irreverent, and wicked."* Noah Webster defines **ungodly** as *"Wicked; impious; neglecting the fear and worship of God, or violating his commands ... Polluted by wickedness. Vines says, not merely irreligious, but acting in contravention of God's demands."* W. R. Newell said, *"It is a bankruptcy of all moral and spiritual inclination toward God and holiness, as well as of power to be or do good."* Before salvation we were spiritually bankrupt and in a state of enmity with God.

We were Hopeless

For scarcely for a righteous man will one die: yet peradventure for a good man some would even dare to die. (Romans 5:7) Talk about a hopeless situation. If we had been righteous, there would at least be some scarce hope.

For scarcely for a righteous man will one die. But the Bible says, **There is none righteous, no, not one. (Romans 3:10)** Even if there were some good to be found in us we would have had hope. **yet peradventure for a good man some would even dare to die.** But again the Bible says of all of us, **They are all gone out of the way, they are together become unprofitable; there is none that doeth good, no, not one. (Romans 3:12)** Godet says that these verses *"describe the miserable condition in which we were at the time when divine love was extended to us."*

We were Helped

But God commendeth his love toward us, in that, while we were yet sinners, Christ died for us. (Romans 5:8) Notice the contrast. Paul says, **But.** Instead of leaving us helpless, horrible, and hopeless Christ stepped in and provided salvation for us. Why? Because of His **love** for us. This is a precious kind of love—it is Calvary love. It is a love that sacrifices for the one who is loved. The word **commendeth** means to *"declare, demonstrate, or prove."* Calvary's cross is the undeniable proof of God's love to this world. The evidence of God's unwavering love is the sacrifice of His Son for the sin of a lost world Man could in no way bring himself to God, so God brought Himself to man. What love!

A PROSPECT FOR OUR SALVATION

Much more then, being now justified by his blood, we shall be saved from wrath through him. For if, when we were enemies, we were reconciled to God by the death of

his Son, much more, being reconciled, we shall be saved by his life. (Romans 5:9-10) The phrase **much more** is used five times in chapter five (verses 9, 10, 15, 17, 20). It was a popular Greek idiom often used in the writing of that time. The thought behind the term is *"from the greater to the lesser."* In other words, God has done the greater thing in dying for us when we were His enemies, will He not do the lesser thing and save us from wrath in the day of judgment now that we are His?

We have been Redeemed

Much more then, being now justified by his blood... (Romans 5:9a) It is for certain that our justification was purchased at a great price—the blood of Jesus Christ. God invested the Blood of Jesus in our redemption.

> **Forasmuch as ye know that ye were not redeemed with corruptible things, as silver and gold, from your vain conversation received by tradition from your fathers; But with the precious blood of Christ, as of a lamb without blemish and without spot. (1 Peter 1:18-19)**

There is very little preaching on the blood of Christ in our day. The liberals and modernists downplay the blood atonement. They tell us that the shedding Christ's blood was nothing more than a symbol of His death. However, the Bible is clear when it comes to sin that **without shedding of blood is no remission. (Hebrews 9:22)** Without the shed blood of Jesus Christ, there is no salvation. **In whom we have redemption through his blood, the forgiveness of sins.**

(Ephesians 1:7a) Furthermore, Acts 20:28 tells us that is was **His own blood** It was no ordinary blood that ran in the veins of Jesus, but the blood of God.

We have been Rescued

Paul assures us that **we shall be saved from wrath through him. (Romans 5:9b)** It is the future that Paul has in mind—he is speaking of the finality of our salvation. The word **wrath** carries the idea of *anger in punishment* and speaks of the day of judgment (John 3:16-18, 36). The believer never has to worry about falling under the penal wrath of God so far as his salvation is concerned. **Wherefore he is able also to save them to the uttermost that come unto God by him, seeing he ever liveth to make intercession for them. (Hebrews 7:25)** God didn't save us to lose us—He saved us to keep us. There will be no believers at the Great White Throne Judgment. For those who put their faith in Christ, the wrath of God was forever satisfied on Calvary.

We have been Reconciled

Paul says, **For if, when we were enemies, we were reconciled to God by the death of his Son, much more, being reconciled, we shall be saved by his life. (Romans 5:10)** The word **reconciled** means *"to change or exchange."* Vines says in relation to people it means *"to change from enmity to friendship.* 'Sin has caused separation and enmity between God and man. However, because of the blood of Christ, the separation has been bridged and we now have fellowship. And instead of enmity with God, we are at peace with Him.

A PRAISE FOR OUR SAVIOUR

And not only so, but we also joy in God through our Lord Jesus Christ, by whom we have now received the atonement. (Romans 5:11) As a result of Christ's reconciling atonement, our hearts are filled and overflowing with joy. At one time we could not come into the presence of God, let alone rejoice in His presence. We were enemies and therefore barred from His presence. Now we can come into the very presence of God—the One Whose wrath was previously focused upon us, but now in His presence, there is joy. We are no longer on the outside, we are part of the family.

From Ruin To Redemption
Romans 5:12-21

In the last passage Christ's redeeming work is seen. In this passage, Adam's work is contrasted to Christ's. Jesus Christ is referred to in the Bible as the last Adam. **The first man Adam was made a living soul; the last Adam was made a quickening spirit. (1 Corinthians 15:45)** Adam and Christ are seen as representatives of the human race. They acted on man's behalf. Adam sinned for us and Christ died for us. Through Adam we inherited a sin nature and death. Through Christ we can have the forgiveness of sin and eternal life. What the representative does is imputed to all who follow him. Martin Luther said, *"There are but two men, Adam and Christ, and all other men hang at their girdles."* The truth of the matter is that every man and woman have their identity either in Adam or Christ.

THE ROOTS OF SIN

Wherefore, as by one man sin entered into the world. (Romans 5:12a) Notice the word **entered.** Sin did not begin with Adam. However, sin did enter into the human race by him. Sin had entered into the world through Satan (Isaiah 14:12-15, Ezekiel 28:11-19), but it entered into the human race by Adam. God had clearly instructed Adam what to do and what not to do.

> **And the LORD God took the man, and put him into the garden of Eden to dress it and to keep it. And the LORD God commanded the man, saying, Of every tree of the garden thou mayest freely eat: But**

of the tree of the knowledge of good and evil, thou shalt not eat of it: for in the day that thou eatest thereof thou shalt surely die. (Genesis 2:15-17)

Regardless of God's command, Adam ate the forbidden fruit; he transgressed God's command and he died spiritually that very moment. Here is the origin of all that is sinful and depraved.

THE RESULTS OF SIN

The Bible says **so death passed upon all men. (Romans 5:12b)** Just like a child inherits the nature of his parents, mankind inherited the fallen nature of Adam. Adam's is where the human race was ruined. This was the opposite of what the Devil had promised Eve. The old liar had assured Eve that she not would die. **And the serpent said unto the woman, Ye shall not surely die: For God doth know that in the day ye eat thereof, then your eyes shall be opened, and ye shall be as gods, knowing good and evil. (Genesis 3:4-5)** He can make it sound good! He is described as being **more subtil than any beast of the field. (Genesis 3:1)** The Bible declares that **Satan himself is transformed into an angel of light. (2 Corinthians 11:40)** When it comes to this business of deception Satan is the master deceiver of the ages. He can take the ugliest of sin and make is sound good. Eve listened to him and it was the beginning of ruin for God's creation. All sin can be traced back to when Adam and Eve ate of the forbidden fruit.

THE REALITY OF SIN

Paul makes it clear that **all have sinned. (Romans 5:12c)** Notice the tense of this statement **all have sinned**. Notice that it is past tense. In the context it is still talking about Adam. What Paul is saying us is that when Adam sinned, we sinned. When Adam fell, we fell. When Adam died spiritually, we all died spiritually! Paul is driving the fact home that we have an inborn sin nature. We are born into this world with this sin nature. It is not something that we have to develop, we already have it when we arrive.

In his commentary on Romans From Guilt to Glory, Ray Stedman quotes from a report by the Minnesota Crime Commission that clearly demonstrates what Paul is saying.

> "Every baby starts life as a little savage. He is completely selfish and self-centered He wants what he wants when he wants it—his bottle, his mother's attention, his playmate's toy, his uncle's watch. Deny him these wants, and he seethes with rage and aggressiveness, which would be murderous, were he not so helpless. He is dirty. He has no morals, no knowledge, no skills. This means that all children, not just certain children, are born delinquent. If permitted to continue in the self-centered world of his infancy, given free reign to his impulsive actions to satisfy his wants, every child would grow up a criminal, a thief, a killer, a rapist."

What a vivid truth. We are not sinners because we sin, instead we sin because we are sinners. We sin because we have a sin nature. Earlier Paul said, **For all have sinned, and come short of the glory of God. (Romans 3:23)** Isaiah said it this way. **But we are all as an unclean thing, and all our righteousnesses are as filthy rags; and we all do fade as a** leaf; and our iniquities, like the wind, have taken us away. (Isaiah 64:6)

THE REIGN OF SIN

For until the law sin was in the world: but sin is not imputed when there is no law. Nevertheless death reigned from Adam to Moses, even over them that had not sinned after the similitude of Adam's transgression, who is the figure of him that was to come. (Romans 5:13-14) Once again Paul goes back to before the law to prove his point. He has already proven that men not were saved by the law. Here he adds that breaking the law is not what brings death. He says, **death reigned from Adam to Moses.** There was no law, but there was still death. Death is the result of Adam's sin and we inherited his sin nature.

THE REMEDY FOR SIN

But not as the offence, so also is the free gift. For if through the offence of one many be dead... (Romans 5:15a) Paul explains the remedy for our sin by contrasting the work of Adam with the work of Christ. When Adam sinned every man died spiritually. Notice the present tense, **For if through the offence of one many be dead** Many are physically alive, but spiritually dead **But she that liveth in pleasure is dead while she liveth. (1 Timothy 5:6)** When the Bible speaks of death in this context it is referring to spiritual death. It is also called the second death (Revelation 2:11; 20:6; 20:14; 21:8). We are by nature **the children of wrath. (Ephesians 2:3)** Jesus said, **He that believeth on the Son hath everlasting life: and he that believeth not the Son**

shall not see life; but the wrath of God abideth on him. (John 3:36)

Next Paul says, **much more the grace of God, and the gift by grace, which is by one man, Jesus Christ, hath abounded unto many**. (Romans 5:15a) In contrast to Adam, Jesus Christ is the deliverer of the doomed. Adam brought guilt, but Jesus brought grace. Please take note of the wording here! Paul says. **much more the grace of God, and the gift of grace… hath abounded unto many.** The grace of God, which is the basis of our justification, is contrasted with the sin of Adam. Grace is greater in quality and greater in degree than Adam's sin. In Adam we got what we deserved, condemnation and guilt. In Christ we have received much more of what we do not deserve, mercy and grace.

And not as it was by one that sinned, so is the gift: for the judgment was by one to condemnation, but the free gift is of many offences unto justification. (Romans 5:16) This is another contrast between Adam's sin and Christ's gift. Adam's was one offence that brought judgment and condemnation to man. However, God's grace exceeds and abounds to **many offences**. Adam brought eternal death, grace brings eternal life.

For if by one man's offence death reigned by one; much more they which receive abundance of grace and of the gift of righteousness shall reign in life by one, Jesus Christ. (Romans 5:17) Paul contrasts the reign of death with the reign of life. Adam's reign in the garden of Eden was brief and ended in disaster. We don't know how long Adam lived in the Garden before he sinned, but ever how long it was—that was the extent of his reign. After Adam sinned, death reigned. The fifth chapter of Genesis reads like the obituary section of the local newspaper. It is like a walk through the cemetery where the tombstones reveal the results of Adams failure.

> **And Adam lived ... and he died,**
>
> **And Seth lived ... and he died,**
>
> **And Enos lived ... and he died,**
>
> **And Cainan lived ... and he died,**
>
> **And Mahalaleel lived ... and he died,**
>
> **And Jared lived ... and he died,**
>
> **And Methuselah lived ... and he died,**
>
> **And Lamech lived ... and he died**

Such was the result of Adam's reign. He brought ruin to God's creation. However, Jesus Christ brought restoration to fallen man. That which Adam lost through his disobedience, Christ redeemed through His obedience.

Paul said that we shall **shall reign in life by one, Jesus Christ. (Romans 5:17b)** In Adam our life is one bondage and hopelessness. However, when we are in Christ, we reign with Him and He reigns over death. Jesus said, **I am the resurrection, and the life: he that believeth in me, though he were dead, yet shall he live. (John 11:25)** For the believer, death is an enemy that will be destroyed. **For he must reign, till he hath put all enemies under his feet. The last enemy that shall be destroyed is death. (1 Corinthians**

15:25-26) We can say, **O death, where is thy sting? O grave, where is thy victory? (1 Corinthians 15:55)** Not only do we positionally live and reign with Christ now; but the day is coming when we shall reign with him literally. Adam brought us into bondage, Christ set us free to reign with Him (2 Timothy 2:12; Revelation 22:5).

Therefore as by the offence of one judgment came upon all men to condemnation; even so by the righteousness of one the free gift came upon all men unto justification of life. For as by one man's disobedience many were made sinners, so by the obedience of one shall many be made righteous. (Romans 5:18-19) Paul summarizes what he has been saying. Paul contrasts the judgment that came upon all men with the free gift that is available for all who will receive it.

Moreover the law entered, that the offence might abound But where sin abounded, grace did much more abound. (Romans 5:20) The phrase **much more abound** carries the idea *"super abounding* and means to *surpass by far, exceed immeasurably,* or *overflow beyond."* It speaks of the fact that God's grace far exceeds the offence. In Ephesians Paul says, **In whom we have redemption through his blood, the forgiveness of sins, according to the riches of his grace. (Ephesians 1:7)** Think about that! It is **according to riches of His grace.** What a fathomless thought! Lehman Strauss said, *"No adequate explanation of divine forgiveness can be made apart from those beautiful and precious words."* Redemption and forgiveness of sins are **according to the riches of his grace.** Notice it is not *"from His riches"* but **according to** the riches of His grace.

Bill Gates is one of the richest men in the world with a net worth of over fifty billion dollars. If Bill Gates were to give to a charity, and he wrote a check for $ 200.00, he would only be giving from his riches. But if, instead, he gave a wrote for $ 200,000.00, he would be giving according to his riches. Charles Hodge spoke of this abundance as *"an overflowing abundance of unmerited love, inexhaustible in God and freely accessible through Christ."* God never gives from his riches, but according to His riches. God's grace is as boundless as He is. His grace far exceeds the offence.

That as sin hath reigned unto death, even so might grace reign through righteousness unto eternal life by Jesus Christ our Lord. (Romans 5:21) When we started this section death was reigning, now grace is reigning.

How Dead Men Live
Romans 6:1-14

We saw in the first section of Romans that every human is under **Condemnation**. He is sinful and disposed to evil, and is therefore under the wrath of God. The second section of Romans we saw **Salvation**—the fact that God desires to save sinful man. Chapters four and five dealt primarily with **Justification**. Here we learned that God's justification of the sinner is by faith in Jesus Christ. We learned that God's justification is the act whereby we are declared righteous. To be justified is to stand before God just as if we had never sinned. Here in Romans six and seven Paul takes up the doctrine of **Sanctification**. Paul has dealt with the fact that we have been saved from the penalty of sin in the past. Now Paul emphasizes how we can be saved from the power of sin in the present. We will learn in chapters six and seven that justification is only the starting point—it is the beginning of God's purpose for us. Justification is where the saving process commences; sanctification is where the saving process continues on.

THE PERVERSION ANSWERED

What shall we say then? Shall we continue in sin, that grace may abound? God forbid... (Romans 6:1-2a) There is probably no doctrine more abused than the doctrine of grace. The preceding chapter concluded with the great truth that though **sin abounded, grace did much more abound.**

Paul anticipated the argument that if God's grace is magnified by sin, then shouldn't we sin all the more so God's amazing grace can be seen in a greater way. This is perverted thinking. The same idea is prevalent today. Many are using their brand of liberty to feed and satisfy worldly and ungodly desires. They teach that the grace of God allows their lifestyle. The Scripture warns us of such men.

> **For there are certain men crept in unawares, who were before of old ordained to this condemnation, ungodly men, turning the grace of our God into lasciviousness, and denying the only Lord God, and our Lord Jesus Christ. (Jude 1:4)**

Notice that they are turning the grace of our God into lasciviousness. The word **lasciviousness** means *"unrestrained."* It carries the idea of having a *"license to live as one desires."* Theirs is a corrupting of the grace of God, turning it into nothing more than a license to sin by living an unrestrained lifestyle.

Shall we continue in sin, that grace may abound? God forbid? Paul emphatically answers **God forbid. (Romans 6:2a)** The idea is perish the thought! There is no basis whatsoever for such foolish thinking. Those who are saved and understand the truth of God's grace do not use it as a license to sin. In fact, the Bible teaches the opposite. **For the grace of God that bringeth salvation hath appeared to all men, Teaching us that, denying ungodliness and worldly lusts, we should live soberly, righteously, and godly, in this present world. (Titus 2:11-12)** The depths to which our wickedness and the sufficiency of God's grace to save us have already demonstrated by the adequacy of God's grace, there is no need to add sin upon sin. The true child of God hates sin and wants to escape it rather than remaining captive to it.

THE PRINCIPLE AFFIRMED

How shall we, that are dead to sin, live any longer therein? (Romans 6:2b) Paul introduces a principle here that he will be expounding on in the next several verses. Paul reinforces his argument that a true believer is dead to sin and it is utterly unthinkable that people who have died to sin should be dominated by its power. Notice that Paul says, **we, that are dead to sin.** This is in the present tense, we are dead now. This verse is a statement of fact. It is a present reality. We are dead to sin. It is something that has already happened. It has already been accomplished. In God's mind every believer is dead to sin.

THE PICTURE APPLIED

Know ye not, that so many of us as were baptized into Jesus Christ were baptized into his death? (Romans 6:3) Paul uses baptism as a picture to illustrate the fact that the believer is dead to sin. We **were baptized into his death.** Paul is talking about the spiritual reality that, when Christ died, we died. Paul points to the death of Jesus Christ, and says that the believer died with Him. Paul is saying that if we truly understand baptism, we you could never make this mistake of thinking that abounding grace is an excuse to sin.

Therefore we are buried with him by baptism into death: that like as Christ was raised up from the dead by the glory of the Father. (Romans 6:4a) We notice here that baptism involved a death and a burial. Baptism is a picture of the death and burial of the old man, as well as of the resurrection of the new man. When a child of God is baptized he is put under the water—he is buried Someone has said that baptism is an outward expression of an inward reality. When you were buried in baptism, it served as a picture of what happened to you. Now, when do we bury people? It is when they are dead. In your baptism you said to all around you that you had died to your old life. Your burial in baptism declared that you had died to sin. When someone is dead and buried his life is over with. Paul uses this illustration to show that the believer is just as dead to sin as a dead man is dead and buried. When a man who has lived his life as a slave to alcohol dies, he is buried and his life of drunkenness is over. He is buried and his addiction is over. You can take his corpse to the bar, prop him up on a stool and surround him with liquor and beer, but he will not drink. Why? Because he is dead to that life. He is no longer a slave to alcohol because he is dead! That is exactly what Paul is saying about the child of God. When he was saved he died with Christ. He is dead to the sin and slavery of the old life.

Paul says, **even so we also should walk in newness of life. (Romans 6:4b)** Paul brings out another point. The picture of baptism also illustrates the resurrection of the new life in Christ. We were raised to **walk in newness of life.** The word **walk** speaks of lifestyle. Walk is used in the Bible to speak of walking **after the Spirit. (Romans 8:4)**, of walking **in honesty. (Romans 13:13)**, of walking **by faith. (2 Corinthians 5:7)**, of walking in **good works. (Ephesians 2:10)**, of walking **in love. (Ephesians 5:2)**, of walking **in** wisdom. (Colossians 4:5) When Paul talked about walking in newness of life, he was talking about a changed lifestyle.

For if we have been planted together in the likeness of his death, we shall be also in the likeness of his resurrection. (Romans 6:5) Christ died for sin, and was buried. When he rose again three days later it was not to the former life. He rose to a new and glorified life. We too are changed as a result of dying in Christ. We now live in the likeness of his resurrection. We are different now! **Therefore if any man be in Christ, he is a new creature: old things are passed away; behold, all things are become new. (2 Corinthians 5:17)** We are a new creature. Not the same old man. He died. The new creature in Christ is indeed a new life with new desires. Regeneration effects a change in our life.

Knowing this, that our old man is crucified with him, that the body of sin might be destroyed. (Romans 6:6a) Our old man was crucified. What is the purpose of crucifixion? Why did the evil men of Christ's day crucify Him? They crucified Him because they wanted Him dead. They wanted to stop His life and His work. When God crucified the old man He did so to put a stop to the life and work of the flesh.

Paul says, **that henceforth we should not serve sin. (Romans 6:6b)** Paul is not saying that a true believer will be perfectly sinless. There will be ups and downs as the believer yields to sin. However, is clear that Christians cannot habitually live under its domination of sin. He is no longer a slave to it.

THE PROCESS ADVANCED

Paul concludes his argument by stressing three points. He uses three significant words to teach us how to bring our life in line with what God says. The words are **knowing, reckon, and yield.**

We Must Comprehend

Knowing that Christ being raised from the dead dieth no more; death hath no more dominion over him. For in that he died, he died unto sin once: but in that he liveth, he liveth unto God. (Romans 6:9-10) There is something that we must comprehend—something that we must know. We must understand that Christ died for sin and He rose from the dead. The reason for our confidence is His resurrection. The Bible says, **And if Christ be not raised, your faith is vain; ye are yet in your sins. (1 Corinthians 15:17)** But praise God, He did rise. Since Christ conquered death Paul says, **death hath no more dominion over him.** When He went to the cross, He paid the sin debt in full. And because it does not have dominion over him, it does not have dominion over us, because we died and were raised with him.

We Must Calculate

Likewise reckon ye also yourselves to be dead indeed unto sin, but alive unto God through Jesus Christ our Lord. (Romans 6:11) Now that we know we are dead in Christ, what are we to do with it. Paul says it is our responsibility to **reckon** our own selves dead. The word **reckon** means to "*count, to number,* or *to calculate.*" The idea that of reconciling a checkbook. We take the bank statement and our checkbook, sit down and make the checkbook agree with the bank statement. That is what God is saying when He commands that we *reckon* ourselves to be dead. God has already declared it so, now reckon it to be so.

We Must Comply

Let not sin therefore reign in your mortal body, that ye should obey it in the lusts thereof. (Romans 6:12) Before salvation we were under the dominion of sin. Our depraved natures ruled our souls. Sin was the ruler on the throne of the heart, and we did obey it. **Let not sin therefore reign in your mortal body, that ye should obey it in the lusts thereof.** In fact, we are to do the opposite. **What? know ye not that your body is the temple of the Holy Ghost which is in you, which ye have of God, and ye are not your own? For ye are bought with a price: therefore glorify God in your body, and in your spirit, which are God's. (1 Corinthians 6:19-20)** Is such a life possible? If so, how do we live such a life?

Paul says, **Neither yield ye your members as instruments of unrighteousness unto sin: but yield yourselves unto God, as those that are alive from the dead, and your members as instruments of righteousness unto God For sin shall not have dominion over you: for ye are not under the law, but under grace. (Romans 6:13-14)** The third key word to living the victorious life is to **yield. (13)** The word **yield** means *"to place at the disposal of another."* It carries the idea of *"presenting something to be used in the service of another."* The word for **instruments** is a military word that carries the idea of *weapons.* The **members** here speaks of part of our body—hands, feet, eyes, tongue, etc. This paints a vivid picture. Sin is an evil dictator who wants to use our own bodily members as instruments or weapons by which it can rule over us. Paul said that the key to overcoming the evil tyrant of sin is to not yield to him. If we are driving down the road and come upon a yield sign, we must slow down and give the other guy the right-of-way. We are not to give sin the right-of-way in our life. Instead we are to bring our life in line with what God said. Now that we know the truth of being crucified in Christ, and sin no longer having dominion over us must reckon it to be so. We must put it to practice in our life by refusing to yield and be a slave to sin. When Satan rears his ugly head and temptation starts in on us, we simply say, The man that used to do that stuff died on the cross, he was buried, he has been raised to walk in newness of life. That man no longer exists. I am a new creature now. That is how we reckon ourselves **to be dead indeed unto sin.**

Governed By Grace
Romans 6:15-23

In the first part of this chapter Paul explained that Christ has broken the bonds of sin that enslave the Christian. In the second part he warned that even though we are free, we can become enslaved to sin if we yield to temptation.

OUR SIN IS REPULSIVE

What then? shall we sin, because we are not under the law, but under grace? God forbid. (Romans 6:15) Paul's question here is not a repeat of verse one. There he asked if we could **continue in sin.** Here he asks, **shall we sin?** There he was dealing with our sin nature. Here he deals with specific acts of sin. The answer, however, is the same. **God forbid.** Sin is still repulsive to God. God always hates sin. Sin is a product of the flesh and Christ said, **the flesh profiteth nothing. (John 6:63)**

OUR SUBMISSION IS REQUIRED

Know ye not, that to whom ye yield yourselves servants to obey, his servants ye are to whom ye obey; whether of sin unto death, or of obedience unto righteousness? (Romans 6:16) The word **yield** means *"to place at the disposal of another."* It carries the idea of presenting *"something to be used in the service of another."* The word was used to describe a servant who stood quietly by his master as he awaited orders. Paul is teaching us a very simple principle. We are a servant to whoever we obey. If we serve God we are God's servant. If we serve sin then we are sin's servant. Jesus said, **No man can serve two masters. (Matthew 6:24)** You cannot yield to and serve sin while claiming that Jesus is your Lord. Jesus said, **Whosoever committeth sin is the servant of sin. (John 8:34)** You can't call Christ the lord of your life if you habitually serve sin. **And why call ye me, Lord, Lord, and do not the things which I say? (Luke 6:46)** Now that we are saved we have a new Master. Our orders come from Jesus Christ. When He speaks we are to yield. This is a matter of choice. Christ must have our heart. We must be submissive to His will. John Phillips said:

> "No person can expect victory who doesn't really want victory. No person can expect victory who has a soft attitude toward sin. God expects sincerity as much today as He did when He said to rebellious Israel, And ye shall seek me, and find me, when ye shall search for me with all your heart Jeremiah 29:13 . God is not going to bring us into the blessedness of this new liberty unless we really want it."

Paul instructed the Galatians, **Walk in the Spirit, and ye shall not fulfil the lust of the flesh. (Galatians 5:16)** This is a command to yield ourselves to the Holy Spirit and live under His influence and control. If we walk in the Spirit we will not **fulfil the lust of the flesh.** We will have victory in the Christian life. The question is, Will I yield to the Spirit and allow Christ control of my life? When I yield to someone,

I give him the right-of-way. The key to enjoying a life of victory is to give God the right-of-way in our life.

OUR SERVICE IS RENEWED

But God be thanked, that ye were the servants of sin, but ye have obeyed from the heart that form of doctrine which was delivered you. Being then made free from sin, ye became the servants of righteousness. (Romans 6:17-18) I want to say with Paul, **But God be thanked!** Thank God we are no longer slaves to the depraved nature. We have been set free from the soul damning sin that once held us captive as it slowly dragged us toward Hell's awful pit. Paul traces the history of every believer through four stages:

We Were Enslaved

Paul says, **ye were the servants of sin. (Romans 6:17a)** The whole human race is a family of bankrupt beggars. Man can by no means pay the price for his salvation. The sinner himself cannot make a satisfactory payment for his sin. The curse of the law rests heavy upon us all. We are were under the bondage of sin. **Cursed is every one that continueth not in all things which are written in the book of the law to do them. (Galatians 3:10)** Oh! How impossible it is for sinful and fallen man to satisfy the righteous demands of the law of God.

We Were Enlightened

Next, Paul said, **but ye have obeyed from the heart that form of doctrine which was delivered you. (Romans 6:17b)** These were people who were genuinely born again. They heard the truth of God's saving grace and the text says, **obeyed from the heart.** Their experience was far more than a mere mental agreement. Their profession of faith wasn't based on the head's knowledge, but on heart belief. It is not what happens in the head that changes a man, it is what happens in the heart. **Keep thy heart with all diligence; for out of it are the issues of life. (Proverbs 4:23)**

We are told by many today that doctrine isn't all that important. That we need emphasis on fellowship. We are told that doctrine divides and love unites. But you will notice here that Paul commends the Roman believers because they had believed and received the **doctrine** that was delivered to them. The word **form** is a word that was used to speak of a mold into which molten metal for castings was poured. We still use this word in the same way today. When you are going to pour concrete, you often pour it into a form. When the concrete sets, it takes on the shape of the form. Why does Paul use this particular word? Well, notice that Paul speaks of it as **doctrine which was delivered you.** The idea here is that the doctrine had not just been delivered to them, but they were also delivered into the doctrine. The doctrine was the **form** that was to mold their lives. We conform to the doctrine, we don't try to conform the doctrine to us. This verse teaches us that once we are saved, the doctrine of God begins to form our life.

We Were Emancipated

Being then made free from sin. (Romans 6:18a) Notice the present tense of **being made free.** This is the thought behind the word redemption. It is a word that speaks of the purchase of a slave from the slave block. The poor slave is on the block for auction. He is bound by chains and has no claim to freedom. He has no means by which to purchase his freedom. He is hopeless and is duty bound to serve whoever purchases him. That is exactly what we were before Christ saved us. We were bound by sin and without any means to gain our freedom. However, Jesus Christ did pay the price. **In whom we have redemption through his blood, the forgiveness of sins.** **(Ephesians 1:7a)** Jesus Christ paid the price not only to save us from Hell, but to completely purchase us from slavery. We are no longer slaves to sin. That bondage to sin was broken by Christ.

We Were Established

Finally, Paul said, **ye became the servants of righteousness. (Romans 6:18b)** Aren't those sweet words! We are now **servants of righteousness.** Christ did much more than simply deliver us from the pit—He established us. Like David we can say, **He brought me up also out of an horrible pit, out of the miry clay, and set my feet upon a rock, and established my goings. (Psalms 40:2)** The word **established** means to be "*set up, fixed, and firmed up.*" Paul wrote:

> **As ye have therefore received Christ Jesus the Lord, so walk ye in him: Rooted and built up in him, and stablished in the faith, as ye have been taught, abounding therein with thanksgiving. (Colossians 2:6-7)**

When we were servants of sin we were weak, wavering and sinking in its filth. We weren't free to serve God for we were bound to another master. But when He set us free, He established us.

OUR STANDARD IS RIGHTEOUSNESS

I speak after the manner of men because of the infirmity of your flesh: for as ye have yielded your members servants to uncleanness and to iniquity unto iniquity; even so now yield your members servants to righteousness unto holiness. For when ye were the servants of sin, ye were free from righteousness. (Romans 6:19-20) Verse 20 is an apt description of what were before salvation. We were free with respect to righteousness. We were free from living right and thinking right. We were slaves to unrighteousness. Nothing we did pleased God. **So then they that are in the flesh cannot please God. (Romans 8:8)** We were in every sense of the word slaves to sin. But Praise God for redemption! Now we have a desire and a choice to serve righteousness. Paul says, **even so now yield your members servants to righteousness unto holiness.** The work of Christ freed us from the bondage of sin and we are now servants of righteousness. Now we are **... partakers of the divine nature, having escaped the corruption that is in the world through lust. (2 Peter 1:4)** We no longer have to live according to the dictates of the depraved flesh. We can now live according to the Divine power of God.

OUR SALVATION IS REWARDING

What fruit had ye then in those things whereof ye are now ashamed? for the end of those things is death. (Romans 6:21) There was nothing of any spiritual value produced in the unsaved life. Isaiah said, **But we are all as an unclean thing, and all our righteousnesses are as filthy rags; and we all do fade as a leaf; and our iniquities, like the wind, have taken us away. (Isaiah 64:6)** That is not a pretty picture, but the Bible is honestly written.

But now being made free from sin, and become servants to God, ye have your fruit unto holiness, and the end everlasting life. (Romans 6:22) Now that we are no longer enslaved to sin, we can serve God thereby producing **fruit unto holiness.** Who we serve determines the fruit we bear.

> **Be not deceived; God is not mocked: for whatsoever a man soweth, that shall he also reap. For he that soweth to his flesh shall of the flesh reap corruption; but he that soweth to the Spirit shall of the Spirit reap life everlasting. (Galatians 6:7-8)**

Whatever we do in life results in fruit. If we sin, there will be the resulting fruit of sin. If we live for and serve the Lord, there will be a resulting fruit.

For the wages of sin is death; but the gift of God is eternal life through Jesus Christ our Lord. (Romans 6:23) Sin has its payday and death is the wages. Sin never results in anything but death. James said, **... sin, when it is finished, bringeth forth death. (James 1:15)** Because we are sinners, we must die for our sin. The Bible is clear that **...the soul that sinneth, it shall die. (Ezekiel 18:4)** The wages of sin is death and every lost person will receive the wages they've earned.

Paul says, ... **but the gift of God is eternal life through Jesus Christ our Lord. (Romans 6:23)** Standing in stark contrast to the wages of sin is the free gift of eternal life through Jesus Christ. A gift is the opposite of wages. Wages are earned but a gift is given. Because it is a gift, it can only be accepted, not earned. The gift of **eternal life** has to do with God's grace and is **through Jesus Christ our Lord.** We do not deserve it. We cannot earn it. All we can do is receive it.

Freedom From The Law
Romans 7:1-13

In chapter seven Paul stresses two great truths. 1) the believer's relationship to the law and 2) the absolute failure of the law to sanctify.

THE FATE OF THE LAW

Think not for a moment that the law is null and void. The law defiantly has a purpose.

The Announcement

Know ye not, brethren, for I speak to them that know the law, how that the law hath dominion over a man as long as he liveth? (Romans 7:1) Man's law operates within certain boundaries. The laws of the United States government are not in effect in Mexico. When a traveler crosses over a country line he enters another jurisdiction. Likewise, when a person dies, the law no longer has any claim upon him. Death ends the believer's relationship to the law, both for salvation and for holy living. As long as we are alive in our natural state, we are condemned by the Law of God, but when we die, we are free from its requirement.

The Analogy

For the woman which hath an husband is bound by the law to her husband so long as he liveth; but if the husband be dead, she is loosed from the law of her husband. So

then if, while her husband liveth, she be married to another man, she shall be called an adulteress: but if her husband be dead, she is free from that law; so that she is no adulteress, though she be married to another man. (Romans 7:2-3) These verses are usually lifted out of their context and applied to divorce. However, this passage is not dealing primarily with the subject of divorce. Paul is simply using this one aspect of marriage as an analogy. These two verses are not the Scripture's main teaching on the subject of marriage and divorce.

An analogy must not be taken too far. Analogies, like parables, are designed to communicate a point of truth. This passage teaches us that death breaks the marriage bond. However, death is not the only thing that breaks the marriage bond. So does Scriptural divorce (Matthew 5:31-32; 19:3-12) and desertion by an unbelieving spouse (1 Corinthians 7:10-15). Paul uses this one aspect of marriage law to call attention to the fact that marriage laws are binding only as long as both partners are alive. Marriage to another man while the husband is alive makes a woman an adulteress. But to marry another after the husband dies is legal because death broke the dominion of the law. Therefore the surviving spouse can remarry.

THE FREEDOM FROM THE LAW

Wherefore, my brethren, ye also are become dead to the law by the body of Christ; that ye should be married to another, even to him who is raised from the dead, that we should bring forth fruit unto God. (Romans 7:4) Now Paul makes application of his analogy. A woman is bound by law to her husband as long as he lives, and only when he dies, is she free to marry another.

There is a New Freedom

Paul said, **ye also are become dead to the law by the body of Christ; (Romans 7:4a)** Paul is telling us that we and believers were made to die to the Law through the death of Jesus. Jesus Christ died for our sins and when we came to Christ we were reckoned dead with Him. This is what we learned in chapter 6 of Romans. From the analogy, we see that we died to our old relationship with sin, and that now we are the bride to a new Husband. Paul said, **ye also are become dead to the law.** This is in the aorist tense speaking of completeness and finality. It is already accomplished. Because my old man is dead, my relationship to the law is broken. I do not have to observe the Old Testament rituals and ceremonies. **If the Son therefore shall make you free, ye shall be free indeed. (John 8:36)**

There is a New Family

Paul says, **that ye should be married to another. (Romans 7:4b)** In Christ's death the believer also died. The law didn't die, but the believer died to the law. Paul said that we are **dead to the law by the body of Christ.** Jesus Christ met and satisfied the righteous demands of the law. When He died the believer died with Him (Romans 6:8). Paul says, **that ye should be married to another.** Our death in Christ makes it possible to have a new relationship with a new husband. The believer is now joined to Jesus Christ in a new and wonderful relationship. I am dead to the law and therefore free to enjoy my relationship with Christ.

There is a New Fruitfulness

Paul says, **that we should bring forth fruit unto God. (Romans 7:4c)** As children of God we bring forth a new kind of fruit. In the next verse Paul reminds us of the fruit of the old life. **For when we were in the flesh, the motions of sins, which were by the law, did work in our members to bring forth fruit unto death. (Romans 7:5)** Notice that Paul did not say *"in the body,"* but **in the flesh**. When Paul uses the word flesh in this context he is talking about the old nature. It is the old depravity driven nature that delights in sin and wickedness. The old nature is not in subjection to the law of God. **Because the carnal mind is enmity against God: for it is not subject to the law of God, neither indeed can be. (Romans 8:7)** It is a nature that is an enemy of God and hates everything that is holy and decent. **For I know that in me that is, in my flesh, dwelleth no good thing: for to will is present with me; but how to perform that which is good I find not. (Romans 7:18)** It was the old depraved nature that Jeremiah was speaking of when he said, **The heart is deceitful above all things, and desperately wicked: who can know it? (Jeremiah 17:9)** When we were still unsaved, before we became believers, **the motions of sins, which were by the law, did work in our members to bring forth fruit unto death.** The word **motions** carries the idea of *"influences or passions."* The unsaved man was driven by sinful influences and passions that resulted in death.

But now we are delivered from the law, that being dead wherein we were held; that we should serve in newness of spirit, and not in the oldness of the letter. (Romans 7:6) Paul says, **But now,** that is now that we are saved, we have been **delivered from the law, that being dead wherein we were held.** The word **held** speaks of being *"seized or retained"* That was our relationship to the law. We were hopelessly held captive by it. No matter how hard we tried to obtain righteousness, the passions of the flesh keep driving us to sin and the law continued to condemn. The law could not set us free. It could only show us our sinfulness, pronounce us guilty and condemn us to death.

Paul says, **But now we are delivered from the law … we should serve in newness of spirit, and not in the oldness of the letter.** Now that we have been delivered from the law and identified with Christ we have a new fruitfulness. Since the power of the old nature has been broken in the believer we can serve in **newness of life.** Earlier Paul said it this way, **… that we should bring forth fruit unto God. (Romans 7:4)** Fruit is the outward demonstration that something real has happened in the heart. John the Baptist said to the Pharisees and Sadducees, **Bring forth therefore fruits meet for repentance. (Matthew 3:8)** The word **meet** comes from *"axios"* and refers to a set of balances or scales. The word means, *"having the weight of another thing of like value, worth as much."* The idea here is if you are saved your life will match your profession. There will be some fruit. **But wilt thou know, O vain man, that faith without works is dead? (James 2:20)** James is teaching us that genuine faith will produce good works. Jesus said, **Herein is my Father** glorified, that ye bear much fruit; so shall ye be my disciples. (John 15:8)

THE FRUIT OF THE LAW

What shall we say then? Is the law sin? God forbid. (Romans 7:7a) Having spoke of the laws bondage and inability to save, Paul now sets out to show that the law is good and fruitful. He does not want to be misunderstood as saying that the law is sinful. As he often does, Paul introduces the subject by asking a rhetorical question. **Is the law sin?** To which he emphatically answers **God forbid.** There is nothing wrong with the law. The problem is with man. He can't obey it. Paul points out some positive things about the law.

The Law Reveals Sin

Nay, I had not known sin, but by the law: for I had not known lust, except the law had said, Thou shalt not covet. (Romans 7:7b) Paul is saying, I wouldn't have known what sin was if it wasn't for the law. **But sin, taking occasion by the commandment, wrought in me all manner of concupiscence. For without the law sin was dead. (Romans 7:8)** The word **concupiscence** speaks of *"a lust for that which is carnal and unlawful."* Paul knew what lust was and that it is sinful because the law said, **Thou shalt not covet.** The idea here is that the law exposed the sin of man. **Moreover the law entered, that the offence might abound... (Romans 5:20a)** Noah Webster defines **sin** as *"The voluntary departure of a moral agent from a known rule of rectitude or duty, prescribed by God; any voluntary* *transgression of the divine law, or violation of a divine command..."* We can never understand what sin is unless we have some standard to judge by. The law is that standard. Without the law there is no sin. Without God's commandments there can be no transgression. The law is God's standard of righteousness that enables us to distinguish between good and evil.

The Law Ruins the Sinner

For I was alive without the law once: but when the commandment came, sin revived, and I died And the commandment, which was ordained to life, I found to be unto death. For sin, taking occasion by the commandment, deceived me, and by it slew me. (Romans 7:9-11) The law leaves the sinner hopeless. All the law can do for the unsaved man is find him guilty and condemn him. **For whosoever shall keep the whole law, and yet offend in one point, he is guilty of all. (James 2:10)** The law shows the sinner what he is—a sinner! The law shows the sinner his real state—ruined by sin! Anyone who is attempting to get to Heaven by keeping the law will fail. The law has legal power to convict of sin, but no life giving power to deliver us from sin.

The Law Reflects our Sinfulness

Wherefore the law is holy, and the commandment holy, and just, and good Was then that which is good made death unto me? God forbid But sin, that it might appear sin, working death in me by that which is good; that sin by the commandment might become exceeding sinful.

(Romans 7:12-13) Paul establishes the fact that God's law and commandments are **holy, and just, and good.** Paul now asks another question. **Was then that which is good made death unto me?** Paul is asking, "*How did something so holy, and just, and good make me dead?*" Paul answers his own question, **But sin ... that sin by the commandment might become exceeding sinful.** The law didn't make Paul dead, it only revealed his sinfulness and the fact that he was spiritually dead.

The War Within
Romans 7:14-25

This passage gets to the heart of the believer's daily struggle with sin. The Bible teaches that within every Christian there are two opposite and opposing natures (Galatians 5:16-17). There is a sharp contrast between the Spirit and the flesh. When God saves us He does not destroy the old depraved nature which we receive at our natural birth. It is the old nature that causes the believer a lot of trouble! **Because the carnal mind is enmity against God: for it is not subject to the law of God, neither indeed can be. (Romans 8:7)** It is a nature that is an enemy of God and hates everything that is holy and decent. **For I know that in me that is, in my flesh, dwelleth no good thing: for to will is present with me; but how to perform that which is good I find not. (Romans 7:18)** A. W. Tozer said:

> We Christians are cut from the same bolt as the rest of mankind, and while we have been made partakers of a new nature we have not yet been entirely divested of the old. For this reason we are under constant temptation to lapse into the flesh and manifest the old nature rather than the new.

The Bible tells us that the only method for dealing with the old nature is crucifixion. Paul said, **I am crucified with Christ: nevertheless I live; yet not I, but Christ liveth in me: and the life which I now live in the flesh I live by the faith of the Son of God, who loved me, and gave himself for me. (Galatians 2:20)** Again, to the Romans, Paul wrote,

For if ye live after the flesh, ye shall die: but if ye through the Spirit do mortify the deeds of the body, ye shall live. (Romans 8:13) The old nature must be put off. It can be crucified and controlled, but it cannot be reformed.

MAN'S CONDITION

For we know that the law is spiritual: but I am carnal, sold under sin. (Romans 7:14) Please note that Paul is addressing his present condition. At this writing Paul had been saved for many years, but is writing in the present tense when he said, **I am carnal.** The word **carnal** comes from the Greek *"sarkikos"* and means *"fleshly" or "pertaining to the flesh."* The phrase **sold under sin** carries the idea of being sold into slavery. Paul was saying that his flesh is a slave to sin. That is true of every one of us. Man's depraved condition is his biggest problem. The law is spiritual. There is no problem with the law. Paul had concluded that **the law is holy, and the commandment holy, and just, and good. (Romans 7:12)** Here in verse 14 he says that **the law is spiritual.** The law is God's law—it is holy, just, good and spiritual. The problem is that our old flesh is a slave to sin and when we give way to the flesh we serve sin.

MAN'S CONFUSION

For that which I do I allow not: for what I would, that do I not; but what I hate, that do I. If then I do that which I would not, I consent unto the law that it is good. (Romans 7:15-16) Paul was somewhat perplexed by his own conduct. He could not understand himself, because, though he knew what was right and acknowledged that he ought to do it, he nevertheless did not always obey. Paul said, **Now then it is no more I that do it, but sin that dwelleth in me. (Romans 7:17)** He said that the real problem is his old sin nature. The old nature is wayward, wicked and weak and the Christian can get into a lot of trouble by following it.

MAN'S CONFESSION

For I know that in me that is, in my flesh, dwelleth no good thing... (Romans 7:18a) We often hear people say, "*There is a little good in everyone.*" However, one of the greatest Christians who ever lived said, **For I know that in me that is, in my flesh, dwelleth no good thing.** The Bible further states that, **They are all gone out of the way, they are together become unprofitable; there is none that doeth good, no, not one. (Romans 3:12)** The reality is that man has nothing to brag about. When left to himself, man will follow the dictates of the old depraved nature.

Paul says, **for to will is present with me. (Romans 7:18b)** The phrase **to will** speaks of Paul's personal desire. It was his will to obey the law and do right. He lived to please Christ. He strove for victory and he desired it with all of his heart.

Paul goes on, **but how to perform that which is good I find not. For the good that I would I do not: but the evil which I would not, that I do. Now if I do that I would not, it is no more I that do it, but sin that dwelleth in me. (Romans 7:18c-20)** The desire to do right is not enough. But it is certainly a good place to start. The sad fact is that many people don't even have the desire to do right. However, every believer, like Paul, ought have a burning desire to obey and please Christ. Paul stated that it was not a lack of desire, but the weakness of his flesh that hindered him. Jesus said to His disciples in Gethsemane, **Watch and pray, that ye enter not into temptation: the spirit indeed is willing, but the flesh is weak. (Matthew 26:41)** The flesh is the problem and it is a dominant force. Paul said, **I find then a law, that, when I would do good, evil is present with me. (Romans 7:21)** Paul says, "I want to obey the law, but my old sin nature is ever present with me and I am hindered by it."

MAN'S CONFLICT

For I delight in the law of God after the inward man. (Romans 7:22) The word **delight** comes from the Greek *"synedomai"* and means *"to rejoice in, to feel satisfaction."* Notice that Paul's delight and satisfaction was **after the inward man.** The **inward man** is Paul's new nature. It is the Divine nature that delights in and desires the things of God. It is said of the blessed man of Psalm one, **But his delight is in the law of the Lord; and in his law doth he meditate day and night. (Psalms 1:2)** Such rejoicing and delight in the things of God is a trait of the believer.

But I see another law in my members, warring against the law of my mind, and bringing me into captivity to the law of sin which is in my members. (Romans 7:23) Now notice in this verse that there are two laws mentioned here. 1) **the law of my mind** speaking of the desire to obey God's law, and 2) **the law of sin** speaking of that which wars against the desire to do right. This is the struggle of the Christian life. It is all out war. **For the flesh lusteth against the Spirit, and the Spirit against the flesh: and these are**

contrary the one to the other: so that ye cannot do the things that ye would. (Galatians 5:17) The word **lusteth** speaks of a strong desire. Paul states that the Spirit and the flesh lust **against** each other, meaning they have opposite desires for us. The flesh wants us to yield to sin while the Spirit wants us to live for Christ. Paul goes on to say that **these are contrary the one to the other.** The word **contrary** means to "*oppose and confront.*" The flesh and the Spirit are adversaries! This is the cause of the believer's struggle with sin. The flesh and the Spirit are contending for the believer's will. The flesh dictates that we be one way and the Spirit immediately steps up and opposes the sinful nature and demands that we walk in the Spirit. They are not going to compromise and will never be at peace between the two. We must yield to Christ.

We can almost hear the anguish as Paul cries out, **O wretched man that I am! who shall deliver me from the body of this death? (Romans 7:24)** This is a cry of desperation. We cannot overcome the flesh in our own power. Our own strength is not sufficient to attain victory. We must have God's help. That help has been given to us in the person of the Holy Spirit. Jesus said, **It is the spirit that quickeneth; the flesh profiteth nothing. (John 6:63)**

MAN'S CONSOLATION

I thank God through Jesus Christ our Lord So then with the mind I myself serve the law of God; but with the flesh the law of sin. (Romans 7:25) Paul's consolation is that delivery comes through the Lord Jesus Christ. He alone can deliver us from sin. It is by God's wonderful grace that the sinner is delivered.

When John Newton penned the great hymn *"Amazing Grace,"* he wrote, *"Amazing grace, how sweet the sound, that saved a wretch like me."* The modern day libertines have objected to Newton's terminology saying that the word wretch is *"too strong and offensive."* The song has even be revised using *"less offensive terminology."* But John Newton had it right. When Paul said, **O wretched man that I am!** he was describing every one of us as the poor helpless sinners that we are.

Victory For The Believer
Romans 8:1-39

Up until now, Paul has emphasized the sin and helplessness of man. He has hammered the point that we are sinners, we are condemned and that we are under the wrath of God. On top of that he has proven to us that we are powerless to do anything about it. In the last chapter we got a good look at the hopelessness of the situation. Paul spoke of sin's slavery and power over man. We saw Paul's Desperation. **For the good that I would I do not: but the evil which I would not, that I do. (Romans 7:19)** We saw Paul's Defeat. He said, **when I would do good, evil is present with me. (Romans 7:21)** We saw Paul's Despair as he cried, **O wretched man that I am! who shall deliver me from the body of this death? (Romans 7:24)** What an agonizing cry! However, there is hope! After describing the life of sin and slavery, Paul turns his attention to the new life in Christ. A life empowered by the Spirit of God.

WE HAVE A NEW FREEDOM

Jesus Christ promised, **If the Son therefore shall make you free, ye shall be free indeed. (John 8:36)** Paul expounds on the wonderful liberty that believers enjoy in Christ.

We Are No Longer Condemned For Sin

There is therefore now no condemnation to them which are in Christ Jesus, who walk not after the flesh, but after the Spirit. (Romans 8:1) This word **therefore** ties Paul's statement here to the previous teaching in Romans 7:14-24. Paul is now giving us the answer to the hopeless situation he described earlier when he said, **O wretched man that I am! who shall deliver me from the body of this death? (Romans 7:24)** Praise God! He does not leave us where He finds us.

Here is the testimony of a changed man. Notice the word **now.** It is a word that suggests a past. Paul is not talking about the wretched man of chapter seven, he is talking about the changed man. Paul now has a future with hope. No longer is he a condemned man, but he cries out, **There is therefore now no condemnation to them which are in Christ Jesus...** Now old things have passed away and all things have become new. Paul is no longer imprisoned by the flesh, he is empowered by the Spirit. He is no longer Fettered by Sin, he has been Freed by the Saviour. He is no longer a slave, but a saint.

Paul is emphatic when he states that, there is **no condemnation.** Herein lies a great truth that the believer must get a hold of before he can fully enjoy the Christian life. Too many believers have not accepted the blessed truth of these words. They are living a miserable life under the load and guilt of sin that has already been forgiven. They experience no peace, no prosperity and no power. Theirs is a miserable existence of bondage and carnality! Speaking of the fact that we are no longer condemned, Donald Grey Barnhouse said, *"The awareness of this present glorious liberty and freedom is one of the greatest spiritual forces that can ever be unloosed in the life of a believer."* Why are so many believers living under the guilt of their past?

Because they are living under the law and the law condemns. Many Christians are on a guilt trip when they should be on a grace trip. The Galatian believer's had been saved by the grace of God, but they had allowed the Judiazers to bring them back under the law. Paul wrote to them, **I marvel that ye are so soon removed from him that called you into the grace of Christ unto another gospel. (Galatians 1:6)** Many have trusted the God of grace to remove the penalty of sin, but they do not hand over the guilt. God has freed them, but they remain under bondage. **But now, after that ye have known God, or rather are known of God, how turn ye again to the weak and beggarly elements, whereunto ye desire again to be in bondage? (Galatians 4:9)** Believer, get a hold of this truth! When God justified you, He not only removed the condemnation of sin, He removed the guilt also.

Speaking of Jesus Christ the Bible says, **that through this man is preached unto you the forgiveness of sins: And by him all that believe are justified from all things, from which ye could not be justified by the law of Moses. (Acts 13:37-39)** Notice that through Christ the believer is **justified from all things.** It is also clearly stated that **ye could not be justified by the law of Moses.** The law condemns! It cannot remove the penalty, instead it demands the penalty. The law pronounces us guilty and demands death. When believers attempt to live by the law they remain under guilt. But when God justifies us, that justification extends to the removal of the guilt. If you go out and commit a crime against someone, the victim can choose to forgive you, but you are still guilty of the crime. No amount of forgiveness can change the fact that the law was broken and a crime committed. In other words, the victim can forgive you, but he cannot justify you. However, when a sinner comes to Christ, God does both. He forgives and justifies. Forgiveness removes the penalty, but justification removes the guilt. Justification means that you are not merely a forgiven criminal, but that you are righteous. That is why Paul admonished the Galatians to **Stand fast therefore in the liberty wherewith Christ hath made us free, and be not entangled again with the yoke of bondage. (Galatians 5:1)**

We must grasp the truth of this passage, that there is **no condemnation.** Jesus that this same truth:

> **He that believeth on him is not condemned: but he that believeth not is condemned already, because he hath not believed in the name of the only begotten Son of God. (John 3:18)**

> **Verily, verily, I say unto you, He that heareth my word, and believeth on him that sent me, hath everlasting life, and shall not come into condemnation; but is passed from death unto life. (John 5:24)**

There is **no condemnation.** This particular Greek word for condemnation is *"katakrima"* and appears only in the book of Romans. It is a word that speaks of the sentence handed down for crime. The emphasis is not so much on the verdict as on the penalty that the verdict demands. The penalty has been clearly stated, **For the wages of sin is death ... (Romans 6:23)** However, for the believer there will be no carrying out of the sentence. Instead of being under God's condemnation, we are at peace with Him. **Therefore being**

justified by faith, we have peace with God through our Lord Jesus Christ. (Romans 5:1)

Paul emphasizes our new position **in Christ Jesus.** In chapter seven Paul speaks as a wretched man who needed deliverance. Here in chapter eight he speaks as a new man in Christ. The believer is no longer under the law, but **in Christ.** Christ satisfied the demands of the law on the believer's behalf. **By whom also we have access by faith into this grace wherein we stand, and rejoice in hope of the glory of God. (Romans 5:2)** As believers we have this new standing in Jesus Christ. **Being justified freely by his grace through the redemption that is in Christ Jesus. (Romans 3:24)** As we have already learned, the word **justified** means *"to be declared righteous."* Webster defines justification as meaning *"to pardon and clear from guilt; to absolve or acquit from guilt and merited punishment, and to accept as righteous on account of the merits of the Savior, or by the application of Christ's atonement to the offender."* Justification is the act of God whereby He declares the forgiven sinner to be righteous. If you are saved, you are justified. Justification means that you are not merely a forgiven criminal, but that you are righteous. This is our standing in Christ. When God looks at us He sees the imputed righteousness of Christ. He sees us **in Christ.**

Paul identifies us as those, **who walk not after the flesh, but after the Spirit. (Romans 8:1b)** Nearly every commentary that you pick up will tell you that this part of the verse does not belong here. Their assertion is that some *"careless Scribe copied it to this line by mistake."* But rather than casting doubt on God's word, let's just take it as it is. It must be understood that this is not a qualifying statement. We are not at peace with God and free from condemnation due to our walk. Such a position would be salvation by works. Justification has nothing to do with the saint's walk, but is wholly dependent upon the Saviour's work. **Being justified freely by his grace through the redemption that is in Christ Jesus. (Romans 3:24)** Paul is not giving us a condition for being saved, but a fact concerning one who has been saved. The condemnation was not removed because of our conduct, but due to our new position in Christ. When we were placed in Christ, we were given the Holy Spirit. Now being endued with power from on high, He has liberated us from the power of the flesh and now we **walk in newness of life. (Romans 6:4)** We **walk not after the flesh, but after the Spirit.** We are no longer <u>**Condemned by Sin**</u>, next …

<u>We Are No Longer Controlled By Sin</u>

For the law of the Spirit of life in Christ Jesus hath made me free from the law of sin and death. (Romans 8:2) Here we see a higher and more powerful law at work. By the **law of the Spirit of life** the believer is delivered from the **law of sin and death.** By the **law of sin and death** I must die for my sin (Romans 7:23-25), but by the **law of the Spirit of life in Christ Jesus** I am able to live a life that pleases God. **This I say then, Walk in the Spirit, and ye shall not fulfil the lust of the flesh. (Galatians 5:16)** There is a more powerful force at work in the believer. John declared **greater is he that is in you, than he that is in the world. (1 John 4:4)** No wonder

Paul said, **Now thanks be unto God, which always causeth us to triumph in Christ... (2 Corinthians 2:14)**

For what the law could not do, in that it was weak through the flesh. (Romans 8:3a) Notice that the problem with the law is our flesh. We are the problem. The problem is not the law. Paul said earlier, **Wherefore the law is holy, and the commandment holy, and just, and good. (Romans 7:12)** Paul establishes the fact that God's law is **holy, and just, and good.** The trouble is the wicked and depraved flesh. **Because the carnal mind is enmity against God: for it is not subject to the law of God, neither indeed can be. (Romans 8:7)** The law is a religion of perfection. If you offend on one point, you offend on all (James 2:10). The law demands perfection and our flesh is incapable of that.

Now Paul points out that Jesus conquered sin. He lived a perfect life and in so doing He satisfied the righteous demands of the law. Paul says, **God sending his own Son in the likeness of sinful flesh, and for sin, condemned sin in the flesh. (Romans 8:3b)** Here we see three major doctrines concerning Christ.

First, **His Virgin Birth. God sending his own Son in the likeness of sinful flesh.** This is the Virgin Birth, the incarnation of the Son of God. **And without controversy great is the mystery of godliness: God was manifest in the flesh, justified in the Spirit, seen of angels, preached unto the Gentiles, believed on in the world, received up into glory. (1 Timothy 3:16)** When Jesus was on earth He was God in human flesh. **But when the fulness of the time was come, God sent forth his Son, made of a woman, made** under the law. (Galatians 4:4) John said, **And the Word was made flesh, and dwelt among us, and we beheld his glory, the glory as of the only begotten of the Father, full of grace and truth. (John 1:14)** Since it impossible for the Law to produce righteousness in man, God sent His Son in our likeness, that is in a body of flesh, to meet the law's requirements on our behalf. Notice that Jesus did not come in *sinful flesh,* but in the **likeness** of sinful flesh. He was 100% man and 100% God. Christ did not simply become human, but became a unique person, fully God, and at the same time, fully man.

Second, **His Vicarious Atonement**. He didn't just come to visit. The text says that He came **for sin.** Jesus Christ came as a sacrifice for the sins of the world. **For he hath made him to be sin for us, who knew no sin; that we might be made the righteousness of God in him. (2 Corinthians 5:21)** He has no sin of His own—His is perfectly sinless. He died as the Lamb of God in our place. **And he is the propitiation for our sins: and not for ours only, but also for the sins of the whole world. (1 John 2:2)** Noah Webster defines **propitiation** as, *"The act of appeasing wrath and conciliating the favor of an offended person."* Christ's work on the cross atoned for all men and provided full satisfaction to God—the offended party.

Third, **His Victorious Resurrection**. When Jesus came out of the tomb, He **condemned sin in the flesh.** Had Jesus been a sinner death could have laid claim on Him. The Bible says, **the soul that sinneth, it shall die. (Ezekiel 18:4)** Jesus had no sin therefore the grave could not hold Him. This is the gospel. **For I delivered unto you first of all that which I** also received, how that Christ died for our sins according to the scriptures; And that he was buried, and that he rose again the third day according to the scriptures. (1 Corinthians 15:3-4) Paul clearly defines the Gospel message as the death, burial, and resurrection of Christ. Paul makes it clear that Jesus literally lived, He literally died, and He literally rose from the dead. After all, What good is a dead Saviour? Many today are trying to destroy the doctrine of Christ's resurrection, but the infallible word of God proclaims it to be true. Man's salvation is dependent upon the resurrection of Christ.

We are no longer **Condemned by Sin**, we are no longer **Controlled by Sin**, and ...

We No Longer Continue In Sin

That the righteousness of the law might be fulfilled in us, who walk not after the flesh, but after the Spirit. (Romans 8:4) At the moment of salvation we become a new creature and a partaker of divine nature. As we grow in Christ putting off the old man and putting on the new, we begin to experience victory in Christ. We no longer live according to the dictates of the depraved nature, but according to the power and leadership of the Holy Spirit.

Again the point is made that we have a *New Position*. Paul speaks of **righteousness of the law (Romans 8:4a)** being fulfilled in us. When a sinner is saved, the whole righteousness of the Law is fulfilled in him. That is when a sinner trusts Jesus Christ as Saviour, he is made right with God—he is declared righteous.

We also have a ***New Power***. Paul speaks of us those who **walk not after the flesh, but after the Spirit. (Romans 8:4b)** Notice in the first part of the verse that righteousness of the law is fulfilled **in us**, not *by us.* The Power of the Holy Spirit makes it possible for me to live the way Christ wants me to live. This is something God does in me by His power. The flesh is that which I do in and of myself. It speaks of that which I produce with my own ability. The Spirit refers to that which God does in me by the Person of the indwelling Holy Spirit.

And we have a ***New Priority***. Paul said that we **walk not after the flesh, but after the Spirit. (Romans 8:4c)** The Bible always takes the position that new life produces a new direction. The person who is born of God is not satisfied to wallow in the sinful mire of the world. The whole idea of repentance is a turning from sin to God. Bible repentance does not mean that one gets immediate victory over all the sin of his life, but it does involve an attitude of being fed up with sin and having a desire for the Christ-life. Repentance says, *"stop doing what you are doing and start doing right."*

WE HAVE A NEW FIGHT

The Christian life is a war zone. The war between the Spirit and the flesh rages as each battle for control of the believer's heart and life. Paul describes our new fight with the flesh.

The Contrast

For they that are after the flesh do mind the things of the flesh; but they that are after the Spirit the things of the Spirit. For to be carnally minded is death; but to be

spiritually minded is life and peace. (Romans 8:5-6) Paul contrasts the person who lives **after the flesh** with those **that are after the Spirit.** The word **mind** comes from the Greek *"phroneo"* and means *"to set ones heart upon something, interest oneself in, set the affection on."* Those who mind the things of the flesh are controlled and directed by the corrupt fallen nature. Their thoughts and affection are upon their own selfish interests. They seek their own gratification. They live for self. Those who walk **after the Spirit** set their mind upon the things of God. They are concerned with His will for their lives. The priorities and principles of God are important to them. They are faithful in their Bible study, prayer, giving, attending Church, soul-winning, etc.

The Conflict

Because the carnal mind is enmity against God: for it is not subject to the law of God, neither indeed can be. So then they that are in the flesh cannot please God. (Romans 8:7-8) The word **enmity** comes from *"echthra"* and speaks of *"hostility and opposition."* The idea is that of a battlefield where opposing armies are engaged in battle. **For the flesh lusteth against the Spirit, and the Spirit against the flesh: and these are contrary the one to the other: so that ye cannot do the things that ye would. (Galatians 5:17)** The word **lusteth** speaks of a strong desire. Paul states that the Spirit and the flesh lust **against** each other, meaning they have opposite desires for us. The flesh wants us to succumb to sin while the Spirit wants us to live for Christ. Paul goes on to say that **these are contrary the one to the other.** The word **contrary** means to *"oppose or confront."* Here is the reason for the conflict that Christians have in their life as they struggle to put off the old and put on the new. The flesh dictates that we be one way and the Spirit immediately steps up and opposes the sinful nature and demands that we walk in the Spirit. The old carnal nature is an enemy of God and hates everything that is holy and decent.

The Companion

But ye are not in the flesh, but in the Spirit, if so be that the Spirit of God dwell in you. Now if any man have not the Spirit of Christ, he is none of his. (Romans 8:9) Every believer has received the Holy Spirit as his companion. The Holy Spirit came the moment we were saved and we have the promise of God that He will never leave (Ephesians 4:30). This verse states that if we do not have the Holy Spirit, we do not belong to God. Paul says, **ye were sealed with that holy Spirit of promise, Which is the earnest of our inheritance until the redemption of the purchased possession, unto the praise of his glory. (Ephesians 1:13-14)** The word **earnest** speaks of *"a pledge or a guarantee."* The word is a legal and commercial term that refers to a *"down payment"* made as a pledge of full payment. It is the guarantee of the purchaser's intent to follow through on the entire transaction. The Holy Spirit God's guarantee to see us through to Heaven. **Being confident of this very thing, that he which hath begun a good work in you will perform it until the day of Jesus Christ: (Philippians 1:6)**

The Conquest

But if the Spirit of him that raised up Jesus from the dead dwell in you, he that raised up Christ from the dead shall also quicken your mortal bodies by his Spirit that

dwelleth in you. (Romans 8:11) The same Spirit that raised up Christ from the dead resides in the believer. Think about that! The same power that raised Jesus Christ from the dead has been given to the believer to empower him to live the victorious life. He is the One who brings life and the One who will raise us from the grave.

Therefore, brethren, we are debtors, not to the flesh, to live after the flesh. For if ye live after the flesh, ye shall die: but if ye through the Spirit do mortify the deeds of the body, ye shall live. (Romans 8:12-13) The child of God is no longer in debt to the flesh to live after its dictates. Believers have been given the Holy Spirit and by His power are no longer bound by the chains of sin. The word **mortify** means *"to kill, to put to death."* By the Holy Spirit's power we can overcome the flesh, putting its deeds to death.

WE HAVE A NEW FAMILY

To be a child of God means more that merely escaping Hell. Praise God that those who know Him have escaped Hell and will never have to face His penal wrath. However, there is more to it than that. Those who come to Christ receive the adoptions of sons and become members of the family of God.

Our Affinity

For as many as are led by the Spirit of God, they are the sons of God. (Romans 8:14) As a member of this new family we are **led by the Spirit of God.** The word **led** carries the idea of *"directing and guiding."* The same word is used of the Spirit leading Jesus. **And Jesus being full of the Holy Ghost returned from Jordan, and was led by the Spirit into the** wilderness. (Luke 4:1) There is a great need in our day for God's people to surrender to the Lordship of Christ and the leadership of His Spirit. The normal Christian life, according to the word of God, is the Spirit-filled life. We are to follow God's leadership.

> **Trust in the LORD with all thine heart; and lean not unto thine own understanding. In all thy ways acknowledge him, and he shall direct thy paths. (Proverbs 3:5-6)**

> **Shew me thy ways, O LORD; teach me thy paths. Lead me in thy truth, and teach me: for thou *art* the God of my salvation; on thee do I wait all the day. (Psalms 25:4-5)**

Paul said, **And be not drunk with wine, wherein is excess; but be filled with the Spirit. (Ephesians 5:18)** To be filled with the Holy Spirit does not mean that we have more of Him, but that He has more of us at His will. Every child of God has all of the Holy Spirit that he will ever have. The issue is not that we get more of Him, but that he gets more of us. We must yield ourselves to Him allowing Him to take over and control us.

We also see that those who are led by the Spirit are called the **sons of God.** There is the false doctrine held by many today that teaches the fatherhood of God and the brotherhood of man. Their assumption is that God is the Father of all and all are His children. However, we know that such a theology does not line up with Scripture. Jesus said to the Pharisees, **Ye are of your father the devil... (John 8:44)** The Pharisees were religious, but they were lost. They remained children of the Devil. One becomes a son by birth.

Jesus said, **Verily, verily, I say unto thee, Except a man be born again, he cannot see the kingdom of God. (John 3:3)** Peter said, **Blessed be the God and Father of our Lord Jesus Christ, which according to his abundant mercy hath begotten us again unto a lively hope... (1 Peter 1:3a)** The phrase **begotten us again** means that we have been born again into the family of God. We sometimes hear folks scoff at this wonderful Bible phrase. The term **born again** is a good Bible term and believers need not shy away from it just because the world doesn't like it. But one thing is for sure. Being born again means a changed life. When a baby is born a new life enters the world. The same is true of the spiritual birth. When a sinner turns from his sin to Jesus Christ as his personal Savior, a new life enters the world. **But as many as received him, to them gave he power to become the sons of God, even to them that believe on his name: Which were born, not of blood, nor of the will of the flesh, nor of the will of man, but of God. (John 1:12-13)** At the very moment of salvation the Holy Spirit came into my life and I was born again. I became a child of God.

Our Adoption

For ye have not received the spirit of bondage again to fear; but ye have received the Spirit of adoption, whereby we cry, Abba, Father. (Romans 8:15) Now Paul deals with the Bible doctrine of adoption. This is a wonderful and assuring truth.

Adoption means that we are *Released From Fear.* **For ye have not received the spirit of bondage again to fear... (Romans 8:15a)** The word **bondage** speaks of slavery. The finished work of Christ freed us from such bondage to fear. **Forasmuch then as the children are partakers of flesh and blood, he also himself likewise took part of the same; that through death he might destroy him that had the power of death, that is, the devil; And deliver them who through fear of death were all their lifetime subject to bondage. (Hebrews 2:14-15)** There is a contrast here between slaves and sons. Under the law men were slaves living under the fear of God's judgment. God delivers us from the slavery of sin and makes us children. After the new birth we are sons living in His favor. Our new relationship is free from any kind of slavery. We do not fear God as the slave fears his master. Rather, we love Him as a son loves his father. The slave obeys his master for fear of punishment. We serve the Lord without such fear, as a son lovingly serves his father.

Adoption means that we are ***Recognized By The Father***. Paul says, **... but ye have received the Spirit of adoption, whereby we cry, Abba, Father. (Romans 8:15b)** Adoption indicates a family relationship. In our day, adoption is the act of legally bringing someone into our family who was not brought in by the process of birth. However, that is not what Paul is talking about here. All who are born again are already children of God by way of the new birth.

The word **adoption** comes from the Greek *"huiothesia"* and means *"to be placed as a son."* In the Roman world children of a man were acknowledged as his children and part of the family by birth. However, when the children began to come of age, usually 12 or 13 years old, the father would chose one of them as heir to continue his name and inherit his estate. There would be a big ceremony and celebration—this was called an adoption. So then we see that adoption has to do with our privileges, not with our relationship to God. **Adoption** is the act of God, whereby He bestows upon us all the rights and privileges of sonship.

Paul says, **whereby we cry, Abba, Father.** So much so are we the children of God that we can address Him as **Abba, Father.** The word **Abba** is the Aramaic word for *"Father."* It is similar to the English word *"Daddy or Papa,"* a term of endearment used by small children in addressing their fathers. Jesus used this term when praying in the garden of Gethsemane. **And he said, Abba, Father, all things are possible unto thee; take away this cup from me: nevertheless not what I will, but what thou wilt. (Mark 14:36)** It is a term that overflows with the thoughts of love, grace, and compassion and expresses the precious relationship we have with God **And because ye are sons, God hath sent forth the Spirit of his Son into your hearts, crying, Abba, Father. (Galatians 4:6)**

Our Assurance

The Spirit itself beareth witness with our spirit, that we are the children of God. (Romans 8:16) The relationship between the believer and the Holy Spirit was designed by Jesus Himself.

> **And I will pray the Father, and he shall give you another Comforter, that he may abide with you for ever; Even the Spirit of truth; whom the world cannot receive, because it seeth him not, neither knoweth him: but ye know him; for he dwelleth**

with you, and shall be in you. I will not leave you comfortless: I will come to you. (John 14:16-18)

One of the greatest assurances we have as Christians is the personal indwelling witness of the Spirit of God. If you are genuinely saved, you will know it because the Spirit of God will hold communion with you. He will speak to your heart. He will warn you. He will lead you. He will comfort you. He will teach you the truth.

Our Abundance

And if children, then heirs; heirs of God, and joint-heirs with Christ; if so be that we suffer with him, that we may be also glorified together. (Romans 8:17) In this new family relationship as God's children, we becomes **heirs of God**. Peter said:

> **Blessed be the God and Father of our Lord Jesus Christ, which according to his abundant mercy hath begotten us again unto a lively hope by the resurrection of Jesus Christ from the dead, To an inheritance incorruptible, and undefiled, and that fadeth not away, reserved in heaven for you. (1 Peter 1:3-4)**

An **inheritance** is wealth that one receives as a member of a family. We already have the **earnest of our inheritance. (Ephesians 1:14)**, which is the Holy Spirit (2 Corinthians 1:22, 5:5). As noted before, the word **earnest** speaks of *"a pledge of a part given in advance."* The Holy Spirit is the Divine pledge of our future inheritance. Not only are we an heir of God, but we are also **joint-heirs with Christ.** Jesus said, **All things that the Father hath are mine... (John**

16:15) As joint-heirs we share in everything that God the Father has given to Jesus Christ. If we have the Son, we have everything.

WE HAVE A NEW FUTURE

In this section we are reminded of an important truth. The truth that although we are saved, we still live in a world that is under the curse of God. As a result of the curse there is a lot of groaning and turmoil. In the midst of this world's trouble it would be easy to just throw up our arms and quit. But Paul speaks of **the glory which shall be revealed in us. (Romans 8:18)** As we compare our present suffering with our future glory we quickly see that there is no real comparison.

A Groaning Creation

For the earnest expectation of the creature waiteth for the manifestation of the sons of God. (Romans 8:19) It is not only the believer who looks forward to our adoption and glorification. All of nature longs for that day of final deliverance. **For the creature was made subject to vanity, not willingly, but by reason of him who hath subjected the same in hope. (Romans 8:20)** We can only imagine what a beautiful place this earth must have been when it first came from the hands of God. Several times throughout creation the Bible speaks of God's work as **good (Genesis 1:4; 10; 10; 12; 18; 21; 25; 31).** Upon completion of creation we have the testimony of God on the matter. **And God saw every thing that he had made, and, behold, it was very good ... (Genesis 1:31)** There were no deserts, no earthquakes, no tsunamis, no thorns, no thistles, no death, and no vicious animals. What a place it must have been! It was paradise for sure. But when Adam sinned and disobeyed God, the entire creation came under the curse. God said, **cursed is the ground for thy sake. (Genesis 3:17)** Instead of a peaceful paradise, the world is in awful turmoil. Today we have earthquakes shaking the world, volcanoes erupting, tornadoes and hurricanes destroying whole cities. Wild and vicious beasts roam the world. Poisonous snakes and insects are everywhere. God never intended for this to be.

Because the creature itself also shall be delivered from the bondage of corruption into the glorious liberty of the children of God. (Romans 8:21) Though nature as we know it today, is not in its original condition, Paul says that someday the curse will be lifted and all creation, which shared in the effects of man's sin, will someday share in the effects of man's redemption.

For we know that the whole creation groaneth and travaileth in pain together until now. (Romans 8:22) The whole creation groans and is longing for the day of restoration. Scientists tell us that all the sounds of nature are in the minor key. They have a mournful tone. The winds, the storms, the tides, and even the songs of the birds. Isaiah said the same thing.

> **The earth mourneth and fadeth away, the world languisheth and fadeth away, the haughty people of the earth do languish. The earth also is defiled under the inhabitants thereof; because they have transgressed the laws, changed the ordinance, broken the everlasting covenant. Therefore hath**

the curse devoured the earth, and they that dwell therein are desolate: therefore the inhabitants of the earth are burned, and few men left. (Isaiah 24:4-6)

The phrase **groaneth and travaileth in pain** is very descriptive. The analogy is that of giving birth and is used to describe the sufferings of man and creation. During labor there is usually awful pain, but at the same time the comforting expectation that a new life will soon be born. We have the Divine promise that the curse will be lifted. **And there shall be no more curse … (Revelation 22:3)** Also see (Isaiah 11:1-10; 65:17-25). We have to deal with sufferings and pains of a sin cursed world, but we have God's promise that there is a new day dawning. At this time order will be restored to nature.

A Glorified Christianity

And not only they, but ourselves also, which have the firstfruits of the Spirit, even we ourselves groan within ourselves, waiting for the adoption, to wit, the redemption of our body. (Romans 8:23) Not only does all nature wait for the time of deliverance from the effects of the curse, but Christians also eagerly await **the redemption of our body.** All of the pain, the diseases, the hurts, the disorders, the cancers and death are the results of sin and the curse.

For we are saved by hope: but hope that is seen is not hope: for what a man seeth, why doth he yet hope for? But if we hope for that we see not, then do we with patience wait for it. (Romans 8:24-25) Someday God will deliver our bodies from disease and death, and give us new bodies like the resurrected body of Jesus. What a blessed hope we have! The word **hope** speaks of something yet in the future, a future expectancy. When people use the word **hope** today it often carries with it the idea of uncertainty. They say, I hope I have enough money to pay my bills. I hope gas prices come down. However, in the Bible the word **hope** carries the idea of certainty because when God says something is going to happen we can expect it to happen without any doubt. As believers we have the assurance that because we stand justified, we will someday be glorified.

These old weary and worn out bodies will be exchanged for perfect and glorified ones. Blind eyes will see. Deaf ears will hear. The lame will walk again. My hope is not in science. It is not in the armies of the world. It is not even in religion. My friend, our hope lies in the coming of King of kings and the Lord of lords. **So when this corruptible shall have put on incorruption, and this mortal shall have put on immortality, then shall be brought to pass the saying that is written, Death is swallowed up in victory. (1 Corinthians 15:54)**

A Gracious Companionship

Likewise the Spirit also helpeth our infirmities: for we know not what we should pray for as we ought: but the Spirit itself maketh intercession for us with groanings which cannot be uttered. (Romans 8:26) Notice, first all that the Holy Spirit **helpeth our infirmities.** The word **helpeth** carries the idea of coming to one's aid to give support. This particular word is used only one other time in Scripture. It is the word used in Luke 10:40 of Martha's plea for her sister

Mary to help her. This word carries the idea of one helping another to bear a heavy load. The word **infirmities** means *"weakness, feebleness, and frailty."* We don't like to admit it, but we are weak, feeble and frail at times. How often we get in a place where we are utterly helpless.

Paul said at those times, **we know not what we should pray for as we ought.** One of the great struggles in the Christian life is to be consistent in our prayer life. Prayer is the one thing that everyone can do and yet, many do not have a prayer life. The only thing the disciples ever asked Jesus to teach them was how to pray. Every believer encounters some difficulty in prayer. Sometimes the burden is so heavy that we can't bare it. Sometimes there are no words to express the hurt of our heart. The load on our heart goes beyond our ability to cry out to God. Under the crushing weight of our circumstances the Holy Spirit cries out to God making **intercession for us with groanings which cannot be uttered.** R. Kent Hughes says, *"The Holy Spirit does not give armchair advice. He rolls up his sleeves and helps us bear our weakness. That is real help."*

A Glorious Confidence

And we know that all things work together for good to them that love God, to them who are the called according to his purpose. (Romans 8:28) This verse speaks of God's providence. Our confidence is not in our own ability, but in God. We are assured that all things will work together for good. Notice that it says **all things.** This includes the pleasant and the unpleasant; the good days as well as bad days; hard times as well as the good times. All things work together for good. Paul began this verse with the words,

And we know. We believers have a sure thing in Jesus Christ. We can face every situation with the confidence that God is in charge and we will prevail. In Darwin's Origin of Species he used the phrase we suppose over 800 times. How sad! As children of God, we do not have to suppose, **we know**! Paul said, **For the which cause I also suffer these things: nevertheless I am not ashamed: for I know whom I have believed, and am persuaded that he is able to keep that which I have committed unto him against that day. (2 Timothy 1:12)** R. A Torrey called Romans 8:28 *"a soft pillow for a tired heart."*

A Great Cause

For whom he did foreknow, he also did predestinate to be conformed to the image of his Son, that he might be the firstborn among many brethren. Moreover whom he did predestinate, them he also called: and whom he called, them he also justified: and whom he justified, them he also glorified. (Romans 8:29-30) These verses deal with the glorification of the believer. John declared, **we shall be like Him. (1 John 3:2)** So many jump on the word **predestinate** and miss the word **conformed** losing sight of the fact that God's ultimate purpose in predestination is to bring about in the believer Christ-likeness. God has predestined that every believer be conformed to the image of Christ. The word **predestinate** comes from the word *"horizoo"* and means *"to determine before, or to establish one's boundaries."* It is the word from which our English word *"horizon"* is derived. Perfection is just over the horizon for believers. The

Christian's ultimate destiny has been predetermined by God. We will be like Christ.

WE HAVE A NEW FOUNDATION

From verse 31 to the end of the chapter Paul asks and answers a series of questions that prove the believer's security. Robert Mounce said"

> "Nowhere in the annals of sacred literature do we find anything to match the power and beauty of this remarkable paean of praise."

William Newell calls this section:

> "...the mountaintop of the Christian position."

Everything that Paul has said in Romans prior to this chapter has led up to this great pinnacle.

Our Resources Are Inexhaustible

What shall we then say to these things? If God be for us, who can be against us? (Romans 8:31) The word **if** does not imply doubt. The word is not speaking of a mere possibility, but a fulfilled condition. The idea is, *"Because or Since God be for us."* Paul is not questioning whether or not God is for us, but he is stating the fact that God is for us! God in His great love gave His Son to save us. He gave us the Holy Spirit! He justified us! He adopted us! He granted us a wonderful inheritance! Now we see that He guarantees our future glorification! With all of this in mind Paul asks, **who can be against us?** The obvious answer is no one! This is a rhetorical question that emphasis the fact that God is for us, therefore all opposition is of none effect. The Father is for us and proved it by giving His Son (Romans 8:32). The Son makes intercession for us (Romans 8:34), and the Spirit is for us as well (Romans 8:26).

He that spared not his own Son, but delivered him up for us all, how shall he not with him also freely give us all things? (Romans 8:32) The words **spared not** carries the idea of giving it all. God did not hold back or refrain from giving His best in order to save us. Oliver B Green said, *"God who is rich in mercy, spared nothing in providing man's salvation. Heaven was emptied of God's best to provide our redemption."* God gave Heaven's best for the world's worst. God turned His back on Christ as He died on Calvary so that He could turn His face to us when we came to the cross.

If God would do that, **how shall he not with him also freely give us all things? (Romans 8:32b)** Robert Mounce said, *"The argument is from the greater to the lesser. A God who sacrificed his own Son on our behalf will certainly not withhold that which by comparison is merely trivial."* God gave His best to save us, surely He will see it through. **Being confident of this very thing, that he which hath begun a good work in you will perform it until the day of Jesus Christ: (Philippians 1:6)** Our resources are inexhaustible! Everything that God has, He has put into our salvation. The believer will remain saved and will arrive safely into Heaven someday.

Our Redeemer Is Incontestable

Who shall lay any thing to the charge of God's elect? It is God that justifieth. (Romans 8:33) The phrase **lay any thing to the charge of** comes from *"enkaleokata"* and means *"to bring a charge against, call to account, accuse, arraign for prosecution."* It carries the idea of coming forward with evidence as an accuser in a court case. We know that there is no shortage of accusers. Christians are often condemned and criticized by the ungodly. Satan also accuses us before God. However, these are often accusations without evidence. Paul says, **It is God that justifieth. (Romans 8:33b)** God has already justified the believer. As we learned earlier Justification means to stand before God just as if we have never sinned. The believer is clothed in Christ's righteousness.

> **For he hath made him to be sin for us, who knew**
> **no sin; that we might be made the righteousness of**
> **God in him. (2 Corinthians 5:21)**

To bring a charge against a believer is to bring a charge against Christ. Sin has been taken to the Cross. The debt has been paid. The believer has been justified and Christ's righteousness imputed to him. Our Redeemer accomplished all this for us and He is incontestable.

Our Redemption is Irrefutable

Who is he that condemneth? It is Christ that died, yea rather, that is risen again, who is even at the right hand of God, who also maketh intercession for us. (Romans 8:34) This verse is loaded! Peter Pell, the Plymouth Brethren teacher said, *"The four great facts in vs. 34 stand out like the horns of the brazen altar ready to be gripped by any trembling soul."* The rhetorical question is asked, **Who is he that condemneth? (Romans 8:34a)** Since it is God that justifies us, the obvious answer is no one. Notice the four great truths.

First, **_Christ's Substitution_. It is Christ that died (Romans 8:34b)** Christ died on the cross taking upon Himself our sin and condemnation. We cannot be condemned because He has already been condemned for us. **There is therefore now no condemnation to them which are in Christ Jesus ... (Romans 8:1)**

Second, **_Christ's Success_. Christ is risen again. (Romans 8:34c)** Even the grave couldn't hold Jesus Christ. His resurrection is proof of His victory over sin and death. The fact that the Father raised Him from the grave shows that He was satisfied with Christ's sacrifice. **But for us also, to whom it shall be imputed, if we believe on him that raised up Jesus our Lord from the dead; Who was delivered for our offences, and was raised again for our justification. (Romans 4:24-25)**

Third, **_Christ's Sovereignty_. Christ at the right hand of God. (Romans 8:34d)** Jesus is right now seated at the right hand of God. He is the exalted Christ. **But unto the Son he saith, Thy throne, O God, is for ever and ever: a sceptre of righteousness is the sceptre of thy kingdom. (Hebrews 1:8)** Jesus Christ is seen as the Sovereign God who's throne will last forever. We cannot be condemned because it is impossible to condemn the work of our Sovereign Saviour. We are eternally secure based upon Christ's position.

Fourth, **_Christ's Supplication_.** Christ also **maketh intercession for us. (Romans 8:34e)** This intercessory ministry of the living Christ is another guarantee that God will never change the verdict by which He declared us justified. This is the great High Priestly work of Christ.

> **Wherefore he is able also to save them to the uttermost that come unto God by him, seeing he ever liveth to make intercession for them. (Hebrews 7:25)**

> **Who being the brightness of his glory, and the express image of his person, and upholding all things by the word of his power, when he had by himself purged our sins, sat down on the right hand of the Majesty on high. (Hebrews 1:3)**

Notice the text says that when Jesus entered Heaven, He **sat down.** That is a very interesting statement. Now there were no seats in the Temple. The sacrifices made there by the priests were never finished. Their work was a continuing one. **And every priest standeth daily ministering and offering oftentimes the same sacrifices, which can never take away sins. (Hebrews 10:11)** However, Jesus' work as our Great High Priest was different. Speaking of Jesus, the Bible says, **But this man, after he had offered one sacrifice for sins for ever, sat down on the right hand of God. (Hebrews 10:12)**

We may fail, but our Intercessor will not. **My little children, these things write I unto you, that ye sin not. And if any man sin, we have an advocate with the Father, Jesus Christ the righteous: And he is the propitiation for our sins: and not for ours only, but also for the sins of the whole world. (1 John 2:1-2)** Because His prayers for us will be answered, we will never lose our salvation. No one can condemn us because Christ died for us. Christ arose for us, Christ is at the right hand of God for us, Christ intercedes for us. What a Saviour!

Our Relationship Is Inseparable

Who shall separate us from the love of Christ? (Romans 8:35a) Paul now moves on to the subject of Christ's great love for us. Paul speaks of one peril after another that we might face. Paul asks **shall tribulation, or distress, or persecution, or famine, or nakedness, or peril, or sword? (Romans 8:35)**

1) **Tribulation**—this is a word that carries the idea of pressure. It means to be squeezed in. It is a word that is used to describe the difficult and stressful situations that we face.

2) **Distress**— this word means *"narrowness of room, calamity, anguish."* The idea is that of being helplessly hemmed in with no way of escape.

3) **Persecution**—this speaks of affliction suffered for the sake of Christ. William Newell points out that, *"Its verb means, to make to run, or to run swiftly to catch those pursued; so, to persecute."* It speaks of someone carrying on a campaign against the believer.

4) **Famine**—this words speaks of *"a scarcity of food, dearth, hunger."* Many believers were severely persecuted for their faith. As a result they were driven from their jobs and families where they literally went hungry and some even starved to death.

5) **Nakedness**—this word does not necessarily speak of stark nudity. The word carries the idea of being *"scantily clad."* The idea is being inadequately coved thereby being exposed to the elements.

6) **Peril**—This word means *"to be exposed to danger."* Paul well understood this word. He used it eight times in one verse. **In journeyings often, in perils of waters, in perils of robbers, in perils by mine own countrymen, in perils by the heathen, in perils in the city, in perils in the wilderness, in perils in the sea, in perils among false brethren. (2 Corinthians 11:26)**

7) **Sword**—Here Paul is referring to death. Some will die for Christ's sake. Untold thousands have died a martyrs death. Paul did!

One of the first things many folks do in trials is question God's love. Yet we are assured that no one or nothing can separate us from the love of Christ. Trials are not a sign that Christ no longer loves us. God's people have always suffered for their faith.

As it is written, For thy sake we are killed all the day long; we are accounted as sheep for the slaughter. (Romans 8:36) God's people have always been hated and despised by the Devil and the world. The believer is nothing more than **sheep for the slaughter** so far as this world is concerned. The enemies of God despise the children of God. Paul quotes Psalm 44:22 to express that there will always be opposition to God's people and the work of God in the world. In Paul's sufferings he said, **But none of these things move me, neither count I my life dear unto myself, so that**

I might finish my course with joy, and the ministry, which I have received of the Lord Jesus, to testify the gospel of the grace of God. (Acts 20:24)

Nay, in all these things we are more than conquerors through him that loved us. (Romans 8:37) Paul concludes by stating that in all these things we can have the victory. The present distress is only temporary! Our present suffering is nothing compared to the glory that will someday be ours.

For I am persuaded, that neither death, nor life, nor angels, nor principalities, nor powers, nor things present, nor things to come, Nor height, nor depth, nor any other creature, shall be able to separate us from the love of God, which is in Christ Jesus our Lord. (Romans 8:38-39) Notice the words, **I am persuaded**. This is an expression of deep conviction. Paul is not setting forth a mere theory. This far more than religious rhetoric. Paul has experienced tribulation, distress, nakedness, peril, and sword, but none of these thing separated him from Christ's love. This is a powerful conviction. Paul lists five more things that cannot separate us from the love of Christ.

1) **Neither death nor life...** Even death is powerless to hurt the child of God. The Lord Himself died, and by His resurrection destroyed death's power. Because He lives, the believer will live. **Therefore we are always confident, knowing that, whilst we are at home in the body, we are absent from the Lord: For we walk by faith, not by sight: We are confident, I say, and willing rather to be absent from the body, and to be present with the Lord. (2 Corinthians 5:6-8)**

Paul mentions **life** is in contrast of death. The most trying experiences of life are unable to break the bond of love between God and us.

2) **Nor angels, nor principalities, nor powers...** This refers to supernatural beings. The kingdom of Satan with its principalities and powers have already been conquered by Jesus Christ. Jesus **having spoiled principalities and powers, he made a shew of them openly, triumphing over them in it. (Colossians 2:15)** Satan and his gang are defeated enemies. They can never separate us from the love of God.

3) **Nor things present, nor things to come...** This refers to the scope of time. Most things change with time, but throughout all eternity the unchanging God who loves us will still be the Sovereign God. He is the Lord of time and eternity.

4) **Nor height, nor depth...** Nothing in the vastness of space can separate the believer from Christ. Height and depth are astrological terms. The word **height** *"hypsoma"* refers to the time a star was at its zenith, when its influence was greatest, and **depth** comes from *"bathos"* referring to a star at its lowest point. Even in the infinity of space, there is nothing that can separate us from Christ's marvelous love.

5) **Nor any other creature.** That settles it! The word **creature** means *"that which is created."* There is absolutely nothing in all the universe that can separate us from God's love in Christ.

Oh! How God's love for us has been proven! **For God so loved the world, that he gave his only begotten Son, that whosoever believeth in him should not perish, but have everlasting life. (John 3:16)** The greatest demonstration of love this world has ever known is the cross of Calvary. The evidence of His unwavering love is the sacrifice of His Son for the sin of a lost world. **But God commendeth his love toward us, in that, while we were yet sinners, Christ died for us. (Romans 5:8)** Calvary demonstrates God's unconditional love for us. God's love will never change or diminish in any way. Our salvation is secure. We have an eternal salvation.

Paul's Heart For Israel
Romans 9:1-5

The Jews were God's chosen people. They were the apple of God's eye and still have a special place in God's plan. However, when God sent them His Son, they failed to receive Him. They rejected and crucified the Messiah. God set Israel aside. In AD 70, Titus attacked Jerusalem, the Temple was destroyed and the Jewish people were scattered. A new dispensation had started and God was calling out a Gentile people for His bride. Gentiles were accepting the Messiah, while the Jews as a nation had rejected Him. How do we reconcile the Old Testament promises to Israel as a nation—with the setting-aside of the nation? Did God's plan fail? What happens to Israel now? Romans 9-11, answers these questions and deals with the fact that God still has a plan for Israel. Israel's failure does not thwart God's sovereignty.

THE HONESTY DECLARED

I say the truth in Christ, I lie not, my conscience also bearing me witness in the Holy Ghost. (Romans 9:1) Paul really pours his heart out here. He is broken because of Israel's rejection of the Messiah. Because of his conversion and ministry to the Gentiles, Paul had probably been accused of turning his back on his own people—the Jews. Paul pleads for his people to believe him and receive his message as from God.

THE HEAVINESS DISPLAYED

That I have great heaviness and continual sorrow in my heart. (Romans 9:2) The word **heaviness** comes from *"lype"* and carries the idea of *"grief and mourning."* The word

sorrow is from *"odyne"* and carries the idea of *"intense pain, anguish and torment."* On top of all of the torment and grief we are told that is was **continual.** The word **continual** means *unceasing.* This was something that Paul couldn't shake. There was constant grief over the fact that people were lost and going to Hell. Bear in mind that Paul has just taken us to the mountaintop of the Christian position, to the pinnacle of praise in Romans chapter 8. He has just assured the believer of the wonderful security we enjoy and guaranteed glorification that we will soon realize. However, in the midst of all the joy Paul couldn't forget the fact that Israel was lost.

For I could wish that myself were accursed from Christ for my brethren, my kinsmen according to the flesh. **(Romans 9:3)** Paul's desire for Israel's salvation was so strong that if it were possible, he would have went to Hell in their place. The tragedy of the day is that believer's seem to be able go about enjoying their salvation while the world goes to Hell. Christian, it is the norm for us to be grieved over the lost. It is the example of Scripture. Jeremiah the weeping Prophet, like Paul was broken over the lost. **Oh that my head were waters, and mine eyes a fountain of tears, that I might weep day and night for the slain of the daughter of my people! (Jeremiah 9:1)** And consider the Lord Himself as He stood broken hearted over Jerusalem crying, **O Jerusalem, Jerusalem, thou that killest the prophets, and stonest them which are sent unto thee, how often would I have gathered thy children together, even as a hen gathereth her chickens under her wings, and ye would not! (Matthew 23:37)** If we as believers can muddle through life with little or no concern for the lost, there is definitely something wrong! We need to stay focused on our mission. How can we truly believe in a place so awful as Hell and not be grieved that multitudes are going there.

THE HERITAGE DISCUSSED

Who are Israelites; to whom pertaineth the adoption, and the glory, and the covenants, and the giving of the law, and the service of God, and the promises; Whose are the fathers, and of whom as concerning the flesh Christ came, who is over all, God blessed for ever. Amen. (Romans 9:4-5) Paul points out that God had bestowed upon Israel many wonderful privileges and blessings.

The Adoption. The first privilege the Israelites enjoyed was adoption by God. The Old Testament has much to say about the fact that God chose Israel to be His people. Throughout the word of God we find that Israel enjoys a unique and privileged relationship with God. No other nation had been called the people of God as were the Jews.

The Glory. This refers to the manifested glory of God's presence. When the Israelites left Egypt God's glory was in their midst in the form of a cloud by day and a pillar of fire by night. The Shekinah glory appeared as a cloud filling the Tabernacle, and later filling the Temple in the same way (1 Kings 8:10-11). No other nation enjoyed the visible presence of God in such a way.

The Covenants. God made covenants with Abraham, Moses, David, and the nation as a whole. These covenants promised material and spiritual blessings to the people of Israel such as land, protection, and prosperity. No other nation on earth received promises from God like those received by Israel.

Giving of the Law. The giving of the Law at Sinai was to Israel, and only to Israel. Romans 2:14 distinctly declares, **the Gentiles, have not the law.** No nation or people has had the law delivered to them directly from the finger of God. Israel alone received the law (Deuteronomy 4:7-8; Psalm 147:19).

The service of God. This refers to the privilege Israel had enjoyed as God met and dwelt with them in the services of the Tabernacle and then in the Temple. No other people enjoyed the presence and partnership of God in such a way.

The promises. Besides the covenants, God gave many precious promises to the Jewish nation. These promises assured them of His love, protection and other blessings on them.

The fathers. The fathers were the patriarchs: Abraham, Isaac, Jacob, Joseph, Moses and King David What a great heritage the Israelites enjoyed.

Of whom as concerning the flesh Christ came. The greatest privilege of all was the Saviour. His mother, Mary, was a Jewess. His nation, was Israel; His people, the Jews. God gave them the highest privilege in allowing the Messiah to come through their nation.

In spite of Israel's tremendous privilege and blessings, they missed the Messiah. When the Saviour came, Israel rejected Him. Instead of embracing Him, they crucified Him. Paul's heart was broken for his people and his greatest desire was for their salvation. So much so that he would have gone to Hell in their place. This is the soul-winner's heart.

God's Sovereignty And Israel's Failure
Romans 9:6-29

Some define election as meaning that certain people are born to be saved and certain others are born to be lost. However, such an interpretation is definitely contrary to the heart of God and Paul. Israel was the elect of God, but not all of Israel was saved. God's election of Israel did not automatically make them children of God. The problem was not with God, but with Israel.

GOD'S SELECTION—ISRAEL'S PROMISES

Not as though the word of God hath taken none effect. For they are not all Israel, which are of Israel: (Romans 9:6) God made many wonderful promises to Israel. He promised them that they would be a great nation (Genesis 12:2). He promised them the land (Genesis 15:18; 17:8). He promised a future kingdom age when there would be justice in all the earth (Jeremiah 23:5). He promised them the Messiah (Isaiah 33:17-22). However, because of God's present dealings with the Gentiles, some might falsely conclude that God's plan for Israel had come to nothing. Paul corrects that falsehood. He says it is, **Not as though the word of God hath taken none effect ... (Romans 9:6a)** The phrase **none effect** comes from the Greek *"ekpipto"* and means to *"drop off or fall short."* God assures the Jew that His word has not failed. God's promises have not fallen short of being accomplished. The promises made to Israel are still good and will be fulfilled just as the word of God proclaims.

Neither, because they are the seed of Abraham, are they all children: but, In Isaac shall thy seed be called. (Romans 9:7) The Jews had the idea that every descendant of Abraham, because he was an Israelite by birth, would inherit the blessings of God. Paul corrects this false thinking when he explains that not all of Abraham's natural descendants are his spiritual descendants. To illustrate Paul asks, **are they all children: but, In Isaac shall thy seed be called**. The point Paul is stressing here is that not all Jews in fact belong to God's kingdom. Only Jews with Abraham's faith are his true children. He quotes from Genesis 21:12 to make that point. **In Isaac shall thy seed be called**. Isaac was the son of promise as Abraham, in faith, took God at His word. The point Paul is making here is that God's promise to Abraham would follow the lineage of faith, not physical ancestry.

That is, They which are the children of the flesh, these are not the children of God: but the children of the promise are counted for the seed For this is the word of promise, At this time will I come, and Sara shall have a son. (Romans 9:8-9) Paul continues to expand and expound on this truth. Ishmael was a child of the flesh, but Isaac was the child of promise. **For it is written, that Abraham had two sons, the one by a bondmaid, the other by a freewoman. But he who was of the bondwoman was born after the flesh; but he of the freewoman was by promise. (Galatians 4:22-23)** The birth of Ishmael was a natural thing accomplished in the power of the flesh (Genesis 16). Ishmael was not the product of Abraham trusting and obeying God, but because he trusted and followed his wife. It was a fleshly attempt to accomplish what God had promised. Therefore, Ishmael was the child of the flesh. However, Isaac was the son of promise. **For this is the word of promise, At this time will I come, and Sara shall have a son. (Romans 9:9)** God kept His promise in a way that only He could. The birth of Isaac was supernatural (Genesis 18:14). It was a miraculous birth. God promised Isaac and God miraculously provided. Paul's point is that though Abraham had two sons, only one of the sons partook of the covenant promise and became part of the chosen line which would become a great nation and out of whom the Messiah would come.

And not only this; but when Rebecca also had conceived by one, even by our father Isaac; For the children being not yet born, neither having done any good or evil, that the purpose of God according to election might stand, not of works, but of him that calleth; (Romans 9:10-11) Paul illustrates with another example. In the case of Isaac's sons, there was no such distinction. There were different mothers and different births, but **conceived by one**. They had the same father. God chose between them before they were born, **neither having done any good or evil, that the purpose of God according to election might stand, not of works, but of him that calleth;** The point is that the choice was based on the will of God alone. The firstborn was rejected and the second born was chosen. This is completely contrary to what man would do. If man were doing the choosing then Esau would have been chosen because the firstborn son was the preferred son in Jewish culture. **And Isaac loved Esau, because he did eat of his**

venison: but Rebekah loved Jacob. (Genesis 25:28) The point is that the choice belonged to God not to man. Man is removed from the equation.

The Calvinists love to jump into this chapter in an attempt to prove their position on salvation. They delight in the word **election**. Election is a good Bible word. We who disagree with Calvinism are often maligned as not believing in election. Such a statement is not true. It is not that we don't believe in election, it is that we don't agree with Calvin's brand of election. The Bible nowhere teaches that God arbitrarily predestines certain ones to be saved while at the same time predestinating others to go to Hell. An honest examination of this text shows that salvation is not even the issue here. **It was said unto her, The elder shall serve the younger. (Romans 9:12)** The context clearly teaches that service is the issue—not salvation. This refers back to God's words to Rebekah. **And the LORD said unto her, Two nations are in thy womb, and two manner of people shall be separated from thy bowels; and the one people shall be stronger than the other people; and the elder shall serve the younger. (Genesis 25:23)** There is not one single reference in any of these passages about Jacob or Esau's salvation. The context is very clear that this has nothing to do with Heaven and Salvation, but nations and service. It is not dealing with individual election, but to the corporate election of a nation.

As it is written, Jacob have I loved, but Esau have I hated. (Romans 9:13) Paul is quoting from the book of (Malachi 1:1-4; 3:6). Again, the context clearly shows that the issue is not Jacob and Esau as individuals, but as nations which descend from them. The teaching is clear. Jacob is Israel and Esau is Edom. Some actually take this verse out of context and teach that God hates the non-elect. They make God out to be an unloving monster rather than the loving God of the Bible. God is simply using the term **hate** in a relative sense. This same idea is found elsewhere in the Scriptures. You will remember in the book of Genesis when Leah spoke of being hated by her husband (Genesis 29:33). However, back in verses 30 we learn that Jacob **loved Rachel more than Leah. (Genesis 29:30)** It wasn't that Jacob hated Leah, but that he loved Rachel so much more. Jesus used the same idea in His teaching. **If any man come to me, and hate not his father, and mother, and wife, and children, and brethren, and sisters, yea, and his own life also, he cannot be my disciple. (Luke 14:26)** Think about it! Does Jesus literally want us to hate our mother and father? No! The idea here is that of giving Christ first place. It refers to desiring something less than something else. As disciples of Christ, we are to put Him first. God's choice was to put Jacob first.

GOD'S SOVEREIGNTY—ISRAEL'S POTTER

What shall we say then? Is there unrighteousness with God? God forbid. (Romans 9:14) God's choice of Isaac rather than of Ishmael, and of Jacob rather than Esau, may lead some to call God's righteous character into question. Paul says, **God forbid**. As we learned before, this phrase is the strongest negative Greek expression and carries the idea of an absolute impossibility. Moses asked the rhetorical question, **Shall not the Judge of all the earth do right?**

(Genesis 18:25) Of course He will. Whatever He does, whatever happens, whatever He allows, whatever decisions He makes, although we may not be able to understand it with our finite minds, God is right. There is absolutely no unrighteousness and no injustice with Him. As the Psalmist said, **the LORD is upright ... there is no unrighteousness in him. (Psalms 92:15)**

For he saith to Moses, I will have mercy on whom I will have mercy, and I will have compassion on whom I will have compassion. (Romans 9:15) Notice that the subject here is mercy, not salvation. Paul is quoting from Exodus 33:19 and it is important to understand the context of this passage. In Exodus chapter 32 the children of Israel quickly and wickedly turned aside out of the way which God commanded them (Exodus 32:8). They took their gold and fashioned a golden calf and gave it the glory for delivering them from Egypt (Exodus 32:2-4). They were guilty of violating the second commandment and they all deserved to be judged and destroyed (Exodus 32:10) . But Moses as a faithful leader interceded on their behalf (Exodus 32:11-13). God granted Moses his request and spared the people (Exodus 32:14). Here is the point! **So then it is not of him that willeth, nor of him that runneth, but of God that sheweth mercy. (Romans 9:16)** God could have righteously destroyed them all. But he made a decision to show mercy instead. The mercy was in no way based upon man's merit, in fact they deserved the judgment. The Israelites were spared solely because God chose to show them mercy.

For the scripture saith unto Pharaoh, Even for this same purpose have I raised thee up, that I might shew my power

in thee, and that my name might be declared throughout all the earth. Therefore hath he mercy on whom he will have mercy, and whom he will he hardeneth. (Romans 9:17-18)** Now Paul illustrates by using Pharaoh as an example. Pharaoh was a man who was known for his pride and stubbornness against God. He was great in his own eyes, but to God he was a vessel fit for wrath. **And in very deed for this cause have I raised thee up, for to shew in thee my power; and that my name may be declared throughout all the earth. (Exodus 9:16)** Again, the issue here is not salvation, but service. Pharaoh was a wicked man and an open enemy of God, yet God raised him up as king to fill a divine purpose.

The Calvinists trip all over this passage and especially the phrase, **whom he will he hardeneth. (Romans 9:18b)** Their understanding is that God arbitrarily forced upon Pharaoh a hard and stubborn heart. In making such a claim they make God the author of sin. This cannot be so. **Let no man say when he is tempted, I am tempted of God: for God cannot be tempted with evil, neither tempteth he any man: But every man is tempted, when he is drawn away of his own lust, and enticed. (James 1:13-14)** When man sins, it comes from his own depraved heart—not from God. There are two things that must be remembered in the hardening of Pharaoh's heart.

First, God already foreknew that Pharaoh was stubborn and would not let the people go. **And I am sure that the king of Egypt will not let you go, no, not by a mighty hand. (Exodus 3:19)** This is God's foreknowledge. In His foreknowledge God knew that Pharaoh would not cooperate.

Second, when God hardened Pharaoh's heart He was only responding to what Pharaoh had already done to himself. Yes, it is clear that God said He would and He did harden Pharaoh's heart. However, it was not some arbitrary hardening whereby Pharaoh had no freewill. Pharaoh had a choice to make as to whether or not he would obey God or resist Him. He made the conscious choice to resist. Notice these verses:

> **But when Pharaoh saw that there was respite, he hardened his heart, and hearkened not unto them; as the LORD had said. (Exodus 8:15)**

> **And Pharaoh hardened his heart at this time also, neither would he let the people go. (Exodus 8:32)**

> **And when Pharaoh saw that the rain and the hail and the thunders were ceased, he sinned yet more, and hardened his heart, he and his servants. (Exodus 9:34)**

The fact of the matter is that Pharaoh hardened his own heart and God only responded to him in kind. **He, that being often reproved hardeneth his neck, shall suddenly be destroyed, and that without remedy. (Proverbs 29:1)** The analogy of hardening the neck is taken from the stubborn mule or ox that turns away from and stiffens his neck to rebel against the yoke. This analogy is applied to all who stubbornly resist the gracious call of God to repent of their sins.

Thou wilt say then unto me, Why doth he yet find fault? For who hath resisted his will? (Romans 9:19) Paul either anticipates or answers another objection. **Why doth he yet find fault?** In other words, How can God judge Pharaoh if God Himself is responsible for hardening Pharaoh's heart? People have trouble reconciling the sovereignty of God with the free agency of man. When the hyper-Calvinist says that God arbitrarily hardened Pharaoh's heart, instead of glorifying a Sovereign God, they make Him out to be the author of sin. Often God is portrayed as someone playing cat and mouse games with man. On one hand He orders them to repent and on the other He hardens them so that they can't repent. That is not the God of the Bible.

The Arminians go to the other extreme claiming that man in his free will can thwart the plans of God. This too is wrong. The whole idea of this passage is that the Sovereign God of Heaven will not be defeated. His purposes and plans will come to fruition even though stubborn and rebellious man refuses to cooperate.

For who hath resisted his will? (Romans 9:19b) God's Sovereignty does not destroy the free will of man. When confronted with the will of God, man has a choice to make. If he submits and surrenders, he has God's blessing. If he resists and continues in his stubbornness, he becomes hardened and brings upon himself the wrath of God. Either way God is seen as Sovereign and glorified. The question **For who hath resisted his will?** does not mean that God can't be resisted or opposed, but that no one resists Him successfully. God will accomplished His purpose in spite of man's opposition. God's purpose was to deliver His people from the bondage of Pharaoh. If Pharaoh had submitted to God, the people would have been delivered and God would have received the glory for their deliverance. However, Pharaoh hardened himself and said, ... **Who is the LORD, that I should obey his voice to let Israel go? I know not the LORD, neither will I let Israel go. (Exodus 5:2)** Pharaoh's problem was clear, he didn't care what God said. He was profiting from the bondage of God's people and he wasn't going to let them go. However, the resistance of Pharaoh did not frustrate the plan and power of God. God delivered the children of Israel and received the glory when He drowned the mighty Pharaoh and his army in the red sea. God wins every time!

When Pharaoh stubbornly resisted the mercy and judgments of God he became so hardened that God finally gave him over to his own ways. Three times in the Romans chapter one we see this tragic truth.

> **Wherefore God also gave them up ... (Romans 1:24a)**
>
> **For this cause God gave them up ... (Romans 1:26a)**
>
> **God gave them over to a reprobate mind... (Romans 1:28)**

The phrases **gave them up** and **gave them over** comes from a word that carries the idea of *"handing over, or delivering to another."* Douglas Moo said, *"Like a judge who hands over a prisoner to the punishment his crime has earned, God hands over the sinner to the terrible cycle of ever-increasing sin."* Because of their rebellion against God, He in effect says, *"Have it your way. Do your own thing."* When God gives the sinner up, He withdraws His Divine restraint, allowing him to hopelessly sink deeper and deeper into the moral quagmire he has chosen for himself. This isn't God's choice. It is the sinner's choice.

Nay but, O man, who art thou that repliest against God? Shall the thing formed say to him that formed it, Why hast thou made me thus? Hath not the potter power over the clay, of the same lump to make one vessel unto honour, and another unto dishonour? (Romans 9:20-21) Paul drives his point home with the illustration of a potter. A piece of pottery has no power to make charges against its maker. What right does man have to reply against God? Is man smarter than God? Is the creature wiser than the Creator? Who are we to question the righteousness of what God does? The potter has every right to take a lump of clay and make it into whatever vessel he chooses.

Again, this does not say that God arbitrarily fits someone as a vessel of wrath. If we are going to use the illustration of the Potter we must take it as a whole. The point folks almost always miss here is that the clay is involved. While the Potter has His Sovereign right to do as He chooses, it does not change the fact that the clay can resist the Potter. Often there are hard lumps that hinder the Potter's work with the clay. The clay must be softened. The Potter will work with the clay rolling and kneading it until it becomes soft and pliable. However, there are times when the clay will not work out to be used as the Potter desires. Jeremiah got a hold of this truth when God sent him to the Potter's House for an object lesson concerning Israel's future. The Bible says, **And the vessel that he made of clay was marred in the hand of the potter: so he made it again another vessel,**

as seemed good to the potter to make it. (Jeremiah 18:4) The clay was marred. It couldn't be used for the purpose that the Potter originally intended. However, it could be made into **another vessel, as seemed good to the potter to make it.** This is what happened in Pharaoh's case. If Pharaoh had softened up and surrendered to God he could have been used that way. But he refused, so God hardened him and made him **again another vessel** and God's Sovereign purpose was accomplished. Pharaoh could have been a vessel for **honour**, but he ended up a vessel of **dishonour**.

What if God, willing to shew his wrath, and to make his power known, endured with much longsuffering the vessels of wrath fitted to destruction: (Romans 9:22) Pharaoh prepared himself for destruction by refusing to repent. He was proud, puffed up and obstinate. He was a vessel of wrath. Paul is drawing a parallel with the nation Israel who were opposing the gospel. God was patient and merciful with them giving them space for repentance. **And thinkest thou this, O man, that judgest them which do such things, and doest the same, that thou shalt escape the judgment of God? Or despisest thou the riches of his goodness and forbearance and longsuffering; not knowing that the goodness of God leadeth thee to repentance? (Romans 2:3-4)**

And that he might make known the riches of his glory on the vessels of mercy, which he had afore prepared unto glory, Even us, whom he hath called, not of the Jews only, but also of the Gentiles? (Romans 9:23-24) God chose to make known the riches of his glory on the vessels of

mercy, which he had afore prepared unto glory. Paul is referring to the gentiles to whom the gospel had been opened up to. Upon Israel's continued stubbornness and now failure to receive their Messiah God made a sovereign choice to reach to the gentiles.

As he saith also in Osee, I will call them my people, which were not my people; and her beloved, which was not beloved And it shall come to pass, that in the place where it was said unto them, Ye are not my people; there shall they be called the children of the living God. **(Romans 9:25-26)** Paul quotes several Old Testament passages (Hosea 1:10, 2:23) to show that God had already prophesied that only a remnant of Israel would be saved, and not the whole nation. What a blessed privilege we Gentiles enjoy. We who were on the outside with no hope have been called by God unto salvation.

> **Wherefore remember, that ye being in time past Gentiles in the flesh, who are called Uncircumcision by that which is called the Circumcision in the flesh made by hands; That at that time ye were without Christ, being aliens from the commonwealth of Israel, and strangers from the covenants of promise, having no hope, and without God in the world: But now in Christ Jesus ye who sometimes were far off are made nigh by the blood of Christ. (Ephesians 2:11-13)**

We were **aliens from the commonwealth of Israel.** The word **aliens** comes from *"apallotrioo"* and means *"estranged, foreign; not belonging to the same country, land* or government. *not allied; adverse to."* The word **commonwealth** comes from *"politeia"* and means *"citizenship."* We were on the outside with no entrance, no help, no place to belong. As a result we had **no hope** and we were **without God in the world**. What a mess we were in, but God in His mercy said, **I will call them my people, which were not my people; and her beloved, which was not beloved ... there shall they be called the children of the living God**. (Romans 9:25-26)

Esaias also crieth concerning Israel, Though the number of the children of Israel be as the sand of the sea, a remnant shall be saved: For he will finish the work, and cut it short in righteousness: because a short work will the Lord make upon the earth. (Romans 9:27-28) Isaiah warned that only a remnant would survive and return to the land after judgment. **The remnant shall return, even the remnant of Jacob, unto the mighty God For though thy people Israel be as the sand of the sea, yet a remnant of them shall return: the consumption decreed shall overflow with righteousness. (Isaiah 10:21-22)** God had promised Abraham, **That in blessing I will bless thee, and in multiplying I will multiply thy seed as the stars of the heaven, and as the sand which is upon the sea shore; and thy seed shall possess the gate of his enemies; (Genesis 22:17)** God's promises had not failed. Everything that God promised to Israel as a nation had been fulfilled, including the assurance that the number of Israelites would be **as the stars of the heaven, and as the sand which is upon the sea shore.** As Murray says, *"the covenant promise did not contemplate or guarantee the salvation of all ethnic Israel."*

The fact that only a remnant of Israel were saved in no way means that God failed. **And as Esaias said before, Except the Lord of Sabaoth had left us a seed, we had been as Sodoma, and been made like unto Gomorrha. (Romans 9:29)** Paul says that it is only by God's grace that even the remnant out of Israel is saved.

GOD'S SALVATION—ISRAEL'S PRESUMPTION

What shall we say then? That the Gentiles, which followed not after righteousness, have attained to righteousness, even the righteousness which is of faith. But Israel, which followed after the law of righteousness, hath not attained to the law of righteousness. (Romans 9:30-31) The word **righteousness** as it is used here is not dealing so much with right living as to a right standing with God. The Gentiles were not God's chosen people and were known for their sinfulness down through the generations. But they came into a place of blessing, while the Jews, who were devout and religious failed. The Jews failed because they refused the Redeemer.

Wherefore? Because they sought it not by faith, but as it were by the works of the law. For they stumbled at that stumblingstone; As it is written, Behold, I lay in Sion a stumblingstone and rock of offence: and whosoever believeth on him shall not be ashamed. (Romans 9:32-33) The Jew believed that he could have a relationship with God by earning it. He thought that his strict obedience to the law would result in salvation. It was this philosophy that led to a rejection of Jesus Christ as their Messiah. As long as man believes that he can earn salvation by his own works, he will reject the message of salvation by faith in Jesus Christ. After all, he doesn't need Jesus if he can save himself. The thought of needing a Saviour is offensive to one who thinks that he is good enough to go to Heaven on his own merit. Israel stumbled over Christ. Instead of accepting Jesus as their Messiah, He became to them a **stumblingstone and rock of offence**.

God's Plan Of Salvation
Romans 10:1-21

As we begin the study of chapter ten, let us keep in mind that chapters 9-11 are one long parenthesis, and that they have to do with Israel's past (chapter 9), present (chapter 10), and future (chapter 11). Also keep in mind that chapters 1-8 are **Doctrinal**, chapters 9-11 are **Dispensational** and chapters 12-16 deal with our **Duty** as believers. Chapters 1-8 show us how God has provided His gift of salvation. Chapters 9-11 show how Israel, as a nation, has rejected God's gift of salvation. Chapters 12-16 show those who accept God's salvation how to live it out in our daily lives.

In chapter 9 we saw that, because of Israel's rejection of the Messiah, God temporally set her aside for a time, as a nation. During that time, known as the Church Age He is offering salvation to the Gentiles. Although God has set Israel aside, Individual Jews are being saved during the Church age. In chapter 11 we learn that when Christ comes again, He will once again deal with Israel as a nation. **For I would not, brethren, that ye should be ignorant of this mystery, lest ye should be wise in your own conceits; that blindness in part is happened to Israel, until the fulness of the Gentiles be come in. (Romans 11:25)** When the Church is raptured out of this world God will gather Israel into their homeland and deal with them as a nation once again. **And so all Israel shall be saved: as it is written, There shall come** out of Sion the Deliverer, and shall turn away ungodliness from Jacob: (Romans 11:26)

THE SAVIOUR REVEALED

Here Paul points out that Israel being ignorant of God's righteousness, set out to establish their own. He continues to establish that Christ is the end of the law and that is by calling on Christ that men are saved.

The Desire Of Paul

Brethren, my heart's desire and prayer to God for Israel is, that they might be saved. (Romans 10:1) Paul had a burning desire to see the Jew saved. Notice how the heart guides the life. Paul had a **heart's desire** that motivated him in **prayer to God** for his kinsman's salvation. The word **desire** speaks of a *"deep longing, yearning, or craving."* Paul had an indescribable yearning to see his people come to Christ.

The Dilemma Of Israel

For I bear them record that they have a zeal of God, but not according to knowledge. For they being ignorant of God's righteousness, and going about to establish their own righteousness, have not submitted themselves unto the righteousness of God. (Romans 10:2-3) Paul points out that Israel's ignorance of God's righteousness led to their false theology of self-righteousness based on the keeping the law. Let's keep in mind here that Israel's ignorance was not due to a lack of information from God on the matter of righteousness. Paul argued earlier, **that unto them were**

committed the oracles of God. (Romans 3:2) The word **oracles** speaks of the supernatural utterances of God. God's word was committed to the Jews. They knew that Abraham **believed in the LORD; and he counted it to him for righteousness. (Genesis 15:6)**They well knew that Noah was saved by grace. **But Noah found grace in the eyes of the LORD. (Genesis 6:8)** They weren't just ignorant of God's way. They were willingly ignorant. **For this they willingly are ignorant of, that by the word of God the heavens were of old, and the earth standing out of the water and in the water: (2 Peter 3:5)** Like the people of the last days, Israel had fallen into apostasy and refused to hear the word of God on the matter. They were religious, but lost.

Notice Paul points out that they had a submission problem. Israel had **not submitted themselves unto the righteousness of God. (Romans 10:3b)** Paul has just spent a whole chapter talking about God's Sovereignty and election. Now he deals with the other side of the coin—human responsibility and submission to God! Israel had been a stubborn and rebellious people. In his sermon to the Jews Stephen pointed this out when he said, **Ye stiffnecked and uncircumcised in heart and ears, ye do always resist the Holy Ghost: as your fathers did, so do ye. (Acts 7:51)** Israel's problem was rebellion.

The Design Of Christ

For Christ is the end of the law for righteousness to every one that believeth. For Moses describeth the righteousness which is of the law, That the man which doeth those things shall live by them. (Romans 10:4-5) The word **end** comes from *"telos"* and carries the idea of completion. Jesus said, **Think not that I am come to destroy the law, or the prophets: I am not come to destroy, but to fulfil. (Matthew 5:17)** Jesus fulfilled or completed the law. Remember that the law was a schoolmaster to bring us to Christ. **Wherefore the law was our schoolmaster to bring us unto Christ, that we might be justified by faith. But after that faith is come, we are no longer under a schoolmaster. (Galatians 3:24-25)** The law as a School master teaches us that we are incapable of obeying its righteous demands. Every time we try, we fail. This schoolmaster was designed **to bring us unto Christ, that we might be justified by faith.** Once we realize that we can't be justified by the law we turn to Christ for salvation. Jesus Christ is God's righteousness. Jesus Christ is the One who puts an end to man having to seek righteousness through the law. Paul said, **Christ is the end of the law for righteousness to every one that believeth.**

THE SAVIOUR RECEIVED

Here Paul deals with the fact that their Messiah had already come. He had walked among them, they had seen His works and yet they rejected Him when all they had to do was receive Him.

The Reasoning Of Scripture

But the righteousness which is of faith speaketh on this wise, Say not in thine heart, Who shall ascend into heaven? (that is, to bring Christ down from above:) Or, Who shall descend into the deep? (that is, to bring up

Christ again from the dead). (Romans 10:6-7) In these two verses Paul draws from Deuteronomy 30:11-14 to make a point that the Jews should have been well aware of.

> **For this commandment which I command thee this day, it is not hidden from thee, neither is it far off. It is not in heaven, that thou shouldest say, Who shall go up for us to heaven, and bring it unto us, that we may hear it, and do it? Neither is it beyond the sea, that thou shouldest say, Who shall go over the sea for us, and bring it unto us, that we may hear it, and do it? But the word is very nigh unto thee, in thy mouth, and in thy heart, that thou mayest do it. (Deuteronomy 30:11-14)**

Moses and Paul were teaching Israel that what they needed, God had already provided. Now notice that Moses says, **it is not hidden from thee, neither is it far off. (Deuteronomy 30:11)** The Jews were notorious for seeking after signs. They even came to Jesus demanding signs. **Then certain of the scribes and of the Pharisees answered, saying, Master, we would see a sign from thee. But he answered and said unto them, An evil and adulterous generation seeketh after a sign; and there shall no sign be given to it, but the sign of the prophet Jonas: (Matthew 12:38-39)** They were looking for a sign when the Messiah stood right there with them. All they had to do was believe the word of God. In seeking a sign they rejected both the written word and the living Word. They were looking for something they could do, when in fact, it had already been done. **This is a faithful saying, and worthy of all**

acceptation, that Christ Jesus came into the world to save sinners; of whom I am chief. (1 Timothy 1:15) What the Jews were looking for was right under their nose and they couldn't discern it. God became flesh and dwelt among them and they missed it. They knew what the word of God said, but they didn't know what it meant. **But what saith it? The word is nigh thee, even in thy mouth, and in thy heart: that is, the word of faith, which we preach; (Romans 10:8)** Christ has already come to the earth. He died in our place and was raised for our justification. Everything that is necessary for the salvation has already been completed. God's righteousness through faith in Jesus Christ is not distant and difficult, it is present and practical. Paul is telling them to just surrender to the truth they have. God has already provided the Messiah.

The Reception Of Salvation

That if thou shalt confess with thy mouth the Lord Jesus, and shalt believe in thine heart that God hath raised him from the dead, thou shalt be saved For with the heart man believeth unto righteousness; and with the mouth confession is made unto salvation. (Romans 10:9-10) Christ has accomplished the work of salvation. We are simply responsible to believe and confess it. Paul hones in on the essence of the gospel message. We learn here that the gospel includes a mouth confession, heart belief, and Divine assurance.

First, there is *__Confession—The Speaking Of The Lips__*. **That if thou shalt confess with thy mouth the Lord Jesus … (Romans 10:9a)** The word **confess** comes from the Greek "homologeo." It is a compound word. "*Homo*" means "*the same*" and "*logeo*" means "*to say or speak.*" Therefore, the word **confess** means "*to speak the same thing.*" We are to confess or speak the same thing about Christ as God the Father speaks. It means that in order for one to be saved he must confess that Jesus is God's substitute for sin, that He is Lord and Saviour, that He is Deity and that He rose from the grave. It is important to read this passage just as God wrote it. Please note that Paul did not simply say to confess Jesus. He specifically stated the **Lord** Jesus. The curse of the day is salvation without Lordship. Unfortunately there are extremes at both ends. There are those who teach that the repeating of a little prayer saves, while others go so far to the other side with repentance that they end up with a works salvation. However, there is a balance in Scripture. Someone has said, "*The pendulum swings, ridiculous extreme, bypassing the truth which lieth between.*" The truth of the matter is that Lordship is clearly taught here within the context of salvation. The sinner does not have to and cannot make Jesus Lord of every area of his life in order to be saved. The sinner can repent himself all the way to the grave and still go to hell. Repentance does not save. Christ saves! To actually make Jesus Christ Lord of our lives is the process of sanctification. It is a lifelong process. To make Christ Lord of our lives is something we can do only after we have been saved and given the Holy Spirit.

However, to be saved it's clear that one must do more than simply repeat a prayer. He must hear the gospel, understand that he has offended a Holy God, recognize His Lordship, and ask forgiveness. The sinner being dealt with may not understand everything about Lordship, but he must receive Christ as Lord. The word Paul uses for **Lord** is *"kurios."* To the Jew that word meant God. It spoke of the One Who is supreme over all—the Lord God of Heaven.

Second, there is ***Conviction—The Sincerity Of The Heart***. Paul says that one must also **...believe in thine heart that God hath raised him from the dead, thou shalt be saved. (Romans 10:9b)** Saving faith goes beyond what the tongue says to what the heart believes. Paul says, **For with the heart man believeth unto righteousness ... (Romans 10:10a)** This is a heart conviction. Salvation is more than a mere profession of faith. Confession without conviction does not produce salvation. **Thou believest that there is one God; thou doest well: the devils also believe, and tremble. (James 2:19)** A mere intellectual belief is not enough to be saved; there must be a heart belief.

The Christian life is lived from the heart, not from the head. **And Philip said, If thou believest with all thine heart, thou mayest. And he answered and said, I believe that Jesus Christ is the Son of God. (Acts 8:37)** Paul said, **For with the heart man believeth unto righteousness ... (Romans 10:10)** The word **believeth** comes from *"pisteuo."* It speaks of a deep seated faith and confidence. When Paul speaks of the heart here he is talking about the very core of our being. When Paul talks about heart belief he is saying that one must believe from the very depths of his soul that Jesus was sent from the Father, He died in a sacrificial and substitutionary death and He rose from the grave. That is heart belief.

Third, **_Confidence—The Security Of The Believer._ For the scripture saith, Whosoever believeth on him shall not be ashamed. (Romans 10:11)** Eternal security is important to the victorious life of the believer. The word **ashamed** carries the idea of *"being shamed, confounded or dishonored."* This is a promise. By believing on Christ, the Christian receives a salvation that cannot be taken away or forfeited. Nothing can separate the believer from the love of Christ. Jesus said:

> **And I give unto them eternal life; and they shall never perish, neither shall any man pluck them out of my hand. (John 10:28)**

There are folks who love to argue against eternal security. Their profession is unsure and unsecure. Their salvation is one of doubt and disappointment. Though they have made a profession of faith, they are fearful of losing it. Jesus said, **All that the Father giveth me shall come to me; and him that cometh to me I will in no wise cast out. (John 6:37)**, The believer's salvation comes with security.

The Reach Of The Saviour

For there is no difference between the Jew and the Greek: for the same Lord over all is rich unto all that call upon him. (Romans 10:12) God's offer of salvation extends to whosoever will. It makes no difference who you are nor how much you've sinned. Your nationality and skin color are irrelevant. No matter who we are, Jew or Gentile, rich or poor, black or white. When we come to Christ, we receive the same treatment. He is **rich unto all that call upon Him**.

The metaphor of riches is used many times to speak of God's grace and salvation.

> In whom we have redemption through his blood, the forgiveness of sins, according to the riches of his grace; (Ephesians 1:7)

> And that he might make known the riches of his glory on the vessels of mercy, which he had afore prepared unto glory, (Romans 9:23)

> O the depth of the riches both of the wisdom and knowledge of God! how unsearchable are his judgments, and his ways past finding out! (Romans 11:33)

> The eyes of your understanding being enlightened; that ye may know what is the hope of his calling, and what the riches of the glory of his inheritance in the saints, (Ephesians 1:18)

> That in the ages to come he might shew the exceeding riches of his grace in his kindness toward us through Christ Jesus. (Ephesians 2:7)

> That he would grant you, according to the riches of his glory, to be strengthened with might by his Spirit in the inner man; (Ephesians 3:16)

> But my God shall supply all your need according to his riches in glory by Christ Jesus. (Philippians 4:19)

> To whom God would make known what *is* the riches of the glory of this mystery among the

Gentiles; which is Christ in you, the hope of glory: (Colossians 1:27)

God's grace is seen in His riches poured out upon those who come to Him for salvation.

The Reality Of Simplicity

For whosoever shall call upon the name of the Lord shall be saved. (Romans 10:13) This is one of the great salvation promises of the Bible. The gift of salvation is available to anyone who will call upon the Lord in faith. C K. Barrett said,

> "Calling upon the name of the Lord' is far more than knowing how to use the right religious formula; it means trusting the one whose name you invoke, looking to him for salvation. But faith is a big thing, not to be exercised lightly; it can exist only in terms of personal relationship."

In this one verse we see the simplicity of salvation. It couldn't be made any clearer. If the sinner will call upon the Lord for salvation, he will be saved.

THE SAVIOUR REPRESENTED

Having just presented the plan of salvation, Paul asks a series of rhetorical questions stressing the fact that the Saviour must be represented by soul-winners, preachers and missionaries. Notice the four questions.

The Prayer

How then shall they call on him in whom they have not believed? (Romans 10:14a) There must be a belief in God before there can be a calling upon God. **But as many as**

received him, to them gave he power to become the sons of God, even to them that believe on his name: (John 1:12) The sinner's call for salvation must be preceded by believing on the Lord.

The Proclamation

... how shall they believe in him of whom they have not heard? (Romans 10:14b) Neither can the sinner believe the Gospel until he hears the Gospel. Hearing comes before believing, and hearing and believing come before calling. The world needs to hear about Jesus Christ. They cannot believe on Him until they hear of Him. Charles Spurgeon said, *"The preacher must take his text and run straight to Jesus."* Jesus Christ is to be the main subject of every sermon.

The Preacher

... how shall they hear without a preacher? (Romans 10:14c) There must be a preacher. Someone must go with the gospel. **For after that in the wisdom of God the world by wisdom knew not God, it pleased God by the foolishness of preaching to save them that believe. (1 Corinthians 1:21)** God calls and equips men to preach the Gospel to the lost. There is a drift away from preaching in our day.

Recently I heard a man say, *"If you want your Church to grow, get rid of the 40 minute sermons and just teach about 20 minutes."* This man went on to say that, *"In our culture 20 minutes is about the attention span of the average person."* There is a major flaw in that fellow's theory. You will notice that they don't make 20 minute movies. Ball games last longer than 20 minutes. The problem is not man's attention span. The problem is man's heart. Man devotes time to that which he desires. God help us if we can sit and watch a 2 hour movie or a 2 hour ball game, but only have 20 minutes to devote to the preaching of God's word. No wonder the world is on a fast slide into Hell. The Word of God must be preached. **For after that in the wisdom of God the world by wisdom knew not God, it pleased God by the foolishness of preaching to save them that believe. (1 Corinthians 1:21)**

The Providence

... how shall they preach, except they be sent? (Romans 10:15a) Here is the great Bible truth that God calls and sends preachers to preach the word. The responsibility of calling and sending preachers is up to God alone. God calls His men at all ages and from all walks of life. A Divine call is a must. Nothing else will do. Not education, not talent, not even desire will make a man a preacher if he does not have God's call to the ministry. Paul said:

> **For though I preach the gospel, I have nothing to glory of: for necessity is laid upon me; yea, woe is unto me, if I preach not the gospel! For if I do this thing willingly, I have a reward: but if against my will, a dispensation of the gospel is committed unto me. (1 Corinthians 9:16-17)**

This was a Divine compulsion to preach the Word of God. You will notice that Paul took no credit whatsoever for his preaching ministry. He had been apprehended by God, and the compulsion was such that he had no choice but to preach. Not only has God called preachers into the ministry, but He has also called and commissioned every believer to witness and win souls to Christ.

If you reverse the order of Paul's question you get a perfect blueprint of the great commission.

1) God calls and sends preachers.

2) Preachers preach the Gospel.

3) People hear the Gospel and some believe.

4) Those who believe call on the Lord for Salvation.

THE SAVIOUR REJECTED

But they have not all obeyed the gospel. For Esaias saith, Lord, who hath believed our report? (Romans 10:16) Sadly, many who hear the gospel reject it and remain in unbelief. Paul says, **But they have not all obeyed the gospel. They** refers to unbelieving Israel. Israel bore the responsibility for being set aside. **He came unto his own, and his own received him not. (John 1:11)** The Jews heard the Message of a coming Messiah all their life. From a child they were trained up in the Word of God. They were devoutly religious, but they did not believe Christ. The message of salvation through Jesus Christ is available to everyone, but it is of no value to those who reject it.

So then faith cometh by hearing, and hearing by the word of God. (Romans 10:17) The seed of faith is rooted in the Word of God. That is why Satan hates the Bible. If a man will hear the word and heed the word, he will get help from the word.

But I say, Have they not heard? Yes verily, their sound went into all the earth, and their words unto the ends of the world. (Romans 10:18) Paul made it clear that Israel had heard the message. They couldn't plead ignorance. They had no excuse. In Paul's day the gospel had already been preached throughout the Roman world.

But I say, Did not Israel know? First Moses saith, I will provoke you to jealousy by them that are no people, and by a foolish nation I will anger you. (Romans 10:19) Paul quotes the Old Testament to show that the Jews did know the Scriptures. They weren't turning away from the Gospel because they didn't understand it; they were turning away because of willful stubbornness.

But Esaias is very bold, and saith, I was found of them that sought me not; I was made manifest unto them that asked not after me. (Romans 10:20) Here is a powerful argument against Israel. The Gentile nations had responded to the gospel message and they were ignorant of the Scriptures. If the Gentiles could hear and understand, surely Israel ought to understand as well.

But to Israel he saith, All day long I have stretched forth my hands unto a disobedient and gainsaying people. (Romans 10:21) What a verse! God's love toward Israel is seen in His constant efforts to save them. The word **gainsaying** comes from the Greek *"antilego"* means *"to dispute, refuse, contradict, deny, gainsay, speak against."* The Jews were a miserable and disobedient people. Yet, over and over again, God sought to save them. **All day long I have stretched forth my hands.** In spite of their defiance God stood with outstretched arms bidding His people to come, but they refused Him. **O Jerusalem, Jerusalem, thou that killest the prophets, and stonest them which are sent unto thee, how often would I have gathered thy children together, even as a hen gathereth her chickens under her wings, and ye would not! (Matthew 23:37)** This is why God turned to the Gentiles.

Hope For Israel
Romans 11

From the beginning of God's call to Abraham to leave Ur of the Chaldees, God has dealt with this nation in a special way. The Jewish people were blessed above all the people of the earth, but in spite of all that God did for them, they failed Him over and over again. Yet, there is hope for Israel as they continue to hold a privileged place in the program of God.

ISRAEL'S REJECTION IS NOT FINAL

Israel's failure did not exhaust God's grace. I am thankful that His grace never runs out. We learned earlier that **Where sin abounded, grace did much more abound. (Romans 5:20)** Regardless of the enormity of one's sin, God's grace. Is sufficient to deal with it. Concerning Israel and God's grace we see three truths presented.

God's Grace is Consistent

I say then, Hath God cast away his people? God forbid For I also am an Israelite, of the seed of Abraham, of the tribe of Benjamin. God hath not cast away his people which he foreknew ... (Romans 11:1-2a) Paul asks the question, **Hath God cast away his people?** And he forcefully answers **God forbid**. Again Paul uses this phrase **God forbid** stressing with the strongest possible language the idea of absolute impossibility. **For I also am an Israelite, of the seed of Abraham, of the tribe of Benjamin.** Paul uses himself as proof that Israel has not been cast away and forsaken by God. Paul is saying, *"here I am. I'm a Jew and God saved me."* His own conversion served as proof that God's grace was still available.

God's Grace is Continued

… Wot ye not what the scripture saith of Elias? how he maketh intercession to God against Israel, saying, Lord, they have killed thy prophets, and digged down thine altars; and I am left alone, and they seek my life. But what saith the answer of God unto him? I have reserved to myself seven thousand men, who have not bowed the knee to the image of Baal. (Romans 11:2b-4) Paul offers another proof this time from the life and ministry of Elijah. Elijah had just seen the mighty power of God fall and defeat the false prophets of Baal. Jezebel, the wicked heathen queen of the northern kingdom, was furious. She vowed to kill Elijah within twenty-four hours. **Then Jezebel sent a messenger unto Elijah, saying, So let the gods do to me, and more also, if I make not thy life as the life of one of them by to morrow about this time. (1 Kings 19:2)** Elijah took off running to get away from Jezebel. He found himself sitting under a juniper tree depleted, distressed, and even depressed. In despair he complained to God. **And he said, I have been very jealous for the LORD God of hosts: for the children of Israel have forsaken thy covenant, thrown down thine altars, and slain thy prophets with the sword; and I, even I only, am left; and they seek my life, to take it away. (1 Kings 19:10)** Notice Elijah said, **I, even I only, am left.** Elijah felt like he was the only one left to which God replied, **Yet I have left me seven thousand in Israel, all the knees which have not bowed unto Baal, and every mouth which hath not kissed him. (1 Kings 19:18)**

Even so then at this present time also there is a remnant according to the election of grace. (Romans 11:5) Paul's argument is that just as there were seven thousand in Elijah's day who had not bowed their knee to Baal, there were many Jews who had received Christ. God was continuing His work of grace among the Jews. While there were many Jews who rejected the Messiah, there were many who had received Him and were saved. No matter how wicked the times are, God always has His remnant. In Elijah's day there were seven thousand who had remained loyal to God. In Isaiah's time there was **a very small remnant. (Isaiah 1:9)** During the captivity there were men like **Daniel**, **Shadrach**, **Meshach**, and **Abednego**. Praise God, there are others who are committed to staying true to God.

And if by grace, then is it no more of works: otherwise grace is no more grace. But if it be of works, then is it no more grace: otherwise work is no more work. (Romans 11:6) Grace and works are two principles that are utterly opposed to each other. They are contrary one to the other. Salvation cannot be the result of grace and works. It must be one or the other—not a mixture of both.

God's Grace is Cast off

What then? Israel hath not obtained that which he seeketh for; but the election hath obtained it, and the rest were blinded. (Romans 11:7) There are two groups mentioned here. One group is called **the election** the other group is called **the rest**. The **election** of verse 7 is the **remnant** of verse 5. The election are those Jews who have put their trust in Christ. **The rest** refers to all of the other Jews who had not received Christ.

Paul says, **and the rest were blinded. (Romans 11:7b)** **Blinded** comes from *"poroo"* and carries the idea of *"hard, callous and numb."* It refers to spiritual blindness that comes from unbelief. The writer of Hebrews warned about such hardness. **Wherefore (as the Holy Ghost saith, To day if ye will hear his voice, Harden not your hearts, as in the provocation, in the day of temptation in the wilderness: (Hebrews 3:7-8)**

(According as it is written, God hath given them the spirit of slumber, eyes that they should not see, and ears that they should not hear;) unto this day. (Romans 11:8) As we learned in Romans chapter one and nine, there comes a point when God just lets go and turns the stubborn and hard hearted over to a reprobate mind (Romans 1:24, 26, 28). They refuse God until He gives them over to the desires of their heart and it is the end. They cross the deadline. Even as Pharaoh hardened his heart and then God in turn hardened his heart.

And David saith, Let their table be made a snare, and a trap, and a stumblingblock, and a recompence unto them: Let their eyes be darkened, that they may not see, and bow down their back alway. (Romans 11:9-10) Paul quotes David from Psalm 69:22-23. This is a Messianic Psalm that speaks of the suffering Saviour. The Jewish nation rejected Christ and they accepted full responsibility for it. Pilate was spineless and without character. He gave in to the people and crucified Christ.

> **When Pilate saw that he could prevail nothing, but that rather a tumult was made, he took water, and washed his hands before the multitude, saying, I am innocent of the blood of this just person: see ye to it. Then answered all the people,**

and said, **His blood be on us, and on our children.** (Matthew 27:24-25)

The judgment of God fell upon the nation Israel like never before. God set them aside and grafted in the wild branch. He begin to call unto Himself a Gentile bride. Their Temple was destroyed in AD 70. Israel as a nation is blind to this day.

ISRAEL'S REJECTION IS NOT FUTILE

Because Israel rejected their Messiah, God gave them the **spirit of slumber. (Romans 11:8)** This slumber is also referred to as blindness and is not permanent, but will last until God is finished with the Gentiles (see Romans 11:25). Israel's rejection is not futile, but instead used by God to bring salvation to the Gentiles.

The Consequences Of Rejection

I say then, Have they stumbled that they should fall? God forbid: but rather through their fall salvation is come unto the Gentiles, for to provoke them to jealousy. (Romans 11:11) Concerning Israel Paul asks the question, **Have they stumbled that they should fall?** The word **fall** carries the idea of a permanent and irrecoverable fall. Israel did stumble but it was not a permanent fall. Paul answers his own question with **God forbid.**

...but rather through their fall salvation is come unto the Gentiles, for to provoke them to jealousy. (Romans 11:11b) God in His providence used Israel's rejection of the Messiah to bring His salvation to the Gentiles. The word **jealousy** means "*excite to rivalry.*" In our culture jealously is basically a negative term, but that is not always the case. God's aim was to use Israel's jealousy of the Gentiles as a stimulus to draw them back to Himself.

Now if the fall of them be the riches of the world, and the diminishing of them the riches of the Gentiles; how much more their fulness? (Romans 11:12) Paul argues that if the riches of God's grace has come to the Gentiles through Israel's failure, how much greater will the riches of grace be when, in a future time, Israel turns to God in faith? Though Israel failed, God still has a place for her in the future. Just prior to Christ's second coming Israel will praise and bless their Messiah. **For I say unto you, Ye shall not see me henceforth, till ye shall say, Blessed is he that cometh in the name of the Lord. (Matthew 23:39)** The present rejection will be followed by a future reception.

The Cause Of Reconciliation

For I speak to you Gentiles, inasmuch as I am the apostle of the Gentiles, I magnify mine office: (Romans 11:13) Though Paul's heart ached for the salvation of his Jewish brethren, he still realized his calling to the Gentiles. Paul said, **I magnify mine office.** The word **magnify** means *"to glory or to honor."* In other words, Paul was going to minister just as seriously and preach just as fervently to the Gentiles as he would to the Jews.

If by any means I may provoke to emulation them which are my flesh, and might save some of them. (Romans 11:14) Paul's labor of taking the gospel to the Gentiles did not mean that he had lost hope for the salvation of the Jews. See Romans 9:1-4; 10:1. Paul's desire was to stir his Jewish brethren to jealousy, as they saw Gentiles entering into the blessings of God, thereby resulting in the salvation of many of them.

For if the casting away of them be the reconciling of the world, what shall the receiving of them be, but life from the dead? (Romans 11:15) Paul says that the Jews being cast aside has resulted in the **reconciling of the world**. The word **reconciling** speaks of bringing two opposing parties together. It means to be brought into friendship from a state of disagreement or enmity. Such was the result of Israel being set aside. According to the old covenant the Jews were God's favored people. Under the law the only way for the blessing of God to be imparted to a Gentile was for the Gentile to become a Jewish convert. Even then there was special requirements and restrictions. The convert had to travel to Jerusalem three times a year and they were not allowed in the main Temple. However, with the setting aside of Israel, Gentiles have entered into a special relationship with God having been reconciled to Him. **And all things are of God, who hath reconciled us to himself by Jesus Christ, and hath given to us the ministry of reconciliation; To wit, that God was in Christ, reconciling the world unto himself, not imputing their trespasses unto them; and hath committed unto us the word of reconciliation. (2 Corinthians 5:18-19)**

Paul says, **... what shall the receiving of them be, but life from the dead? (Romans 11:15b)** Paul compares the casting off of Israel to the death of a man, but he points out that there would be resurrection from the dead. Someday the Lord Jesus Christ will ride out of Heaven in all of His glory and descend onto the Mount of Olives and set up His Kingdom.

The Concept Of Reaping

For if the firstfruit be holy, the lump is also holy… (Romans 11:16a) Paul uses the concept of the firstfruit and reaping to further illustrate the future national restoration of Israel. The **firstfruit** is the first loaf of bread to come from the oven. The **lump** refers to the large lump of dough from which it was taken. The idea that Paul is stating is that if the bread is good, then the dough must be good also. If the dough was bad it certainly would not result in good bread.

… and if the root be holy, so are the branches. (Romans 11:16b) The metaphor of the root and branches expresses the same thought as the dough and bread. The nation of Israel is compared to an olive tree. The root is Abraham and the individual Israelites make up the branches. Israel was rooted in the covenant promises made to Abraham. They had been set apart for God and belonged to Him. In that sense Israel is a holy nation.

Paul goes on to develop his illustration. **And if some of the branches be broken off, and thou, being a wild olive tree, wert graffed in among them, and with them partakest of the root and fatness of the olive tree; (Romans 11:17)** Paul illustrates the putting aside of the Jew and the receiving of the Gentile by using an illustration drawn from the world of horticulture. He speaks of some branches being **broken off** and other branches being **graffed in among them.** Grafting is the process of taking a young branch and inserting it into another tree at a place where its branch has been cut off. The trunk of the tree into which the branch has been grafted provides the necessary nourishment, but the branch bears fruit after its own kind. In our text the root represents Abraham to whom was given the covenant promises of God. The branches that are **broken off** refer to the individual Jews who were **broken off** as a result of unbelief. The branches from the **wild olive tree** which have been **grafted in**, represent Gentile believers who have received Christ.

Boast not against the branches. But if thou boast, thou bearest not the root, but the root thee. Thou wilt say then, The branches were broken off, that I might be graffed in. (Romans 11:18-19) Paul issues a strong warning here. He said, **thou bearest not the root, but the root thee.** The word **bearest** carries the idea of *"supporting or to sustain."* The Gentiles do not support the root but the root supports them. We have nothing to brag about. We are grafted in not because of any merit or goodness on our part, but only because of our relationship to Abraham. **Therefore it is of faith, that it might be by grace; to the end the promise might be sure to all the seed; not to that only which is of the law, but to that also which is of the faith of Abraham; who is the father of us all, (Romans 4:16)**

Well; because of unbelief they were broken off, and thou standest by faith. Be not highminded, but fear: For if God spared not the natural branches, take heed lest he also spare not thee. (Romans 11:20-21) We are warned about becoming puffed up and proud lest we end up in the same fix as the Jew. If God didn't spare the Jews, why would He spare the Gentiles? If God judged unbelief in Israel, He will certainly judge unbelief among the Gentiles. If the apple of

God's eye, His chosen people fell into unbelief, shouldn't we **take heed** lest the same thing happen to us?

Behold therefore the goodness and severity of God: on them which fell, severity; but toward thee, goodness, if thou continue in his goodness: otherwise thou also shalt be cut off. (Romans 11:22) This is an eye opening statement. Paul warns us to carefully consider both the **goodness and severity** of God. We hear a lot about God's goodness and love today, but we don't hear much about His justice and judgment. We are warned not to get out of balance by focusing on God's goodness and failing to remember that He is a God of judgment and justice. The word **severity** speaks of dealing sternly with someone. God's severity is seen in His dealing with unbelieving Israel. They have been cut off from the place of blessing. On the other hand, God's goodness is seen in His dealings with the Gentiles. Gentiles are warned that they must remain in belief so as to continue in the goodness of God, or else they will be cut off like Israel was. This in no way lends any support whatsoever to the false doctrine of falling from grace. God is speaking here of a nation and a people as a whole, not of individuals losing their salvation.

And they also, if they abide not still in unbelief, shall be graffed in: for God is able to graff them in again. For if thou wert cut out of the olive tree which is wild by nature, and wert graffed contrary to nature into a good olive tree: how much more shall these, which be the natural branches, be graffed into their own olive tree? (Romans 11:23-24) What a message of hope for the Jew. Paul says, **for God is able to graff them in again.** Paul longed for the day when the Jews would be restored again into God's favor. The Scriptures consistently teach that Israel will turn from her unbelief.

ISRAEL'S REJECTION IS NOT FRUITLESS

The day is coming when Israel will recognize the Messiah and become the great and mighty nation that God promised Abraham.

The Promise

For I would not, brethren, that ye should be ignorant of this mystery, lest ye should be wise in your own conceits; that blindness in part is happened to Israel, until the fulness of the Gentiles be come in. (Romans 11:25) Paul speaks here of a **mystery**. In the New Testament a **mystery** is that which was previously unknown. It refers to the doctrine which is specific for the Church Age. It is called **the mystery** because its truths were never revealed in Old Testament scriptures. The mystery is that of the Jew being set aside and the Gentiles grafted in. Paul spoke of this same mystery several times.

> **Even the mystery which hath been hid from ages and from generations, but now is made manifest to his saints: To whom God would make known what is the riches of the glory of this mystery among the Gentiles; which is Christ in you, the hope of glory: (Colossians 1:26-27)**
>
> **If ye have heard of the dispensation of the grace of God which is given me to you-ward: How that by revelation he made known unto me the mystery; (as I wrote afore in few words, Whereby, when ye read,**

ye may understand my knowledge in the mystery of Christ) Which in other ages was not made known unto the sons of men, as it is now revealed unto his holy apostles and prophets by the Spirit; That the Gentiles should be fellow-heirs, and of the same body, and partakers of his promise in Christ by the gospel: (Ephesians 3:2-6)

Paul says, **that blindness in part is happened to Israel. (Romans 11:25b)** We are assured that Israel's blindness is a temporary condition. Someday in the future Israel as a nation will turn to Christ. **He shall cause them that come of Jacob to take root: Israel shall blossom and bud, and fill the face of the world with fruit. (Isaiah 27:6)**

Paul says, **until the fulness of the Gentiles be come in. (Romans 11:25c)** The word **until** speaks of time and places a limit on Israel's blindness. The phrase **fulness of the Gentiles** speaks of the completion of the body of Christ at which time the rapture will take place and God will begin to deal with Israel as a whole once again.

The Prophecy

And so all Israel shall be saved: as it is written, There shall come out of Sion the Deliverer, and shall turn away ungodliness from Jacob: For this is my covenant unto them, when I shall take away their sins. (Romans 11:26-27) Paul draws on Old Testament prophecy and God's covenant with Israel. Isaiah prophesied the salvation of Israel.

And the Redeemer shall come to Zion, and unto them that turn from transgression in Jacob, saith the LORD As for me, this is my covenant with them, saith the LORD; My spirit that is upon thee, and my words which I have put in thy mouth, shall not depart out

of thy mouth, nor out of the mouth of thy seed, nor out of the mouth of thy seed's seed, saith the LORD, from henceforth and for ever. (Isaiah 59:20-21)

David said:

Oh that the salvation of Israel were come out of Zion! when the LORD bringeth back the captivity of his people, Jacob shall rejoice, and Israel shall be glad. (Psalms 14:7)

Also see Jeremiah 31:31-35. The Word of God will be fulfilled. The salvation of Israel carries with it a divine guarantee. Every promise that God made to Abraham will be fulfilled.

The Principle

As concerning the gospel, they are enemies for your sakes: but as touching the election, they are beloved for the fathers' sakes. (Romans 11:28) You will notice here that God's elect are seen as His enemies because they have rejected the gospel. God is gracious and merciful, but He will deal with rebellion in His people. We see this in Isaiah.

In all their affliction he was afflicted, and the angel of his presence saved them: in his love and in his pity he redeemed them; and he bare them, and carried them all the days of old But they rebelled, and vexed his holy Spirit: therefore he was turned to be their enemy, and he fought against them. (Isaiah 63:9-10)

What a terrifying thought—to become the enemy of God. Paul had once been an enemy of the gospel. He persecuted and killed Christians. He put them in prison. He took part in

Stephen's killing. He did everything he could to stop Christianity. But God got a hold of him on the Damascus road and he did an about face for the Lord.

For the gifts and calling of God are without repentance. (Romans 11:29) Israel remains God's elect and beloved nation because His gifts and call **are without repentance**. God will not cast Israel off forever. She has a place in His Divine plan and purpose. This is God's principle and God will not break it.

The Prerogative

For as ye in times past have not believed God, yet have now obtained mercy through their unbelief: Even so have these also now not believed, that through your mercy they also may obtain mercy. (Romans 11:30-31) Here's the argument. Because of her unbelief, Israel was set aside and the gospel extended to the Gentiles. So, if God would offer His grace to pagan Gentiles in their unbelief, how much more will He extend His grace again to His chosen people Israel while they are in unbelief? This is God's prerogative. He will show mercy to the Jews.

For God hath concluded them all in unbelief, that he might have mercy upon all. (Romans 11:32) We are all in the same mess. **For all have sinned, and come short of the glory of God; (Romans 3:23)** Jew or Gentile. Black or white. Rich or poor. It matters not. We are all sinners.

The Praise

O the depth of the riches both of the wisdom and knowledge of God! how unsearchable are his judgments,

and his ways past finding out! (Romans 11:33) Paul breaks out in praise to God. There is no comparison of God to anyone or anything else. His **riches both of the wisdom and knowledge** go far beyond what we can ever imagine.

For who hath known the mind of the Lord? or who hath been his counsellor? Or who hath first given to him, and it shall be recompensed unto him again? (Romans 11:34-35) The answer is no one! Praise God we can know Him through reading the Word of God, but no man can fully know the mind of God. His mind transcends our ability to comprehend. **For my thoughts are not your thoughts, neither are your ways my ways, saith the LORD For as the heavens are higher than the earth, so are my ways higher than your ways, and my thoughts than your thoughts. (Isaiah 55:8-9)** He is the Omniscient God and we can never fully understand Him or His ways.

For of him, and through him, and to him, are all things: to whom be glory for ever. Amen. (Romans 11:36) Everything in this world exists because God created it and he sustains it.

> **For by him were all things created, that are in heaven, and that are in earth, visible and invisible, whether they be thrones, or dominions, or principalities, or powers: all things were created by him, and for him: And he is before all things, and by him all things consist. (Colossians 1:16-17)**

Why did God call Abraham? Why is Israel His chosen nation? Why were they then blinded and the Gentiles given the gospel? Why are they going to be restored? God Almighty is the Sovereign Creator and Sustainer, He has a plan that we cannot even begin to fully understand.

> **Which doeth great things and unsearchable; marvellous things without number: (Job 5:9)**

> **Canst thou by searching find out God? canst thou find out the Almighty unto perfection? It is as high as heaven; what canst thou do? deeper than hell; what canst thou know? The measure thereof is longer than the earth, and broader than the sea. (Job 11:7-9)**

> **O LORD, how great are thy works! and thy thoughts are very deep. (Psalms 92:5)**

The idea here is that although we will never fully understand God's plans and purposes, we are to trust Him. He is powerful and He will bring it to pass.

The Consecrated Life
Romans 12:1-2

In the last four chapters of Romans Paul takes up the matter of our duty as children of God. He kicks this chapter off by dealing with the believer's consecration. Noah Webster defines consecration as *"the act of separating from a common to a sacred use, or of devoting and dedicating a person or thing to the service and worship of God."* We learn here that consecration is not only the will of God, but also the reasonable service of His children.

THE APPEAL TO A CONSECRATED LIFE

I beseech you therefore, brethren, by the mercies of God... (Romans 12:1a) The **therefore** refers to the believer reckoning himself dead to sin and alive unto God as established in the previous chapters. The word **beseech** means *"to entreat; to supplicate; to implore; to ask or pray with urgency."* Paul begged these believers to die to self, forsake their sin, and sell out to Christ.

Note that Paul makes his appeal based upon the **mercies of God**. When we were lost God extended His mercy to us and forgave us of our sins, made us new creatures in Christ Jesus and adopted us into His family. Paul argues that if God's mercy was sufficient to do all of that, certainly His mercy is sufficient to enable us to consecrate ourselves to Him. It is by the mercy of God that we enter into the consecrated life. It is not by force or fear that we are manipulated into serving God. Consecration is not attained by some list of rigid rules and regulations, but by the mercy of God. It is His mercy that motivates us to consecration.

THE ACT OF A CONSECRATED LIFE

... that ye present your bodies a living sacrifice, holy, acceptable unto God. (Romans 12:1b) The picture that Paul had in mind here was that of an altar and sacrifice. The terminology Paul uses contrasts the New Testament Christian to the Old Testament sacrifice. He is exhorting Christians to wholly offer themselves to God with the same attitude that the Old Testament worshiper presented his offering to God.

A Compliant Offering

Paul said, **... that ye present your bodies.** The idea here is that of making a presentation. This is to be a willing, voluntary, and submissive act. The Christian is simply to comply with the Lord's desire and present himself to Christ. There is no arm twisting, no high pressure maneuvering to get folks down the aisle. This not something that is worked up in the flesh. Rather, it is the voluntary submission of the believer to his Lord.

A Complete Offering

It is to be a **sacrifice.** The sacrifice which God demands must be a complete sacrifice. Nothing can be held back. In the Old Testament the sacrifice did not have to be great, but it did have to be complete. In the Old Testament, if a man could not afford a bullock God allowed him to bring a lamb. If a man was too poor to be able to afford a lamb, God allowed him to bring a turtledove or even a pigeon. However, God never accepted a part of anything. It had to be the whole bullock, or a whole lamb. It had to be the whole turtledove. God never accepted a partial sacrifice. The only sacrifice acceptable to God is a complete sacrifice. This is where many Christians mess up. Many believers have a bits-and-pieces philosophy where they will give God a piece of their life, but will not fully surrender. God requires a complete sacrifice with nothing held back.

A Consumed Offering

The sacrifice was to be **holy, acceptable unto God**. There is a finality here. In the Old testament a sacrifice belonged wholly to God. Once a sacrifice was accepted by God, it was once and for all His. It was consumed by Him and never used for a common purpose again. We do not sacrifice to God today, and then take it all back tomorrow. A living sacrifice means that a person dedicates himself wholly to God and sticks with his commitment.

THE ARGUMENT FOR A CONSECRATED LIFE

Paul says, **... which is your reasonable service. (Romans 12:1c)** The word reasonable comes from the Greek *"logikos"* and means *"reasonable, rationale or logical."* Considering all that God put into redeeming us, it is only **reasonable** that we give ourselves back to Him for service. It is important to realize that the Christian belongs to Christ anyway.

> **What? know ye not that your body is the temple of the Holy Ghost which is in you, which ye have of God, and ye are not your own? For ye are bought with a price: therefore glorify God in your body, and in your spirit, which are God's. (1 Corinthians 6:19-20)**

To present ourselves to the Lord for service is the least that we can do. Adam Clarke said:

> "Nothing can be more consistent with reason than that the work of God should glorify its Author. We are not our own, we are the property of the Lord, by the right of creation and redemption; and it would be as unreasonable as it would be wicked not to live to his glory, in strict obedience to his will."

God will never ask you to do something that is unreasonable. **For this is the love of God, that we keep his commandments: and his commandments are not grievous. (1 John 5:3)** God's commands only become unreasonable when His children are selfish and fail to surrender to His will.

THE ATTITUDE OF A CONSECRATED LIFE

And be not conformed to this world: but be ye transformed by the renewing of your mind ... (Romans 12:2a) Christians have nothing in common with this world. Our command is to come out and be separate. Separation is an important part of the Christian life. Paul warned the Ephesians:

> **For ye were sometimes darkness, but now are ye light in the Lord: walk as children of light: (For the fruit of the Spirit is in all goodness and righteousness and truth;) Proving what is acceptable unto the Lord And have no fellowship with the unfruitful works of darkness, but rather reprove them. (Ephesians 5:8-11)**

The Christian is no longer a creature of darkness, but of light. The admonition here is that believers align their walk to match their position in Christ. We can't play in the world and walk with Christ at the same time. **If we say that we have fellowship with him, and walk in darkness, we lie, and do not the truth. (1 John 1:6)** A Christian will prove to be a true follower of Christ when he is no longer conformed to the world. James warns, **Ye adulterers and adulteresses, know ye not that the friendship of the world is enmity with God? whosoever therefore will be a friend of the world is the enemy of God**. **(James 4:4)** God uses strong language to describe those who claim with their lips to love Him, but with their life serve the world. The terms **adulterers and adulteresses** are used to describe unfaithfulness to the Lord. Consecrated Christians are separated from the world.

Paul describes this process as a transformation. He says, **be ye transformed by the renewing of your mind**. Notice that our transformation is the result of renewing our mind. The Christian's mind is renewed and his life transformed as he takes in the Word of God and surrenders to the Holy Spirit's leadership in his life. **Thy word have I hid in mine heart, that I might not sin against thee. (Psalms 119:11)** The mind is important in living the Christian life. Peter warned us to, **gird up the loins of your mind. (1 Peter 1:13)** There was a custom in Bible days of gathering up one's long robes and tying them around the waist. Men did this when they were going to work or travel so that they wouldn't trip. Peter uses this practice as an analogy to illustrate the need to protect our minds. It is in the thought life that sin is conceived. When Peter said, **gird up the loins of your mind,** he is telling us to gather up the loose ends of our thought life lest it trip us up. Solomon said, **For as he thinketh in his**

heart, so is he. (Proverbs 23:7a) Many believers trip up and fall because they are not thinking right.

THE ACHIEVEMENT OF A CONSECRATED LIFE

... that ye may prove what is that good, and acceptable, and perfect, will of God (Romans 12:2b) The word **prove** carries the idea of *"discernment."* The unsaved man has no discernment. **But the natural man receiveth not the things of the Spirit of God: for they are foolishness unto him: neither can he know them, because they are spiritually discerned (1 Corinthians 2:14)** The natural man is void of spiritual discernment, but it is a different matter with the Christian. We now have the Holy Spirit to enlighten us. The purpose of having a transformed mind is so that we can discern and do the will of God. The renewing of the Christians mind enables him to **prove what is that good, and acceptable, and perfect, will of God**. The world says I will do what suits me. The Christian learns to say, I will do what pleases my Saviour.

Humility And Service

Romans 12:3-8

Having dealt with consecration Paul moves on to the believer's responsibility to serve God. The context demands that consecration come first. It is only after we have offered our self to God, separated from the world, transformed our thinking and conformed to God's will that we can be effective in service.

ATTITUDE CONCERNING MEEKNESS

For I say, through the grace given unto me, to every man that is among you, not to think of himself more highly than he ought to think; but to think soberly, according as God hath dealt to every man the measure of faith. (Romans 12:3) Pride is one of the deadliest sins of man and Devil. It is at the top of the list of the seven abominations in God's hate list (Proverbs 6:16-19). Pride is one of the ugliest sins that man can be guilty of. It is a sin of destruction. **Pride goeth before destruction, and a haughty spirit before a fall. (Proverbs 16:18)** Pride incurs the wrath of God and destroys everything it touches. **The LORD will destroy the house of the proud ... (Proverbs 15:25)** Man has the tendency to over evaluate himself. It happens across the board, even in the ministry. God blesses a ministry and man gets the idea that he accomplished it. Don't forget the context. Paul has just talked about becoming a living sacrifice. We are supposed to be on the altar. We are to be dead to self. The truth of the matter is, it makes no difference how established one may be in the word, or how many souls he wins, or how enthusiastically he serves God, none of this matters until we are on the altar and out of God's way. Anything we accomplish that is of value to the Kingdom is accomplished by God's power and enabling.

ANALOGY CONCERNING MEMBERSHIP

For as we have many members in one body, and all members have not the same office: (Romans 12:4) Paul uses the human body to illustrate unity. Different parts of the body function in different ways. Eyes see, ears hear, noses smell and feet walk. But all are part of one body and all work together. When you walk you use your feet, knees, hips and eyes. All doing a different function yet all working together. Now Paul makes an application. **So we, being many, are one body in Christ, and every one members one of another. (Romans 12:5)** Like the human body, the body of Christ has many members. Each having different functions but still the same body. This emphasizes the importance of each church member.

ASSIGNMENT CONCERNING MINISTRY

Having then gifts differing according to the grace that is given to us ... (Romans 12:6a) When Jesus ascended back into Heaven He **gave gifts unto men. (Ephesians 4:8)** We are told that those gifts were given to us, **For the perfecting of the saints, for the work of the ministry, for the edifying of the body of Christ. (Ephesians 4:12)** Not only did our Lord give gifts, He gave gifts to every believer. **As every man hath received the gift, even so minister the same one to another, as good stewards of the manifold grace of God 1 Peter 4:10 But the manifestation of the Spirit is given to every man to profit withal. (1 Corinthians 12:7)** No believer is without a spiritual gift. These gifts are named in our current passage along with 1 Corinthians 12:8-10, 28-30 and Ephesians 4:11-12. These gifts fall into three separate categories.

Temporal Gifts To Establish God's Authority

During the days of the Apostles there was no New Testament as we have it today. How did people know whether or not the Apostles had authority for what they were preaching? The only way they would know was for God to authenticate their preaching. How did God do that? With these temporal sign gifts.

> **How shall we escape, if we neglect so great salvation; which at the first began to be spoken by the Lord, and was confirmed unto us by them that heard him; God also bearing them witness, both with signs and wonders, and with divers miracles, and gifts of the Holy Ghost, according to his own will? (Hebrews 2:3-4)**

The sign gifts were a visible demonstration that what they spoke was the Word of God. Sign gifts established the fact that these men spoke with God's Authority. Paul deals with the passing of temporal gifts in 1 Corinthians 13 where he explains that love is eternal while the gifts of prophecy, tongues, and knowledge and other sign gifts are temporary. Paul said, **Charity never faileth: but whether there be prophecies, they shall fail; whether there be tongues, they shall cease; whether there be knowledge, it shall vanish away. (1 Corinthians 13:8)** Look at the terms Paul uses to describe the temporal nature of these sign gifts.

Paul says, **they shall fail.** The word **fail** comes from the word *"kataargeo"* and means *"to be entirely idle useless,* *cease, become of no effect, come to naught, vanish away, make void."* From where Paul was standing in time, there would be a day in the future when the temporal gifts would come to naught.

Next he says of tongues, **they shall cease.** The word tongues is *"glocesah"* and refers to a known language. The gift of tongues was not some sort of jabber or unintelligible utterance, but the supernatural ability to speak by the power of the Holy Spirit a language that one had not learned. Paul said that tongues **shall cease.** Cease comes from the word *"powo"* and means *"to stop, restrain, quit, desist, come to an end."* Again, Paul is saying that at some point in the future the gift of tongues would simply come to an end.

He says **knowledge, it shall vanish away.** Knowledge here does not refer to information and education. Paul was speaking here about knowledge that comes from direct revelation. The word for **vanish** is the same one that Paul used for **fail** earlier in this verse. It simply means that the temporal gift of knowledge will come to nothing.

Paul explains that these temporal gifts were only a small part of the big picture. **For we know in part, and we prophesy in part. 1 Corinthians 13:9**

The word **part** comes from *"meros"* and means *"a portion, piece or fragment."* Up until the time Paul was writing there was no completed revelation of God. Over the years the Prophets had only communicated to the people that which God chose to reveal. They only had a **part** of the whole. However, all of that was about to change. Paul continues. **But when that which is perfect is come, then that which is** in part shall be done away. (1 Corinthians 13:10) The word **perfect** means *"to finish or complete so as to leave nothing wanting..." (Webster).* Paul not only told us that the temporal gifts would end, but when they would end . Once the canon of Scripture was complete the temporal gifts would cease. These temporal sign gifts are no longer in operation and are no longer needed because we have the perfect word of God

Teaching Gifts To Explain God's Truth

The gift of teaching is mentioned specifically a number of times in the NT (Romans 12:7; 1 Corinthians 12:28; Ephesians 4:11). The teaching ministry is vital to the strength and stability of the local Church. The mission of the Church goes beyond evangelism. Winning folks to Christ is one of the greatest works we can involve ourselves with. However, if we are just winning them and not going on to disciple them, we are only doing half of the job. The Great Commission is not just to make converts, but to **make disciples. (Matthew 28:18-20)** Evangelism must be coupled with teaching. Every Christian can study the Scriptures and learn, but there are certain ones God has placed among us who are specially gifted not just to understand the Bible, but to communicate what it says in a way that all can understand. This is the gift of teaching.

Team Gifts To Enable God's Work

We call these team gifts because everyone is part of the team. It is not just the Pastor or the Deacons or the Teachers that get everything done. Everyone needs to be part of the team. Someone said, *"Team work is what makes the team work."* The preaching and teaching ministries do not stand alone. If a Church is going to succeed we must work together. God has placed people in the local Church to make up that team. Think about this. One farm horse can pull an average of six tons. So if you team two horses together how much should they be able to pull? You would think twelve tons. But that is not right. One horse can pull six tons, but two horses can pull thirty-two tons! That's teamwork! The Pastor can pull a little with his preaching and the teacher can pull a little with his teaching, but it is not until the people in the pews get a hold of the truth and put their spiritual gifts to work that we are enabled as a local Church to do what God has called us to do. We can get a lot more done if we work as a team. Paul names seven team gifts.

First, the **_Gift To Sermonize_**. Paul begins with **Prophecy … (Romans 12:6)** In the Old Testament the gift of prophecy was the gift to proclaim and explain the will of God and often involved predicting future events. However, upon the completion of God's word that gift of prophecy ceased. In the New Testament the gift of prophecy is not foretelling, but forth telling. The Bible says, **Despise not prophesyings (1 Thessalonians 5:20)**. The word **prophesyings** comes from a word that means "*to speak or proclaim publicly.*" This gift involves preaching the word.

Second, the **_Gift To Serve_**. **Or ministry, let us wait on our ministering: (Romans 12:7a)** The word **ministry** simply means to do service. Ministry is the gift of service. Paul also referred to service as the gift of **helps. (1 Corinthians 12:28)** The word helps carries the idea of taking the burden off someone else and placing it on oneself.

Third, the **Gift To School**. ... **or he that teacheth, on teaching; (Romans 12:7b)** The gift of teaching is specifically mentioned three times in the New Testament (Romans 12:7; 1 Corinthians 12:28; Ephesians 4:11). The gift of teaching is the supernatural ability to explain clearly and make application of the Word of God. Teaching is a major part of carrying out the great commission.

> **And Jesus came and spake unto them, saying, All power is given unto me in heaven and in earth. Go ye therefore, and teach all nations, baptizing them in the name of the Father, and of the Son, and of the Holy Ghost: Teaching them to observe all things whatsoever I have commanded you: and, lo, I am with you alway, even unto the end of the world Amen. (Matthew 28:18-20)**

The Great Commission is not just to win folks to Christ, but to **make disciples.** Disciples are produced through teaching. Jesus said, **Teaching them to observe all things whatsoever I have commanded you.** Someone has well said that, *"Evangelism brings new life, teaching sustains that new life."*

Fourth, the **Gift To Stir**. **Or he that exhorteth, on exhortation: (Romans 12:8a)** Exhortation comes from the word *"paraklesis." "Para"* means *"to the side of"* and *"klesis"* means *"to call."* The idea is that of being called to someone's side for the purpose of helping them. The gift of exhortation consists of advising, encouraging, warning, strengthening, and comforting. This gift is vital to the preaching ministry of the local Church. It is a gift that picks up where preaching leaves off. The preaching instructs as to what is right, the exhorter encourages others to do right.

Fifth, the **_Gift To Share_**. ... **he that giveth, let him do it with simplicity. (Romans 12:8b)** The gift of giving is that of sharing what we have with others. *"The gift of giving is the capacity to give of one's substance to the work of the Lord consistently, liberally, and sacrificially."* R. G. LeTourneau, the great Texas industrialist, was known for his gift of giving. Realizing that not only 10% but 100% belonged to God He said, *"The question is not how much of my money I give to God, but rather how much of God's money I keep."* LeTourneau's gave 90% of his earnings to the Lord.

Sixth, the **_Gift To Supervise_**. ... **he that ruleth, with diligence. (Romans 12:8c)** The word **ruleth** comes from *"proistemi"* and has the basic meaning of *"standing before others."* It carries the idea of leadership or administration. Paul refers to the same gift as **governments** in 1 Corinthians 12:28. Governments comes from the word *"koobernaysis."* It was the word that spoke of a steersman for a ship. The steersman had the responsibility of bringing a ship into the harbor. Steering it through the rocks and sandbars under all types of pressures. The gift of ruling is the ability to lead, organize, and govern. Individuals with this gift are a tremendous help the Pastor.

Seven, the **_Gift To Sympathize_**. ... **he that sheweth mercy, with cheerfulness. (Romans 12:8d)** Mercy means to feel sympathy with or for others. But notice that this gift goes beyond feeling. It says **he that sheweth mercy.** The idea here is that of actively demonstrating sympathy for someone. This is someone who has the ability to minister to people who have needs that most other people feel very uncomfortable working with.

Supernatural Living

Romans 12:9-21

Paul follows his discourse on spiritual gifts with a list of maxims or proverbs for supernatural living.

CONCERNING HONESTY

Let love be without dissimulation. Abhor that which is evil; cleave to that which is good. (Romans 12:9) We are admonished to have an honest and sincere heart concerning the matter of Christian love. There several truths here.

Bible Love Is Sincere

Let love be without dissimulation ... (Romans 12:9a) It is interesting that Paul brings up the subject of Christian love just after dealing with spiritual gifts. He did the same thing right in the middle of his teaching on spiritual gifts in 1 Corinthians. The Bible is clear that love is far more important than any gift we may have.

> **Though I speak with the tongues of men and of angels, and have not charity, I am become as sounding brass, or a tinkling cymbal. And though I have the gift of prophecy, and understand all mysteries, and all knowledge; and though I have all faith, so that I could remove mountains, and have not charity, I am nothing. And though I bestow all my goods to feed the poor, and though I give my body to be**

burned, and have not charity, it profiteth me nothing. 1 Corinthians 13:1-3

The Corinthians were infatuated with the temporary gifts. But Paul stressed the point that no matter what gift one may have, it is worthless if practiced apart from love. Paul says, **Let love be without dissimulation. (Romans 12:9a)** Paul spoke of **love unfeigned. (2 Corinthians 6:6)** Peter used the same terminology. **Seeing ye have purified your souls in obeying the truth through the Spirit unto unfeigned love of the brethren, see that ye love one another with a pure heart fervently: (1 Peter 1:22)** The words **dissimulation** and **unfeigned** come from the same Greek word. It is the word from which we get the English *"hypocrite."* God is telling us to be sincere and genuine in our Christian love. In secular Greek the word hypocrite was an acting term. It spoke of someone who simply played a part. Paul is warning us here not to be an actor playing a part, but to make sure that our love is genuine.

Love is extremely important in Christianity. Our love for one another is a result of Christ's love for us. Jesus said, **Greater love hath no man than this, that a man lay down his life for his friends. (John 15:13)** Jesus Christ put principle into picture. If you want to see true biblical love, look at Christ. Jesus said, **This is my commandment, That ye love one another, as I have loved you. (John 15:12)** The command to love one another was new in the sense that Jesus gave it a new standard. Moses said, **thou shalt love thy neighbour as thyself. (Leviticus 19:18)** The new standard set by Jesus is, **that ye love one another; as I have**

loved you. (John 13:34) To love people the way Jesus did, means to love them unconditionally.

Love for the brethren is proof of salvation, while hate is a good indication that salvation has not taken place. **He that saith he is in the light, and hateth his brother, is in darkness even until now. But he that hateth his brother is in darkness, and walketh in darkness, and knoweth not whither he goeth, because that darkness hath blinded his eyes. (1 John 2:9, 11)** A man who claims to be a Christian and hates others is a deceived man. John looks at the Christian's compassion as a test of his conversion. Our compassion for others proves our Christianity. **A new commandment I give unto you, That ye love one another; as I have loved you, that ye also love one another. By this shall all men know that ye are my disciples, if ye have love one to another. (John 13:34-35)** Only a genuine and sincere love can fill this order.

Bible Love Is Separated

Abhor that which is evil ... (Romans 12:9) Biblical love demands separation. The word **abhor** comes from the Greek *"apostygeo"* and means *"to hate and detest utterly."* Vines defines **abhor** as meaning *"to render foul* and *to turn oneself away from."* We are to hate and separate from evil. Paul said that charity, **Rejoiceth not in iniquity, but rejoiceth in the truth; (1 Corinthians 13:6)** Biblical love finds no satisfaction in that which is evil. David said, **Ye that love the LORD, hate evil: he preserveth the souls of his saints; he delivereth them out of the hand of the wicked. (Psalm 97:10)** Later David said, **A froward heart shall depart from me: I will not**

know a wicked person. (Psalm 101:4) There is not much said about Biblical separation these days. However, the word of God still demands it.

> Wherefore come out from among them, and be ye separate, saith the Lord, and touch not the unclean thing; and I will receive you, (2 Corinthians 6:17)

> Let every one that nameth the name of Christ depart from iniquity. (2 Timothy 2:19)

Biblical separation involves the entire Christian life. There is a lot of confusion as to whether or not you should separate from another Christian. The truth of the matter is that we can get into just as much trouble hanging around a professing Christian who is not living right, as we can by hanging around an unsaved person. That is why the Bible demands that we be careful who we have close fellowship with.

> But now I have written unto you not to keep company, if any man that is called a brother be a fornicator, or covetous, or an idolater, or a railer, or a drunkard, or an extortioner; with such an one no not to eat. (1 Corinthians 5:11)

> Now we command you, brethren, in the name of our Lord Jesus Christ, that ye withdraw yourselves from every brother that walketh disorderly, and not after the tradition which he received of us. (2 Thessalonians 3:6)

The Bible clearly commands the believer to separate from other believers who are in error. In Matthew 18:15-17 concerning a **brother** who has trespassed against us and will not get it right, Jesus said, **let him be unto thee as a heathen man and a publican**. Heathens and publicans were two of the most abhorred and detested people of Jesus' day. To deal with another Christian in such a way would be to separate from him and have no close fellowship with him. This is instruction from the Lord concerning separation from erring brethren.

The problem is that with a lot of people their life centers around their friends, work, hobbies, and social life rather than around Christ. **Let love be without dissimulation. Abhor that which is evil...** What Paul is saying here is simple. If you claim to be a Christian, don't be a hypocrite and a stage player. If something is wrong, render it foul and turn away from it. **Ye adulterers and adulteresses, know ye not that the friendship of the world is enmity with God? whosoever therefore will be a friend of the world is the enemy of God. (James 4:4)** It is impossible to claim we love God when we are in sin or yoked up with those who don't life holy lives. It is like the old saying, *"Your deeds speak so loud that I can't hear your words."* We are not to be Pharisaical, looking down our noses at those who have fallen. However, we must remember that ... **evil communications corrupt good manners. (1 Corinthians 15:33)** God has established the doctrine of separation to protect His people from sin.

Bible Love Is Sanctified

We are to **cleave to that which is good. (Romans 12:9c)** Biblical love is lived out in one's life. Here is the positive aspect of Biblical separation. We **cleave to that which is**

good. When we practice true Bible love, we hate what God hates and we love what God loves. When we love Him as we are supposed to we live that love out in our life. The word **cleave** means *"to stick, join, cohere or glue together."* It carries the idea of permanently fitting and joining two objects together. As God's people we are to join ourselves to **that which is good** in God's eyes.

CONCERNING HONOR

Be kindly affectioned one to another with brotherly love; in honour preferring one another. (Romans 12:10). Having just explained what real Biblical love is Paul calls on us to make application by honoring and preferring others. Jesus stressed the importance of brotherly love. **By this shall all men know that ye are my disciples, if ye have love one to another (John 13:35).** Brotherly love is one of the traits by which the world will know that we are Christians. **Whosoever believeth that Jesus is the Christ is born of God: and every one that loveth him that begat loveth him also that is begotten of him (1 John 5:1).**

The word **preferring** comes from *"proegeomai"* and means *"being in the lead or to go before."* The idea is that we are to allow others to be first. We are to yield the right-of-way. This is true humility. It is letting the other guy be out front. Paul admonished the Philippians, **Let nothing be done through strife or vainglory; but in lowliness of mind let each esteem other better than themselves. (Philippians 2:3)**

CONCERNING HASTE

Not slothful in business; fervent in spirit; serving the Lord (Romans 12:11). Slothful comes from the word *"okernos"* and carries the idea of being *"tardy, slow, or lazy."* The word **business** comes from *"spoude"* and means *"diligence, earnestness and haste."* The idea here is that we are to be diligent in carrying out our duties. We are to be **fervent in spirit; serving the Lord. Fervent** comes from *"zeontes"* and means *"to be hot, to boil, or to be aflame."* The believer is to be enthusiastic in his walk and service for Christ.

CONCERNING HOPE

Rejoicing in hope; patient in tribulation; continuing instant in prayer. (Romans 12:12) Here is a threefold command that will help us to maintain our service for the Lord.

Our Praise

As God's people we are to always be **rejoicing in hope. (Romans 12:12a)** The word **hope** speaks of something yet in the future, a future expectancy. When people use the word **hope** today it often carries with it the idea of uncertainty. However, in the Bible the word **hope** carries the idea of certainty because when God says something is going to happen we can expect it to happen without any doubt. The hope that Paul tells us to rejoice in is our future with God. It entails the rapture with is called the blessed hope. **Looking for that blessed hope, and the glorious appearing of the great God and our Saviour Jesus Christ (Titus 2:13).** It involves the glorification of the believer. We are told, **And every man that hath this hope in him purifieth himself, even as he is pure (1 John 3:3).** Isaiah spoke of the future when, **Thine eyes shall see the king in his beauty: they shall behold the land that is very far off**. (Isaiah 33:17) What a hope! Someday we will see Jesus in all of His beauty. We will share in the splendor of Heaven. With a hope like that we can do a lot of rejoicing.

Our Patience

Next, we are warned to be **patient in tribulation. (Romans 12:12b)** The word **patience** speaks of *"the ability to wait and endure."* This is a word that speaks of patience and endurance under affliction and provocation. It is the ability to keep on keeping on even against strong opposition. Paul exhorted Timothy to ... **endure hardness, as a good soldier of Jesus Christ (2 Timothy 2:3).** One of the greatest needs in Christianity today is for people to just stay by the stuff. **If thou faint in the day of adversity, thy strength is small. (Proverbs 24:10)** Bob Jones Sr. said, *"The test of your character is what it takes to stop you."* Paul is telling us not to quit short of our potential.

We are to stay our course, even in **tribulation**. The word **tribulation** speaks of the troubles and trails that Christians suffer for the sake of the Lord. Jesus said, **In the world ye shall have tribulation: but be of good cheer; I have overcome the world. (John 16:33)** The Christian who has determined to live all out for God will have tribulations. **Yea, and all that will live godly in Christ Jesus shall suffer persecution. (2 Timothy 3:12)**

The word **tribulations** comes from the Greek word *"thlipsis"* and means *"to press, squash, or to squeeze."* It was used in Bible days to describe the squeezing of olives to produce oil and the squeezing of grapes to produce wine.

When tribulations come the pressure is on and we get squeezed. Tribulations aren't fun, but they are necessary. When you squeeze an olive you get oil. When you squeeze a grape you get juice. God allows tribulation to squeeze us so that He can get something out of us. Paul said, **For our light affliction, which is but for a moment, worketh for us a far more exceeding and eternal weight of glory.** (2 **Corinthians 4:17)** The idea is that the product produced is far greater than the problems we have to endure. The Bible says, **We must through much tribulation enter into the kingdom of God. (Acts 14:22)**

Our Prayer

Paul says, **continuing instant in prayer. (Romans 12:12c)** The fact that we have a God who answers prayer can get us through a lot of tough times. **Be careful for nothing; but in every thing by prayer and supplication with thanksgiving let your requests be made known unto God And the peace of God, which passeth all understanding, shall keep your hearts and minds through Christ Jesus. (Philippians 4:6-7)** A solid prayer life will knock the worry and fear out of our tribulation. No wonder we are admonished to **Pray without ceasing. (1 Thessalonians 5:17)** James said, **The effectual fervent prayer of a righteous man availeth much (James 5:16).** Prayer moves the hand of God. Jesus said, **Men ought always to pray, and not to faint (Luke 18:1).**

CONCERNING HOSPITALITY

Distributing to the necessity of saints; given to hospitality (Romans 12:13). The word **distributing** means to share what we have with others. The word **necessity** speaks of that which is necessary or needed. Here we are specifically told that we are to meet the needs of the saints. This is a serious command. The Church has unfortunately turned this responsibility over to the welfare department. However, we need to be involved in feeding, clothing and helping those who are in need, especially believers. James said, **If a brother or sister be naked, and destitute of daily food, And one of you say unto them, Depart in peace, be ye warmed and filled; notwithstanding ye give them not those things which are needful to the body; what doth it profit? (James 2:15-16).** Paul said to the Galatian Church, **As we have therefore opportunity, let us do good unto all men, especially unto them who are of the household of faith (Galatians 6:10).** We are to be a people who help one another. Jesus said, **... Inasmuch as ye did it not to one of the least of these, ye did it not to me (Matthew 25:45).** By the way, this is a hand up not a hand out. We are not to encourage a lifestyle of laziness and mooching.

CONCERNING HOSTILITY

Bless them which persecute you: bless, and curse not (Romans 12:14). The word **bless** is from *"eulogeo."* It is the word from which we get the English eulogy and means to speak well of. We are to not cuss back, but to speak well those who persecute us. This is a hard order to fill, but it is God's way. Jesus said, **Ye have heard that it hath been said, Thou shalt love thy neighbour, and hate thine enemy. But I say unto you, Love your enemies, bless them that curse you, do good to them that hate you, and pray for them which despitefully use you, and persecute you (Matthew 5:43-44).** First Peter was written to believers who were suffering through one of the greatest times of persecution known to the Church. He wrote, **Not rendering evil for evil, or railing for railing: but contrariwise blessing; knowing that ye are thereunto called, that ye should inherit a blessing. (1 Peter 3:9)** When Jesus died, He spoke well of and interceded for the very ones who had crucified Him. **Then said Jesus, Father, forgive them; for they know not what they do. And they parted his raiment, and cast lots. (Luke 23:34)** What an example to live up to.

CONCERNING HAPPINESS

Rejoice with them that do rejoice ... (Romans 12:15a). There are folks who find it difficult to rejoice over another person's success. The natural tendency is more toward jealously than rejoicing. Sometimes it is harder to rejoice with those who rejoice than it is to weep with those who weep. But we are to rejoice and share in the blessings of others.

CONCERNING HEAVINESS

... weep with them that weep (Romans 12:15b). This a trait we ought pick up from God . **In all their affliction he was afflicted, and the angel of his presence saved them: in his love and in his pity he redeemed them; and he bare them, and carried them all the days of old (Isaiah 63:9).** Of Jesus Christ the Bible states, **For we have not an high priest which cannot be touched with the feeling of our infirmities ... (Hebrews 4:15).** This is not sympathy, it is empathy. Empathy is feeling what another person feels.

CONCERNING HUMILITY

Be of the same mind one toward another. Mind not high things, but condescend to men of low estate. Be not wise

in your own conceits (Romans 12:16). We are admonished to **Be of the same mind one toward another.** We are avoid partiality and favoritism in the Church. The ground is level at the cross and we all were saved from sin. There are no big shots in God's house.

> For by one Spirit are we all baptized into one body, whether we be Jews or Gentiles, whether we be bond or free; and have been all made to drink into one Spirit. (1 Corinthians 12:13)

> There is neither Jew nor Greek, there is neither bond nor free, there is neither male nor female: for ye are all one in Christ Jesus. (Galatians 3:28)

We are to recognize the fact that every believer is significant. Everybody is somebody in God's house. Paul says, **Mind not high things, but condescend to men of low estate.** Don't be prideful. We are not to consider ourselves better than someone else. Paul is calling for unity among believers. Paul says, **condescend to men of low estate.** The word **condescend** comes from *"synapago"* and means to *"take off together."* It carries the idea of associating with someone. We are to associate with one another regardless of background or social standing. This was demonstrated in the life of Jesus Christ.

CONCERNING HARMLESSNESS

Recompense to no man evil for evil. Provide things honest in the sight of all men (Romans 12:17). The word **recompense** means *"to pay, reward, or render."* We are not to return evil for evil. It is not up to us to get even with those who wrong us. This is a common truth that is found throughout the New Testament.

> See that none render evil for evil unto any man; but ever follow that which is good, both among yourselves, and to all men. (1 Thessalonians 5:15)

> And labour, working with our own hands: being reviled, we bless; being persecuted, we suffer it: Being defamed, we intreat: we are made as the filth of the world, and are the offscouring of all things unto this day. (1 Corinthians 4:12-13)

> Now therefore there is utterly a fault among you, because ye go to law one with another. Why do ye not rather take wrong? why do ye not rather suffer yourselves to be defrauded? (1 Corinthians 6:7)

> Not rendering evil for evil, or railing for railing: but contrariwise blessing; knowing that ye are thereunto called, that ye should inherit a blessing. (1 Peter 3:9)

Provide things honest in the sight of all men. (Romans 12:17) Paul warns us to do right because others are watching us. When Jesus was wronged He didn't return evil for evil. He could have called twelve legions of Angels (upwards to 72,000) to His side, but He didn't (Matthew 26:53). Instead He prayed ...**Father, forgive them; for they know not what they do. (Luke 23:34)**.

CONCERNING HARMONY

If it be possible, as much as lieth in you, live peaceably with all men (Romans 12:18). The phrase **if it be possible** indicates that believers cannot always be at peace with all men. The world hates the truth. They love darkness and wickedness. Jesus said:

> **And this is the condemnation, that light is come into the world, and men loved darkness rather than light, because their deeds were evil. For every one that doeth evil hateth the light, neither cometh to the light, lest his deeds should be reproved (John 3:19-20)**

Since the world hates truth they also hate the messengers of truth. Hence, the tribulation that Jesus talked about. **These things I have spoken unto you, that in me ye might have peace. In the world ye shall have tribulation: but be of good cheer; I have overcome the world. (John 16:33)** Notice that Paul says, **as much as lieth in you...** We are to make every effort possible to maintain peace and harmony with others. Regardless of what the other guy is doing we are to do everything possible from our side to live peaceably with all men. Some folks are not going to let us live peaceable with them. But we are to go as far as God will allow and enable us. There does however come a time when the wicked must be answered and dealt with (see Proverbs 26:4-5).

CONCERNING HURT

Dearly beloved, avenge not yourselves, but rather give place unto wrath: for it is written, Vengeance is mine; I will repay, saith the Lord (Romans 12:19). When we are wronged, the natural reaction is to take things into our own hands and to try and get even. The old man boils up inside of us we start looking for ways to get even. Paul says, **but rather give place unto wrath.** The phrase **give place** comes from *"didomitopos."* The word *"didomi"* means *"to give"* and *"topos"* means *"room."* The idea is that we are to stay out of God's way and give Him room to work.

When we are all up into things trying to get even, we hinder God's working to bring about His will. The Christian way to deal with it is to give it to God. He said, **Vengeance is mine; I will repay.** We are to stay out of God's way and let Him do as He pleases. **To me belongeth vengeance, and recompence; their foot shall slide in due time: for the day of their calamity is at hand, and the things that shall come upon them make haste (Deuteronomy 32:35).** God is well able to handle it Himself. By turning it other to God we give place to His wrath. We are to be patience and let God's wrath have its course.

CONCERNING HUMANITY

Therefore if thine enemy hunger, feed him; if he thirst, give him drink: for in so doing thou shalt heap coals of fire on his head (Romans 12:20). No matter how wicked the enemy is we are not to stoop to his level. If he is hungry, feed him. If he is thirsty, give him something to drink. What the enemy is and what he does is not to change us. We are to be Christ-like in our dealings with him. Paul says, **...for in so doing thou shalt heap coals of fire on his head.** There are several ideas about the meaning of this phrase. However, in keeping with the context it no doubt to refers to

God's judgment. The idea is that our good deeds to him are like coals of fires in the day of his judgment.

CONCERNING HOLINESS

Be not overcome of evil, but overcome evil with good (Romans 12:21). This verse sums up the whole of chapter twelve. Oliver B Greene says:

> "This chapter is full of human impossibilities. From the natural aspect, it is impossible to live chapter 12 Yet, in the Spirit, this chapter presents practical, normal Christian living. Spiritual victory comes to the believer through a definite yielding or surrendering of the body to God as a living sacrifice. God wants our body—all of it, every member of it; and when we have yielded our body to God in every minute detail, we have not done one thing to boast about. We have done that which is 'OUR REASONABLE SERVICE.'"

This verse rings with victory. Evil is overcome by living the Christ-life. If we practice the commands of chapter 12 we will have victory in our Christian life and live in a way pleasing to God

The Powers That Be
Romans 13:1-10

Now Paul deals with the believer's relation and responsibility to civil government. Every believer has a solemn civil responsibility.

THE PRIORITY OF SUBMISSION

Paul explains that government is established by God and that every citizen is to respect the law of the land.

The Obligation of the Christian

Let every soul be subject unto the higher powers... **(Romans 13:1).** The word **powers** comes from *"exousia"* and carries the idea of *"magistrate, authority and jurisdiction."* It speaks of government authority including our country's legislatures, courts, police officers and all that goes with it. The word **subject** simply means *"submission."* Peter wrote:

> **Submit yourselves to every ordinance of man for the Lord's sake: whether it be to the king, as supreme; Or unto governors, as unto them that are sent by him for the punishment of evildoers, and for the praise of them that do well. For so is the will of God, that with well doing ye may put to silence the ignorance of foolish men: As free, and not using *your* liberty for a cloke of maliciousness, but as the servants of God. Honour all *men*. Love the brotherhood. Fear God. Honour the king. (1 Peter 2:13-17)**

It is popular in some circles to be anti-government. But such is not the case for believer's who want to please God. It is clear that God commands the believer to submit to the law of the land. Please notice here that our submission is not dependent on whether or not we agree with who is the White House. We are to submit! That is the bottom line! Remember that the recipients of 1 Peter were being persecuted by the government. They were forced to flee from their homes, leaving everything behind. They had to abandon their family, clothes and jobs. These were trying and difficult times for God's people. The command of God was, **Submit yourselves to every ordinance of man for the Lord's sake.**

The Ordination of the Government

... For there is no power but of God: the powers that be are ordained of God. (Romans 13:1b) Government authority is delegated authority and we are to obey it because in so doing we are obeying God. Pilate said to Jesus, **... knowest thou not that I have power to crucify thee, and have power to release thee? (John 19:10)** Pilate's position had gone to his head. He thought he would throw his weight around with our Lord. But look at Jesus' answer, **... Thou couldest have no power at all against me, except it were given thee from above: therefore he that delivered me unto thee hath the greater sin. (John 19:11)** Nations and empires rise and fall at the command of God. Keep in mind that God ordained government for man's good. Imagine what it would be like without any government. Think about a land without laws, police, courts and jails. There would be absolute anarchy. Man's depravity would rule instead of organized government. It would be an awful land. It would be safe to stick your head out the door.

THE PERIL OF STUBBORNNESS

Whosoever therefore resisteth the power, resisteth the ordinance of God: and they that resist shall receive to themselves damnation. (Romans 13:2) This verse offers a stern warning to those whole would rise up and rebel against government.

The Resisting

Whosoever therefore resisteth the power... (Romans 13:2a) Man is by nature a rebellious creature. Sadly there are those who call themselves Christians, yet rebel against authority in the most ungodly way. We will not always be in agreement with in authority, but there is a balance to maintain. We must be careful not to cross the line. Praise God that we live in the nation that we do. There is no place on earth like the United States of America. Thank God for free speech. We can openly disagree with our government. We can have a part in the election of government officials. If we don't like what they stand for or what they are doing, we can vote them out. But our stand must be taken in a Christ-like manner.

The Reality

Whosoever therefore resisteth the power, resisteth the ordinance of God... (Romans 13:2b) Because government is ordained of God, those who resist government are rebelling against God. In his classic commentary on Romans, Robert Haldane said, "*The people of God, then, ought to consider* *resistance to the government under which they live as a very awful crime — even as resistance to God Himself."* It is a serious matter to rise up against government.

This is not a blind, anything goes obedience. There are principles by which we must live. There is always a balance and there are instances where we must obey God rather than government. As Christians we are to obey the government as long as it's laws are not in violation of God's law. There are many examples in the Bible of believers disobeying the law, when that law was contrary to the word of God.

When Pharaoh became fearful of the growing population of God's people he ordered two Hebrew midwives, Shiphrah, and Puah to kill all the male children that was born. This was the first government sponsored planned parenthood. However, there was a problem. **But the midwives feared God, and did not as the king of Egypt commanded them, but saved the men children alive (Exodus 1:17)**. These women were commanded by law to do something that violated their conscience and God's law, so they disobeyed

Shadrach, Meshach, and Abednego refused to worship the golden image of Nebuchadnezzar (Daniel 3). The Bible is clear, **Thou shalt have no other gods before me (Exodus 20:3).** Shadrach, Meshach, and Abednego obeyed God rather than man.

Now we must be careful with this. These men opposed law of the land only when it violated the law of God. In such cases we must be prudent in determining where our duty to civil government ends and our duty to God begins. Our

Christianity is supposed to make us better citizens—not rebels and criminals.

The Retribution

Paul warns, **... and they that resist shall receive to themselves damnation.** The word **damnation** comes from *"krima."* It is a judicial term that speaks of penal judgment and penal condemnation. The fact is, the very system that the rebels oppose is what God will use to punish them.

THE POWER OF THE STATE

For rulers are not a terror to good works, but to the evil. Wilt thou then not be afraid of the power? do that which is good, and thou shalt have praise of the same: For he is the minister of God to thee for good But if thou do that which is evil, be afraid; for he beareth not the sword in vain: for he is the minister of God, a revenger to execute wrath upon him that doeth evil (Romans 13:3-4). There is no fear of government authority for those who do right and live according to the law. It is the criminal who hates and fears the law. Paul says, **do that which is good, and thou shalt have praise of the same.** Law abiding people do not hate the law they praise it. Government is a **minister of God to thee for good**. The law serves to protect and keep order as well a **revenger to execute wrath upon him that doeth evil.**

THE PEACE OF SUBJECTION

Wherefore ye must needs be subject, not only for wrath, but also for conscience sake. (Romans 13:5) Another reason we ought to be obedient to governing authorities is for peace of conscience. The **conscience** is the inner witness that God has put within us. In other words, as believers we don't obey simply to escape the wrath of the king, we submit to and obey authority because it is the right thing to do. **Therefore to him that knoweth to do good, and doeth it not, to him it is sin. (James 4:17)**

THE PROVISION OF SUPPORT

For for this cause pay ye tribute also: for they are God's ministers, attending continually upon this very thing. (Romans 13:6) Since we benefit from what the civil government provides, we are commanded and expected to support it. Notice that it is not left to us to decide whether or not we pay our taxes. Jesus gave clear instructions on this matter.

> **Is it lawful for us to give tribute unto Caesar, or no? But he perceived their craftiness, and said unto them, Why tempt ye me? Shew me a penny. Whose image and superscription hath it? They answered and said, Caesar's. And he said unto them, Render therefore unto Caesar the things which be Caesar's, and unto God the things which be God's. And they could not take hold of his words before the people: and they marvelled at his answer, and held their peace. (Luke 20:22-26)**

Render therefore to all their dues: tribute to whom tribute is due; custom to whom custom; fear to whom fear; honour to whom honour. (Romans 13:7) No matter one's opinion on how the government spends money. No matter who is in office. No matter how much the money is needed for something else. The biblical command is that we pay our taxes.

Time To Awake
Romans 13:11-14

In this section Paul stresses several basic principles for Christians living in dark days. He calls for believer's to wake up and live all-out for God.

THERE IS PERCEPTION

And that, knowing the time ... (Romans 13:11a) In the next verse Paul says, **The night is far spent, the day is at hand. (Romans 13:12a)** Paul is talking about an awareness and discernment concerning the times. The lack of discernment we are seeing among God's people is a fearful thing. Every believer ought to be a person of discernment. **But he that is spiritual judgeth all things, yet he himself is judged of no man. (1 Corinthians 2:15)** The flesh is the biggest hindrance to discernment. Many believers are living in bondage to their flesh rather than walking in the Spirit. As a result the world has become so churchy, and the Church has become so worldly, that you can hardly tell them apart.

There is a sad lack of discernment among believers and because of this the world has infiltrated the Church. The devil could fold back his horns, tuck his tail in his pants and join the average Church. Discernment is something that God's people cannot do without. You will remember when the men of war gathered at Hebron in support of David who was establishing his rule over all of Israel. Over 350,000 of the greatest soldiers of the day gathered with David. The Bible says that among them were **the children of Issachar, which were men that had understanding of the times, to**

know what Israel ought to do … (1 Chronicles 12:32) This is discernment; having the understanding to know what to do! David said, **Give me understanding, and I shall keep thy law; yea, I shall observe it with my whole heart. (Psalm 119:34)** Discernment not only enables us to know the difference between right and wrong and good and best, but it enables us to choose the right and the best. Oh, God give us discernment in these dark days!

THERE IS OBLIGATION

Paul says, **… it is high time to awake out of sleep. (Romans 13:11b)** The word **sleep** is used in the sense of spiritual apathy and indifference. Paul often used this analogy. He wrote to the Thessalonians, **Therefore let us not sleep, as do others; but let us watch and be sober. (1 Thessalonians 5:6),** and to the Ephesians as well, **Wherefore he saith, Awake thou that sleepest, and arise from the dead, and Christ shall give thee light. (Ephesians 5:14)** Keep in mind that Paul is speaking to believers. There was a great indifference toward spiritual things on the part of the believers of Paul's day as there is in our own day. We see an overwhelming condition of callousness and lack of concern for God's will and values. We are living in a day when carnal apathy greatly hinders the work of Christ.

Such an indifference toward spiritual things has always been a problem with God's people. You will remember that while our Lord agonized in Gethsemane, His disciples slept. In the parables we see the problem of sleeping. In the parable of the sower Jesus said, **But while men slept, his enemy came and sowed tares among the wheat, and went his way. (Matthew 13:25)** In the parable of the ten virgins we learn, **While the bridegroom tarried, they all slumbered and slept. (Matthew 25:5)** God's people for the most part are asleep with the world. What a tragedy! Paul calls for a great awakening here. America's greatest need is for such an awakening. Leonard Ravenhill said that the tragedy of the day is that *"Hell is burning while the Church sleeps."* The devil is gaining a lot of ground while God's people sleep.

THERE IS ANTICIPATION

Paul points out **... for now is our salvation nearer than when we believed (Romans 13:11c)** This a precious nugget of truth? Paul is speaking clearly to the believer hereto he who is already saved. Paul is pointing to the finality of our salvation—our glorification. He is reminding us that glorious days are ahead. The moment we trusted Christ, we were fully saved. The child of God is Personally Saved, Powerfully Sustained, and Permanently Secured. **Wherefore he is able also to save them to the uttermost that come unto God by him, seeing he ever liveth to make intercession for them. (Hebrews 7:25)** What a wonderful salvation!

However, while we are saved to the uttermost, we have not fully entered into all that our salvation entails. The best is yet to come. John said, **Beloved, now are we the sons of God, and it doth not yet appear what we shall be: but we know that, when he shall appear, we shall be like him; for we shall see him as he is. (1 John 3:2)** When we are caught up in the rapture, we are going to receive glorified bodies. We will be like Jesus. John said, **we shall be like him.** Glorification is the desire and will of God for every believer. **For whom he did foreknow, he also did predestinate to be conformed to the image of his Son, that he might be the** firstborn among many brethren. (Romans 8:29) When that day comes, we will be like Him. Isaiah spoke of that day. **Thine eyes shall see the king in his beauty: they shall behold the land that is very far off. (Isaiah 33:17)** What a hope! Someday we will see Jesus in all of His beauty. We will share in the splendor of Heaven. In that day **we shall be like him** and that day is **nearer than when we believed.**

THERE IS SEPARATION

The night is far spent, the day is at hand: let us therefore cast off the works of darkness, and let us put on the armour of light. (Romans 13:12) There are two phrases that stand out here. We are commanded to **cast off** and to **put on.** This is the essence of separation. It is not just a matter of putting off that which is wrong and separating from the wickedness. It is also putting on that which is right, and separating unto Christ. Paul expounds upon this truth.

Let us walk honestly, as in the day; not in rioting and drunkenness, not in chambering and wantonness, not in strife and envying. (Romans 13:13) Paul points out that it is imperative for us to **...walk honestly, as in the day.** The word **honestly** comes from a word that conveys the idea of *"decently or honorably."* It speaks of honest and honorable behavior. Notice that Paul says **as in the day.** He is simply saying that if we are saved and claim to be children of light, then we are to live accordingly. Next, Paul gives three couplets of sin which are all preceded by the negative **not.**

Carousing and Intoxication

...not in rioting and drunkenness. (Romans 13:13a) The word **drunkenness** means intoxication. It is the sin of being under the influence of alcohol. The word **rioting** comes from *"komos"* and carries the idea of *"letting loose, carousing and partying."* The same word is listed in the works of the flesh, and is translated **revellings (Galatians 5:21)** It is a word used to describe drunken parties filled with sexual promiscuity. It is the party scene of the day. People love carousing. They love to go to night clubs and parties. The world lives to satisfy the desires of the flesh. The Christian is to have no part with such a lifestyle.

Cohabitation and Immorality

...not in chambering and wantonness. (Romans 13:13b) Both of these words refer to immoral sexual conduct. The word **chambering** comes from the word *"koite."* It means *"cohabitation."* The idea is that of shacking up together without being married. The word **wantonness** comes from *"aselgeia"* and means *"licentious, filthy, lascivious behavior."* It conveys the idea of shameless excess and absence of restraint. It speaks of the brazen promiscuity that is rampant and openly accepted in our day.

Conflict and Incense

...not in strife and envying. (Romans 13:13c) The word **strife** is from the Greek *"eris"* and speaks of *"squabbling, wrangling, contention, bickering, petty disagreement."* The word **envying** comes from *"zelos "*and carries the idea of jealousy. Webster defines **envying** as *"Feeling uneasiness at the superior condition and happiness of another."* That pretty much describes the world and, unfortunately, many Church members of today. Strife and envy always go together. Strife is the product of envy. Paul, in dealing with the Corinthian believers, says **For ye are yet carnal: for**

whereas there is among you envying, and strife, and divisions, are ye not carnal, and walk as men? (1 Corinthians 3:3) There is no place for such carnal behavior among God's people.

THERE IS SANCTIFICATION

But put ye on the Lord Jesus Christ, and make not provision for the flesh, to fulfil the lusts thereof. (Romans 13:14) We are to put off the works of the flesh and put on the Lord Jesus Christ. We are to replace the bad with the good. Paul said to the Ephesian Church, **That ye put off concerning the former conversation the old man, which is corrupt according to the deceitful lusts; And be renewed in the spirit of your mind; And that ye put on the new man, which after God is created in righteousness and true holiness. (Ephesians 4:22-24)** We are challenged to walk according to what we are, rather than what we were. The words **put ye on** express the idea of *"being arrayed in or clothed with."* Here we see the sharp contrast between the Spirit-led life and the flesh-led life.

In closing, Paul says, **...and make not provision for the flesh, to fulfil the lusts thereof.** Right here is where most folks fail. The word **provision** comes from *"pronoia"* and means *"forethought."* This is important because the outward life follows the thought life. Solomon said, **For as he thinketh in his heart, so is he. (Proverbs 23:7)** Most sin is committed in the thought life, long before it appears outwardly.

Dealing With Diversity
Romans 14:1-12

In this chapter Paul deals with the relationship between weak and strong Christians. This whole chapter deals with how we, as believers, are to handle the liberty that God has given us. Christian liberty frees us from legalism and the dictates of the flesh, so that we are free to serve God. Christians who fail to grasp the truth of Christian liberty usually do not enjoy an intimate relationship with Christ. Let us remember that ours is not a ***Law Relationship***, whereby we must obey every detail of the Old Testament law in order to gain the favor of God Paul says, **... for ye are not under the law, but under grace. (Romans 6:14b)** Neither is it a ***Loose Relationship***, whereby grace frees us from the commands of God so that we can live in the flesh. **What then? shall we sin, because we are not under the law, but under grace? God forbid. (Romans 6:15)**

When the Bible speaks of liberty, it never means a freedom from restraint that allows the Christian to live as he wishes. Rather ours is a ***Love Relationship***, whereby we obey the Word of God and follow Christ wholeheartedly, because of our love for Him. Jesus said, **If ye love me, keep my commandments. (John 14:15)** Because it is connected to Christ, it is a ***Liberating Relationship***. **If the Son therefore shall make you free, ye shall be free indeed (John 8:36)** Paul said, **For sin shall not have dominion over you ...**

(Romans 6:14a) Christian liberty is a wonderful Bible truth when understood and applied as the Bible teaches it.

In the context of Romans 14, the issue is concerning those who are **weak in the faith. (Romans 14:1)** In this case the **weak** is someone who does not have a full understanding of his Christian liberty. The teaching is that stronger believers are to be careful not to let their liberty destroy weaker Christians.

REQUIRED ACCEPTANCE

Him that is weak in the faith receive ye, but not to doubtful disputations. (Romans 14:1) This is a command There is no room to wiggle out of this. Paul says, **receive ye**. Paul addresses this command to the mature believer. He is speaking to those who are seasoned in the faith. Their desire is not to major on minors. They are more interested in being an example; in encouraging and edifying.

The phrase **doubtful disputations** is important. The word **doubtful** means *"not settled in opinion; undetermined ... Dubious; ambiguous; not clear in its meaning"* (Noah Webster 1828 Dictionary). It is speaking of things that are debatable. The word **disputations** means *"The act of disputing; a reasoning or argumentation in opposition to something, or on opposite sides; controversy in words; verbal contest..."* (Noah Webster 1828 Dictionary). Though what some people believe is debatable, and the seasoned believer may know enough Bible to adequately debate them, they are not to be received for that purpose. The aim is not to debate, but to disciple. This word **receive** is used of Christ receiving us. **Wherefore receive ye one another, as**

Christ also received us to the glory of God (Romans 15:7) That is exactly how we are to receive those who are weak in the faith—just as Christ received us. Paul gives two examples.

Concerning Diet

For one believeth that he may eat all things: another, who is weak, eateth herbs. Let not him that eateth despise him that eateth not; and let not him which eateth not judge him that eateth: for God hath received him. (Romans 14:2-3) There is a lot of debating in our day about diet. What is lawful and what is unlawful to eat? Are we to follow the dietary laws of the Old Testament? Or can we now eat pork and shrimp? Here is a fellow **who is weak.** Paul said that he **eateth herbs.** This poor guy is a vegetarian. Most of us eat and enjoy meat. We can even enjoy those meats from which the Jews had to abstain.

You will remember how the Lord spread a great feast before Peter and told him to eat. But there were some things that Peter considered unclean. He said, **Not so, Lord; for I have never eaten any thing that is common or unclean. (Acts 10:12)** God spoke again ... **What God hath cleansed, that call not thou common. (Acts 10:15)** The next verse says, **This was done thrice...** Peter was so locked into the dietary laws of the Old Testament that he had trouble submitting to God. One thing is for certain here. God is no longer holding us to Old Testament law concerning diet! Paul said, **For every creature of God is good, and nothing to be refused, if it be received with thanksgiving: (1 Timothy 4:4)** The mature believer can argue his case, with

Scripture to back him up, but that is not the purpose of receiving a weaker brother or sister. The goal is to receive them as Christ received us—to encourage and edifying them.

Concerning Days

One man esteemeth one day above another: another esteemeth every day alike. Let every man be fully persuaded in his own mind. (Romans 14:5) Our subject now moves from diet to days. It seems as though there is always plenty to argue about. Someone said, *"The best measure of a man's mentality is the importance of the things he will argue about."* The issue here is whether or not we should regard one day as more holy than another day. Sadly, there have been church splits over holidays. One believer considers certain days holier than other days while another considers each day the same. Paul dealt with this same issue in other places, warning about the legalistic observance of holy days.

> **But now, after that ye have known God, or rather are known of God, how turn ye again to the weak and beggarly elements, whereunto ye desire again to be in bondage? Ye observe days, and months, and times, and years. I am afraid of you, lest I have bestowed upon you labour in vain. (Galatians 4:9-11)**

There is a certain bondage that results from a legalistic observance of days. You will notice in our text that Paul didn't take one side or the other. He simply said, **... Let every man be fully persuaded in his own mind. (Romans**

14:5) It didn't matter one way or the other to Paul. Paul would fight about truths of great importance, but he wasn't going to waste valuable time and energy wrangling about minor things that didn't matter. That is why just before he died he said, **I have fought a good fight, I have finished my course, I have kept the faith: (2 Timothy 4:7)** Paul fought a **good** fight. What he fought for was worth fighting for. Paul is not talking about great questions of morality and holiness. Rather he is dealing matters of lesser importance that often flair up and divide God's people. Too many have the tendency to major on minors. This is what Paul is talking about.

REALISTIC ATTITUDE

He that regardeth the day, regardeth it unto the Lord; and he that regardeth not the day, to the Lord he doth not regard it. He that eateth, eateth to the Lord, for he giveth God thanks; and he that eateth not, to the Lord he eateth not, and giveth God thanks. (Romans 14:6) Paul gets down to the real issue here. Why do we observe certain days? Or why do we not observe certain days? Are we doing it out of a pure conscience as unto the Lord? Or are we doing it for religious reasons, or so that we can be contentious? The Pharisees were good at observing days, but they failed miserably in honoring the Lord. Jesus speaking to the religious crowd of His day said ... **Thus have ye made the commandment of God of none effect by your tradition. Ye hypocrites, well did Esaias prophesy of you, saying, This people draweth nigh unto me with their mouth, and honoureth me with their lips; but their heart is far from**

me. **But in vain they do worship me, teaching for doctrines the commandments of men. (Matthew 15:6b-9)** They were good at observing days, but they were so good at living for the Lord

Paul is simply saying here that those who observe certain days do so **unto the Lord** and those who eat certain foods do so **unto the Lord.** Notice that the fellow who eats meat gives God thanks and the fellow who doesn't eat meat also gives God thanks. Either way, God gets the glory if our hearts and motives are right. The issue is not with certain days or in meat. The real issue is whether or not we are glorifying God in what we do.

> **Whether therefore ye eat, or drink, or whatsoever ye do, do all to the glory of God (1 Corinthians 10:31)**

> **And whatsoever ye do in word or deed, do all in the name of the Lord Jesus, giving thanks to God and the Father by him. (Colossians 3:17)**

> **And whatsoever ye do, do it heartily, as to the Lord, and not unto men; (Colossians 3:23)**

Paul expands what he is saying. **For none of us liveth to himself, and no man dieth to himself. For whether we live, we live unto the Lord; and whether we die, we die unto the Lord: whether we live therefore, or die, we are the Lord's. For to this end Christ both died, and rose, and revived, that he might be Lord both of the dead and living. (Romans 14:7-9)** What we do is important, and how we do what we do is even more important. No man lives unto himself and no man dies unto himself. Our lives shape and influence others. As believers, **we live unto the Lord** and, when we die, **we die unto the Lord.** The things we eat, the days we observe, the places we go, the people we run with, all influence the lives of those with whom we mix and mingle. God help us to live and die as unto the Lord. It is not about us. It is not about our differences, diets or days. It is about the Lord Jesus Christ.

RIGHTEOUS ACCOUNTABILITY

But why dost thou judge thy brother? or why dost thou set at nought thy brother? for we shall all stand before the judgment seat of Christ. For it is written, As I live, saith the Lord, every knee shall bow to me, and every tongue shall confess to God So then every one of us shall give account of himself to God (Romans 14:10-12) Paul points out that it not our place to play God and to pass judgment on our weaker brother. Paul asks ... **why dost thou set at nought thy brother?** The phrase **set at nought** means to *"hold in contempt, to count as nothing."* We have no business judging and treating others as if they are nothing.

We are reminded that **...all stand before the judgment seat of Christ. (Romans 14:10b)** Each of us will someday have to give an account of himself to God. This is the judgment that we need to be the most concerned about. Earlier Paul said, **Who art thou that judgest another man's servant? to his own master he standeth or falleth. Yea, he shall be holden up: for God is able to make him stand (Romans 14:4).** We may not agree with others on some non-essential things. But how are we going to deal with them.

The principle is that we are God's servants and God will deal with us. As we deal with these matters, it is important for us to keep this warning in mind; **So then every one of us shall give account of himself to God. (Romans 14:12)**

Responsibility And Christian Liberty
Romans 14:13-23

We hear a great deal about Christian liberty today. The problem is that much of what we hear is not in line with the Word of God. The principle of Christian liberty is clearly taught in the word of God. However, we must maintain a balance in our liberty. Liberty is never the freedom to ignore the clear commands of God's Word. Liberty is always in line with the Word of God. David said, **And I will walk at liberty: for I seek thy precepts. (Psalm 119:45)** Christian liberty never releases the believer from the moral law of God. Liberty ensures our freedom from sin, it is never freedom to sin.

THERE IS CAUTION

Let us not therefore judge one another any more: but judge this rather, that no man put a stumbling block or an occasion to fall in his brother's way. (Romans 14:13) Here is the major problem with misunderstood liberty. It hurts others. Paul has just stated that we do not live or die to ourselves (Romans 14:7). Paul told the Corinthians:

> **Ye are our epistle written in our hearts, known and read of all men: (2 Corinthians 3:2)**

Most of the people we come in contact with never read the Bible, but they sure read us. Our life has an impact on others. People will judge Christ and Christianity based upon what they see in us. This is a serious responsibility.

Paul tells us that instead of judging others, we would be better off judging ourselves, lest our liberty **put a stumbling block or an occasion to fall** before a brother or sister in Christ. Paul had to deal with the Corinthian Church about the same matter. **But take heed lest by any means this liberty of yours become a stumbling block to them that are weak. (1 Corinthians 8:9)** This was a serious problem in Corinth. The word **stumbling block** carries the idea of an obstacle in the pathway. The picture is that of someone tripping and falling due to such an obstacle. The word **occasion** comes from the Greek *"skandalon"* and means *"to trap, to snare."* The word actually speaks of the trigger that springs the trap. The idea is that of leading an animal into a trap. These are vivid illustrations of what happens when we abuse our liberty. We must realize that our liberties are not important enough to cause a brother to fall or to be lured into a snare.

THERE IS CONVICTION

I know, and am persuaded by the Lord Jesus, that there is nothing unclean of itself ... (Romans 14:14a) The word **unclean** speaks of foods that were forbidden by the law (Leviticus 11, Deuteronomy 14). Paul was fully convinced that nothing was unclean of itself. This was clearly Paul's conviction concerning this matter. In his letter to the Church at Corinth Paul wrote:

> **As concerning therefore the eating of those things that are offered in sacrifice unto idols, we**

know that an idol is nothing in the world, and that there is none other God but one. For though there be that are called gods, whether in heaven or in earth, (as there be gods many, and lords many,) But to us there is but one God, the Father, of whom are all things, and we in him; and one Lord Jesus Christ, by whom are all things, and we by him. (1 Corinthians 8:4-6)

Even in the matter of eating meat offered to idols Paul says to eat it and enjoy it. You say, *"How could Paul say such a thing? How can we eat meat that was offered to pagan gods?"* Because **... we know that an idol is nothing in the world, and that there is none other God but one. (1 Corinthians 8:4)** That idol is nothing more than metal, stone, or wood and there is no need to throw a good steak away just because some knucklehead offered it to his false god.

... but to him that esteemeth any thing to be unclean, to him it is unclean. (Romans 14:14b) Now Paul considers the other fellow. Though we are solid and sure in our conviction that we can eat meat, there are others who do not agree. They are just as sure that such meats are unclean. They have a conviction also, but it is the opposite of ours. A Jew who follows the Levitical dietary laws will not eat pork. He reads Leviticus 11 and is convinced that he should abstain from such meats. If he were to eat pork, he would be going against his conviction. Though a slice of ham is not unclean in itself, to the Jew it would be sin, because eating it violates his conscience. Our liberty in Christ should never be practiced at the expense of another. Others are more important than our liberty.

THERE IS COMPASSION

But if thy brother be grieved with thy meat, now walkest thou not charitably. Destroy not him with thy meat, for whom Christ died. (Romans 14:15) Charity is more important than our liberty. If a weaker Christian is grieved with our practices, then it is no longer a question of liberty, but of love. The word **grieved** comes from the Greek *"lypeo"* and carries the idea of *"grief, distress, to make sorrowful or cause pain."* It is the same word used of our grieving the Holy Spirit with our sin (Ephesians 4:30). Our liberty can cause others a lot of grief. Though we may be able to practice certain liberties with a clear conscience, others could be distressed and grieved by our actions, even to the point of their destruction.

Paul warns, **Destroy not him with thy meat.. (Romans 14:15b)** The word **destroy** comes from *"apollymi"* and carries the idea of *"destruction, ruin or devastation."* Vines defines it as *"the loss of wellbeing."* Paul is warning us that our lifestyle could destroy a weaker brother or sister in Christ.

Paul says, **now walkest thou not charitably.** In other words, if your lifestyle is hurting others, you are not walking in love. Christian love puts others first. **Be kindly affectioned one to another with brotherly love; in honour preferring one another; (Romans 12:10)** The Bible states that real biblical love, **seeketh not her own... (1 Corinthians 13:5)** Love does not insist on its own way. Love does not destroy others for pleasure. **Look not every man on his own things, but every man also on the things of others. (Philippians 2:4)** No personal liberty is more important than the wellbeing of a brother or sister in Christ. Therefore, as believers, we are not to insist on having our liberty at the expense of others.

THERE IS A CONCERN

Let not then your good be evil spoken of: (Romans 14:16) To insist on practicing our liberty at the expense of others, will bring reproach upon our Lord and His work. Some folks allow their convictions to destroy their testimony. They take a good stand, but the manner in which they take their stand does more damage than good. How we take a stand is just as important as the stand we are taking. There is nothing that will hurt the work of Christ more that cold dead orthodoxy. I have met some folks whose theology was right on the mark, but the way they presented it did more harm than good. Paul told Timothy that **... the servant of the Lord must not strive; but be gentle unto all men, apt to teach, patient, (2 Timothy 2:23-24)** We are not going to win folks over by running them over. What we believe may be right and although we have plenty of Bible to back it up, we will never win them if our liberty becomes an offense to them. Someone has well said, *"People don't care how you know until they know how much you care."*

For the kingdom of God is not meat and drink; but righteousness, and peace, and joy in the Holy Ghost. (Romans 14:17) It would be good for us to get a hold of this truth. Paul says, **For the kingdom of God is not meat and**

drink... Do you know what that means? It means that a lot of the things Christians fight over don't amount to a hill of beans in Heaven. It is a sad thing when our preferences becomes the basis of our Christianity. Some folks are so wrapped up in their standards and convictions that they miss out on their relationship with Christ. They have no clue what the kingdom of God is all about. Paul is stressing the fact that the Kingdom of God is not based on external things, but on **... righteousness, and peace, and joy in the Holy Ghost.** Paul lists three blessings of our relationship with God and states that these are far more important than food and liberty.

For he that in these things serveth Christ is acceptable to God, and approved of men (Romans 14:18) When Paul said, **he that in these things serveth Christ,** he is talking about those who obey this passage by not putting a stumbling block before others. Paul says, if you do this, you are serving Christ and you are acceptable to God and approved of men. To live this way does not hurt the kingdom of God; it helps it. **That ye may be blameless and harmless, the sons of God, without rebuke, in the midst of a crooked and perverse nation, among whom ye shine as lights in the world; (Philippians 2:15)**

THERE IS A COURSE

Let us therefore follow after the things which make for peace, and things wherewith one may edify another. (Romans 14:19) The idea here is simple. Instead of majoring on minors and destroying the unity of the local church we are to honor other men's consciences. Our main concern should be that **one may edify another.** The word **edifying** means to *"build up."* Sometimes we might have to give up our liberty in order to salvage and build up a weaker brother.

A COMMAND

For meat destroy not the work of God All things indeed are pure; but it is evil for that man who eateth with offence. (Romans 14:20) Here we are warned not to destroy the work of God with our liberty. Certain liberties make no difference to us, but they can make a big difference in a weaker Christian's life. Paul warned us to be careful lest our liberty become a **stumbling block** to others. Then he says, **It is good neither to eat flesh, nor to drink wine, nor any thing whereby thy brother stumbleth, or is offended, or is made weak. (Romans 14:21)** Even though we have liberty, it is better to forego that liberty than to cause a weaker Christian to fall because of it. Paul warned the Corinthians:

> **But take heed lest by any means this liberty of yours become a stumbling block to them that are weak. For if any man see thee which hast knowledge sit at meat in the idol's temple, shall not the conscience of him which is weak be emboldened to eat those things which are offered to idols; (1 Corinthians 8:9-10)**

A mature Christian, with knowledge that idols are nothing and that eating food offered to them is not wrong in itself, can eat the meat. However, when a weaker brother sees it, he is **emboldened** to eat the food sacrificed to idols. In doing so it goes against his conscience. It is at this point that our liberty becomes a **stumbling block to them that are weak.**

Hast thou faith? have it to thyself before God Happy is he that condemneth not himself in that thing which he alloweth. (Romans 14:22) As individual Christians, we may have certain convictions that other do not share. But we are commanded to **have it to thyself before God**. Paul is saying that these convictions are between the individual and God

And he that doubteth is damned if he eat, because he eateth not of faith: for whatsoever is not of faith is sin. (Romans 14:23) The man who indulges in such eating, against his conscience, is sinning. We must practice our liberty with assurance of heart. If there is any doubt whatsoever—then it is sinful. Paul says that **whatsoever is not of faith is sin.**

Christian Behavior
Romans 15:1-7

Although there is a chapter break here, there is not a break in the theme. Paul continues to instruct concerning diversity and differences in the Church. In chapter 14, Paul instructed the stronger believers to be careful how they exercised their liberty, lest they cause a younger Christian to stumble. Here in chapter 15:1-7, he continues with his instruction.

THE EXPECTATION

We then that are strong ought to bear the infirmities of the weak ... (Romans 15:1a) The word **ought** comes from *"opheilo"* and means *"to owe a debt."* It conveys the idea of having a legal obligation. Notice how this word is used in Scripture.

> **He that saith he abideth in him <u>ought</u> himself also so to walk, even as he walked (1 John 2:6)**

> **Hereby perceive we the love of God, because he laid down his life for us: and we ought to lay down our lives for the brethren. (1 John 3:16)**

> **Beloved, if God so loved us, we <u>ought</u> also to love one another. 1 (John 4:11)**

Not only is it expected of us, but we have a binding obligation to consider the weaker brother or sister in Christ. Our obligation is to **bear the infirmities of the weak.** The word **bear** comes from *"bastazo"* and simply means *"to take up, to carry a load."* The word **infirmities** is from "asthenema" and means "weak or powerless." Paul referred to these folks as **weak. (Romans 14:1)** The weak are those who are young in the faith. They are not grounded in the Word of God. They do not have the spiritual understanding of a more seasoned believer. We want to be careful not to miss the point here. When Paul said we **ought to bear the infirmities of the weak,** he wasn't talking about just putting up with them. This goes beyond merely tolerating weaker brothers. The idea is not to simply put up with them, but to support them. They may not have the standards that we have. Maybe they don't share our convictions in every detail. Why not? Because they are young in the faith. They have to grow,and that takes time. Rather than pushing them away with pharisaical attitudes, we are to bear their infirmities; that is, to support them in their weakness. **Bear ye one another's burdens, and so fulfil the law of Christ. Galatians 6:2)**

THE EXHORTATION

... and not to please ourselves. Let every one of us please his neighbour for his good to edification. (Romans 15:1b-2) There is Scriptural balance to be maintained here. Paul is not talking about being a yes man and about trying to accommodate everyone's views. Paul lived primarily to please God. **For do I now persuade men, or God? or do I seek to please men? for if I yet pleased men, I should not be the servant of Christ. (Galatians 1:10)** Paul is not saying that we should be man pleasers. What Paul is stressing is the forgotten principle of living for others rather than self. He is talking about self-denial. Rather than selfishly insisting on having our way and enjoying our liberties, we must first consider the effect it will have on others, and put them first. Paul was never disloyal to Christ in his dealings with man, but he did put others before himself. **Even as I please all men in all things, not seeking mine own profit, but the profit of many, that they may be saved (1 Corinthians 10:33)** Paul says that we do this **for his good to edification.** Our first concern is for the edification of the weak.

THE EXAMPLE

For even Christ pleased not himself; but, as it is written, The reproaches of them that reproached thee fell on me. (Romans 15:3) Paul quotes from Psalm 69:9 to emphasize the fact that Jesus endured reproach because He lived to please God rather than Himself. Had He been selfish, He would not have tolerated the shame and suffering that befell Him. Jesus had a two-fold purpose while on earth.

He desired to Satisfy the Father

Jesus did not live for himself. He lived for the Father. He said, **... My meat is to do the will of him that sent me, and to finish his work. (John 4:34)** Even as He approached the moment when He would bear the sins of the world, and for the first time be separated from the Father, the Bible says He **...fell on his face, and prayed, saying, O my Father, if it be possible, let this cup pass from me: nevertheless not as I will, but as thou wilt. (Matthew 26:39)** Jesus came to do the Father's will. Just before His crucifixion, the Lord Jesus prayed, **I have glorified thee on the earth: I have finished the work which thou gavest me to do. (John 17:4)** Jesus put the Father first. He denied His rights and accomplished God's will.

He desired to Save the Sinner

For the Son of man is come to seek and to save that which was lost. (Luke 19:10) I can understand Christ denying Himself for the Father, but also for me? **But made himself of no reputation, and took upon him the form of a servant, and was made in the likeness of men: And being found in fashion as a man, he humbled himself, and became obedient unto death, even the death of the cross. (Philippians 2:7-8)** He put sinners before himself and ... **came not to be ministered unto, but to minister, and to give his life a ransom for many. (Mark 10:45)** He left Heaven's glory; took upon Himself our humanity; endured the shame and suffering that was rightfully ours, and never once complained about it. That is self-denial. Jesus Christ is the supreme example of self-denial. He always put others first.

THE ENCOURAGEMENT

For whatsoever things were written aforetime were written for our learning, that we through patience and comfort of the scriptures might have hope. (Romans 15:4) The Old Testament is full of examples of men and women who lived sacrificially, to the glory of God. Noah, who preached for 120 years as he built the ark, didn't have one convert. Yet he persevered in the face of ridicule and opposition to carry out the task that God had given him. Moses denied himself the riches and glory of Egypt so that he could please God. He is spoken of as, **Choosing rather to suffer affliction with the people of God, than to enjoy the**

pleasures of sin for a season; (Hebrews 11:25) We could go on and on with Scriptural examples of self-denial. Daniel suffered for putting God first. Joseph suffered for righteousness sake. Shadrach, Meshach, and Abednego denied themselves and suffered the vengeance of the king. In the Psalms we learn how David suffered at the hand of Saul and others. The bottom line is that the Christian life is one of self denial. It is putting others first.

THE ENDOWMENT

Now the God of patience and consolation grant you to be likeminded one toward another according to Christ Jesus: (Romans 15:5) Here is the cure for what ails so many believers. Such an attitude of self-denial is not something that we can accomplish on our own. By nature, we are depraved and selfish people. The flesh cannot accept and carry out the commands of God. It is only by His enabling that we can deny our self and put others first. Not only is Christ our Example, He is also our Enabler for living a selfless life.

THE EFFECT

That ye may with one mind and one mouth glorify God, even the Father of our Lord Jesus Christ. Wherefore receive ye one another, as Christ also received us to the glory of God. (Romans 15:6-7) When we deny self and put others first we bring glory and honor to God Who doesn't get glory out of our selfish dealings, but out of our self-denial. Jesus lived for others and when we do the same, the world around us sees the love of Christ. **By this shall all men know that ye are my disciples, if ye have love one to**

another. **(John 13:35)** Why do we have to receive these weak brethren?   Because Christ received us.

Now I say that Jesus Christ was a minister of the circumcision for the truth of God, to confirm the promises made unto the fathers: (Romans 15:8) Paul points out that Jesus Christ came to confirm the promises made unto the fathers. The fathers are Abraham, Isaac, and Jacob; the great Patriarchs of the Old Testament. Jesus was the fulfillment of the promised Messiah. However, **He came unto his own, and his own received him not. (John 1:11)** When the Jews rejected Christ, a door was opened to the Gentiles.

And that the Gentiles might glorify God for his mercy; as it is written, For this cause I will confess to thee among the Gentiles, and sing unto thy name. And again he saith, Rejoice, ye Gentiles, with his people. And again, Praise the Lord, all ye Gentiles; and laud him, all ye people. And again, Esaias saith, There shall be a root of Jesse, and he that shall rise to reign over the Gentiles; in him shall the Gentiles trust. Now the God of hope fill you with all joy and peace in believing, that ye may abound in hope, through the power of the Holy Ghost. (Romans 15:9-13) Paul quotes several Old Testament Scriptures to illustrate what he has been teaching (Psalm 18:49, 2 Samuel 22:50, Deuteronomy 32:34, and Isaiah 11:10). Paul shows that God accepted both Jew and Gentile into His family and, therefore, serves as an example of how we should accept others. We are to accept those who love our Lord even though they may differ with us in some areas of lesser importance.

Paul's Vision
Romans 15:14-33

As Paul nears the end of this letter, he begins to pour out his heart to the Romans, concerning his desire to visit them, as well as his future plans and vision to reach the regions beyond.

PAUL'S PURPOSE

Nevertheless, brethren, I have written the more boldly unto you in some sort, as putting you in mind, because of the grace that is given to me of God, That I should be the minister of Jesus Christ to the Gentiles, ministering the gospel of God, that the offering up of the Gentiles might be acceptable, being sanctified by the Holy Ghost. (Romans 15:15-16) Paul has **written the more boldly.** He had faithfully and boldly stated what needed to be. He didn't soften it, sugar it, or skirt it. He spoke the truth. This was Paul's method of preaching. **And how I kept back nothing that was profitable unto you, but have shewed you, and have taught you publickly, and from house to house, (Acts 20:20)** Paul lived to preach the gospel. His one great objective was to reach the lost for Christ.

PAUL'S PLAN

For which cause also I have been much hindered from coming to you. But now having no more place in these parts, and having a great desire these many years to come unto you; (Romans 15:22-23) Paul had a **great desire** to visit the believer's in Rome but he had been **much hindered** from doing so. The word **hindered** comes from the Greek *"enkopto"* and means "to cut, to impede." It was a word used to describe ditches cut in the road to hinder the advancement of enemy troops. Paul later said to the Thessalonians, **Wherefore we would have come unto you, even I Paul, once and again; but Satan hindered us. (1 Thessalonians 2:18)** Satan did everything possible to impede and hinder Paul's ministry. We must keep in mind that Satan is a very real enemy. He will stop at nothing to hinder the work that God has called us to. But regardless of the opposition, Paul forged ahead, and so must we.

Whensoever I take my journey into Spain, I will come to you: for I trust to see you in my journey, and to be brought on my way thitherward by you, if first I be somewhat filled with your company. (Romans 15:24) Regardless of Satan's hindrance, Paul planned to see them as he passed by on his way to Spain. It is one thing to serve the Lord and even continue on serving as long as thing are going well. But to remain committed despite all hindrances and difficulties is another story. Paul would later write, **I press toward the mark for the prize of the high calling of God in Christ Jesus. (Philippians 3:14)** Paul didn't let up in the face of adversity.

PAUL'S PASSION

But now I go unto Jerusalem to minister unto the saints. For it hath pleased them of Macedonia and Achaia to make a certain contribution for the poor saints which are at Jerusalem. It hath pleased them verily; and their debtors

they are. **For if the Gentiles have been made partakers of their spiritual things, their duty is also to minister unto them in carnal things. (Romans 15:25-27)** Again we see Paul's heart for people who are hurting. At a point where many would be focused on their own problems, Paul was concerned for others. The believers in **Macedonia and Achaia** had taken up an offering for the poor in Jerusalem, and Paul was on his way to deliver it. **As we have therefore opportunity, let us do good unto all men, especially unto them who are of the household of faith. (Galatians 6:10)** There were many things vying for Paul's time and attention, but he never lost sight of the need to help the hurting.

PAUL'S PRAYER

Now I beseech you, brethren, for the Lord Jesus Christ's sake, and for the love of the Spirit, that ye strive together with me in your prayers to God for me; (Romans 15:30) Paul calls upon the Roman believers to strive together with him in prayer to God. The word **beseech** means *"to entreat; to supplicate; to implore; to ask or pray with urgency."* The English words **strive together** come from the Greek *"synagonizomai"* and carry the idea of *"struggling in company with someone, to be a partner, to strive together with.* Paul begged these believers to not only enter into a prayer partnership with him, but to put every effort into praying for him.

That I may be delivered from them that do not believe in Judaea; and that my service which I have for Jerusalem may be accepted of the saints; That I may come unto you with joy by the will of God, and may with you be

refreshed. Now the God of peace be with you all. Amen. (Romans 15:31-33) Paul needed prayer for protection from unbelievers (31a); to be accepted of the saints in Jerusalem (31b); and to be able to visit the Romans with joy by the will of God (32). We notice that Paul's heart was consumed with a passion for the Lord and His people. May God help us to develop such a passion!

Paul And His Companions
Romans 16:1-16

Paul ends his epistle by commending many of his friends and fellow laborers in the ministry, as well as by giving a word of warning and instruction concerning the false teachers who threatened the purity and unity of the Church at Rome.

PAUL'S COMMENDATION

I commend unto you Phebe our sister, which is a servant of the church which is at Cenchrea: That ye receive her in the Lord, as becometh saints, and that ye assist her in whatsoever business she hath need of you: for she hath been a succourer of many, and of myself also. (Romans 16:1-2) Paul highly commends **Phebe** as a **sister** a **servant**, a **succourer of many**. Phebe's testimony was that of a great servant of God. She was from the **church which is at Cenchrea,** a port of Corinth. While many suppose her to have been a deaconess, we know that this was not the case, since she could not have met the qualifications. It's hard for a woman to be the husband of one wife (1 Timothy 3:12). She was, however, a tremendous servant of God, and Paul exhorted the Roman Christians to **receive her in the Lord.**

Greet Priscilla and Aquila my helpers in Christ Jesus: Who have for my life laid down their own necks: unto whom not only I give thanks, but also all the churches of

the Gentiles. (Romans 16:3-4) Priscilla and Aquila were a husband and wife team that had labored with Paul at Corinth (Acts 18:1-3). Paul speaks of them as **my helpers in Christ Jesus**. We know that they were wholly committed to the cause of Christ because Paul testified that they had **laid down their own necks** to save his life.

Likewise greet the church that is in their house. Salute my wellbeloved Epaenetus, who is the firstfruits of Achaia unto Christ. (Romans 16:5) Paul speaks of Epaenetus as **wellbeloved** and as the **firstfruits of Achaia.** He was possibly Paul's first convert from Achaia, and he held a special placed in Paul's heart.

Greet Mary, who bestowed much labour on us. Salute Andronicus and Junia, my kinsmen, and my fellowprisoners, who are of note among the apostles, who also were in Christ before me. Greet Amplias my beloved in the Lord Salute Urbane, our helper in Christ, and Stachys my beloved Salute Apelles approved in Christ. Salute them which are of Aristobulus' household Salute Herodion my kinsman. Greet them that be of the household of Narcissus, which are in the Lord Salute Tryphena and Tryphosa, who labour in the Lord Salute the beloved Persis, which laboured much in the Lord Salute Rufus chosen in the Lord, and his mother and mine. Salute Asyncritus, Phlegon, Hermas, Patrobas, Hermes, and the brethren which are with them. Salute Philologus, and Julia, Nereus, and his sister, and Olympas, and all the saints which are with them. Salute one another with an holy kiss. The churches of Christ salute you. (Romans 16:6-16) These names are not mentioned anywhere else in the word of God. Except for Paul referring to them here, they are unknown to us. Paul had met a lot of people along the way. We do know that these were helpers and fellow servants of Paul. They had labored together on the same team, to the glory of Christ. **Wherefore we labour, that, whether present or absent, we may be accepted of him. (2 Corinthians 5:9)** As Paul looked back over his ministry, he enjoyed many fond memories of their ministering together.

PAUL'S CONCERNS

Now I beseech you, brethren, mark them which cause divisions and offences contrary to the doctrine which ye have learned; and avoid them. (Romans 16:17) Paul was concerned about false doctrine and division in the Church. Many times Paul warned his readers about the need to deal with such matters. Paul said to **mark them.** This phrase comes from *"skopeo "*and means to *"fix one's eyes on."* It is the word from which we get our word *"scope."* A microscope or a telescope is used to examine something that can not been seen with a normal glance or with the naked eye. It must be scrutinized and studied. Paul is telling us to keep our eyes on them; to examine and scrutinize them.

.... which cause divisions and offences contrary to the doctrine which ye have learned; and avoid them. (Romans 16:17). Divisions and offences are the natural results of false doctrine. When a Pastor has labored over the Word and has faithfully taught his people the precious truths of Scripture, and someone comes in and begins to oppose him, the result is serious trouble for the Church. Notice the phrase

contrary to the doctrine which ye have learned. Paul is saying, "You have been taught sound doctrine. You hold to the truth. Don't even listen to someone who is teaching contrary to what you have already been taught." These false teachers cause **divisions and offences** in the Church. These false teachers would do well to remember that the Lord hates him **that soweth discord among brethren. (Proverbs 6:19)** Unity is vital to the work of God, and God hates those who disrupt His work.

Notice that the word of God commands that we **avoid them**. The word **avoid** comes from the work *"ekklino"* and means to *"avoid, shun, to go out of the way."* It speaks of absolute separation. Don't go near them. There is a great danger in associating with heretics. **Be not deceived: evil communications corrupt good manners. (1 Corinthians 15:33)** If you associate with them, you will pick up their ways.

For they that are such serve not our Lord Jesus Christ, but their own belly; and by good words and fair speeches deceive the hearts of the simple. (Romans 16:18) Those who bring false doctrine and division into the Church are not servants of the Lord. They are serving themselves. They use **good words and fair speeches** but their aim is to **deceive the hearts of the simple.** They know just what to say and how to say it. They have no integrity. They lie and tell folks what they want to hear. With false words and flattery they **deceive the hearts of the simple.** Like a wolf going after a young lamb, these false teachers single out the young ones in the Lord, those who haven't been saved very long, and those who aren't well established in the faith. And with false words and fair speech they begin to sow their discord. Such people are dangerous and detrimental to the cause of Christ. They must be avoided!

For your obedience is come abroad unto all men. I am glad therefore on your behalf ... (Romans 16:19a) Paul commends the brethren for their obedience to Christ. Though there were some who were teaching false doctrine and causing division, the majority of the Roman Christians were not falling for it. They were loyal to Christ. Paul mentions their **obedience**. This is the key to success in the Christian life! Obedience to Christ must continue regardless of what others are saying and doing.

Paul says **...but yet I would have you wise unto that which is good, and simple concerning evil. (Romans 16:19b)** When Paul admonishes his readers to be **wise unto that which is good,** he is calling on us to know the Word of God; to be students acquainted with the word. Folks get into a lot of trouble because they don't know the Bible. Hosea said, **My people are destroyed for lack of knowledge... (Hosea 4:6)** Unfortunately, their problem was not that there was no knowledge available, but that they had rejected God's knowledge. Jesus said, **Ye do err, not knowing the scriptures. (Matthew 22:29)** Let's determine to be **wise unto that which is good**.

Not only are we to be wise unto that which is good, but we are also to be **simple concerning evil.** The word simple comes from *"akeraios"* and conveys the idea of *"being pure, free from evil, innocent."* It is the same word that is translated harmless when Jesus said, **Behold, I send you** forth as sheep in the midst of wolves: be ye therefore wise as serpents, and harmless as doves. (Matthew 10:16) Now, Paul commanded us to be **wise unto that which is good, and simple concerning evil** and Jesus commanded that we be **wise as serpents, and harmless as doves.** The idea of both commands is for us to know what is right so that we can avoid what is wrong.

And the God of peace shall bruise Satan under your feet shortly. The grace of our Lord Jesus Christ be with you. Amen. (Romans 16:20) Paul assures his readers that the day is coming when the false teachers and rebels will be dealt with. God Himself will deal with Satan and those who do his work. God is identified as the **God of peace.** The believer enjoys the peace of God no matter what he is going through at the time.

PAUL'S COMPANIONS

Timotheus my workfellow, and Lucius, and Jason, and Sosipater, my kinsmen, salute you. I Tertius, who wrote this epistle, salute you in the Lord Gaius mine host, and of the whole church, saluteth you. Erastus the chamberlain of the city saluteth you, and Quartus a brother. (Romans 16:21-23) Paul began this chapter with greetings to his fellow laborers in Rome. Here he sends greetings to them from those who were with him in Corinth.

Timotheus my workfellow... Timothy was Paul's **own son in the faith. (1 Timothy 1:2)** He was very dear to the heart of the Apostle. Timothy was a young preacher who was led to the Lord and trained by Paul. He is called **my workfellow.** Paul told the Philippians, **But I trust in the Lord Jesus to**

send Timotheus shortly unto you, that I also may be of good comfort, when I know your state. For I have no man likeminded, who will naturally care for your state. (Philippians 2:19-20) Timothy was the kind of companion in the ministry that Paul could trust with great responsibility. What an invaluable helper!

Lucius is mentioned in Acts 13:1 as one of the prophets and teachers of the Church at Antioch.

Jason could well be the same man mentioned in Acts 17:5-9 He had faithfully cared for Paul and Silas while they were ministering to Thessalonica.

Sosipater is not mentioned anywhere else in Scripture.

I Tertius, who wrote this epistle, salute you in the Lord (Romans 16:22) Tertius was Paul's secretary. You remember that Paul suffered from bad eye sight (Galatians 4:15, 6:12). **Tertius** served as Paul's assistant. Paul spoke under the inspiration of the Holy Spirit (2 Peter 1:21) and Tertius faithfully transcribed as Paul dictated

Gaius mine host, and of the whole church, saluteth you. Erastus the chamberlain of the city saluteth you, and Quartus a brother. (Romans 16:23) Gaius was a man of great hospitality. He not only hosted Paul, but the whole Church. Here was another of Paul's converts and one of the few that Paul personally baptized (1 Corinthians 1:14).

Erastus is described as **the chamberlain of the city.** The word **chamberlain** comes from the word *"oikonomos"* and means *"one who oversees or manages another's affairs."* He was the city treasurer, a high ranking government official who had come to Christ.

Quartus a brother. Quartus is another one that is not mentioned anywhere else in Scripture. This is all we know about him. He was **a brother.**

The grace of our Lord Jesus Christ be with you all. Amen. (Romans 16:24) Again, as in verse 20, Paul asks for grace from the Lord Jesus Christ for the saints at Rome.

PAUL'S CONFIDENCE

Now to him that is of power to stablish you according to my gospel, and the preaching of Jesus Christ (Romans 16:25a) Paul had confidence that God's power would be sufficient to establish and sustain the believers at Rome. The word **stablish** comes from the Greek *"sterizo"* and means *"to be fixed, to set fast, to strengthen."* It conveys the idea of being immovable. It describes a believer that is grounded in the truth. Paul spoke of being **Rooted and built up in him, and stablished in the faith... (Colossians 2:7)** Paul knew that their help would come from God. It is the Lord Who establishes us. **But the Lord is faithful, who shall stablish you, and keep you from evil. (2 Thessalonians 3:3)**

... according to the revelation of the mystery, which was kept secret since the world began, (Romans 16:25b) The mystery is explained in Colossians where Paul said, **Even the mystery which hath been hid from ages and from generations, but now is made manifest to his saints: To whom God would make known what is the riches of the glory of this mystery among the Gentiles; which is Christ**

in you, the hope of glory: Colossians 1:26-27 A mystery is something that is unknown. Throughout the Old Testament the idea of the Church was unknown. The Jews never even suspected that God would show such grace to the Gentiles. A major part of that mystery was the fact that they would not only know God and walk with Him, but that He would indwell them. Paul said, **which is Christ in you, the hope of glory.** The believer is strengthened and established by Christ, Who abides within.

But now is made manifest, and by the scriptures of the prophets, according to the commandment of the everlasting God, made known to all nations for the obedience of faith: (Romans 16:26) Paul says, **But now is made manifest.** It is no longer a mystery. The secret is out. Christ has come and paid the sin debt and whosoever will, may come and be saved. Regardless of nationality, color, or social standing, the gospel is for all.

Notice that this message is **made manifest, and by the scriptures of the prophets.** Preaching and teaching of the Word of God is God's prescribed method for getting the gospel out. **So then faith cometh by hearing, and hearing by the word of God (Romans 10:17)** Paul says that this message is to be **...made known to all nations for the obedience of faith: (Romans 16:26)** Paul no doubt had the Great Commission in mind here. Salvation is not in any church or religion. It is not in ordinances or ceremonies. Salvation is in Christ alone. To be saved one must simply believe on Jesus Christ, as the only begotten Son of God who died for our sins, and rose for our justification, and receive Him as Lord and Saviour.

To God only wise, be glory through Jesus Christ for ever. Amen. (Romans 16:27) In closing Paul was careful to give glory to God, who in His infinite knowledge saw man's fall and depravity, and in His matchless mercy, provided for us a Saviour.